REV. DR. WILSON

I Love to Tell the Story:

100+ Stories of Justice, Inclusion, and Hope

A Books to Believe In Publication
All Rights Reserved
Copyright 2016 by Nancy Wilson

No part of this book may be reproduced or transmitted in any form or by any means, electronic or mechanical, including photocopy, recording or by any information storage and retrieval system, without permission, in writing from the author.

Proudly Published in the USA by
Books to Believe In
17011 Lincoln Ave. #408
Parker, CO 80134

Phone: (303)-794-8888

Find us on Facebook at
www.facebook.com/Books2BelieveIn

Follow us on Twitter at
@books2believein
@RevNancyWilson

Visit us at
BooksToBelieveIn.com
MccChurch.org

Editors:
Ann Craig and Linda Brenner

Cover Design and Cover Photo by:
Linda Brenner

Author Photo Credit:
DonDalyPhoto.com

ISBN:1530747538

DEDICATION

To my generation of MCC clergy and lay leaders, the first generation, those still living or those enjoying your heavenly reward, those who had the courage to step into the light.

Contents

Introduction   **13**

Weddings, Love and Marriage Equality   **17**
The Judge and her Wife
The Wedding Cake
Our Many Weddings: Let Me Count the Ways
One Love in Jamaica
Wedding Diversities
Maybe *They* Won't Turn Us Down
Cruising Towards Marriage Equality
The Wedding Whisperer
Dave and Bill's Wedding
A Ukrainian Marriage
My Cousin's Catholic Wedding
Thanksgiving for Forty Years
Breaking into the Wedding Chapel at New York City Hall
Funny Wedding Stories

Pastoring the Lost and Found   **37**
And a Little Dog Shall Lead Them
Praise Jesus!
It May as Well Have Been a Million
You Made My Christmas
Tie a Yellow Ribbon
Fat Lady or Angel?
CHIRP! Coming Back to Life
Dumped on the Lawn
Welcome to MCC: She's an Idiot!
Charles Manson and Susan Atkins
To God Be the Glory

Funerals, Death and Grieving 59
Race, Culture and Funerals
Death Drama/Trauma
We Don't Do Funerals for Strangers
Signs of Hope
I Have Everything I Need
New Year's Eve on a Plane
A Funeral to Remember

Hate, Violence and Hate Crimes 71
We Never Called It a Hate Crime
Jamaican Newspapers, Hate and Homophobia
Nate Phelps Helps Heal Hate in Topeka
Terror at a Funeral
Healing the Hate: Virgil Scott's Murder
Matthew Shepard: The Hate Crime that Moved a Nation
Early Hate: Slapped at the Altar
Bomb Threat in San Francisco, 1974
Bomb Threat in Washington DC, 1976
Paying the Price in Jamaica
Hate and Human Rights in The Ecumenical Movement

Laughter is the Best Medicine 91
Pants Down!
Star Struck and Singing Like Ethel Merman
IT IS NOW 1AM!
Martina's Right to Bear Arms
With Jerry Falwell on the Ron Reagan Jr. Show
The Two Jerrys
The Palms
Taking It to the Boom Boom Room
Things in a Pastor's Closet
Ecumenical Humor at MCC Confrence in 1999
Earl's Chest Hairs

Portraits 109
You Too, Grandma?
An Unlikely Friendship
I Have One Good Year Left
Mabel O'Dell Moves In

God Works in Mysterious Ways
Been Coming to MCC All My Life
Just a Minute There, Mr. Schuller!
The Vicar of Brixton
"Mom" Edith Allen Perry
Promoted to Glory
Sweet Hour of Prayer

Babies, Kids and Angels 129
Jamaal's Bread
Easter Inclusion
Caring for Babies with AIDS
The Eagle's Center
The Baby Relay
The Miracle of Miles Isaiah
The Christmas Gift
If You Could Love Johnie
Brighter Days Are Coming

The First Decade 145
Outed by a Gay Pioneer, 1972
My First MCC Service, October 1972
Meeting Troy Perry, 1973
The Homophile Community Health Service
First Pride in Worcester, 1974
Elected Elder, 1976
Elders Meetings, Troy Fasts, Jeff's Couch and Sweatshops
No on 6
Let My Books Go
A Queer Christmas Dinner
To Retreat or Not to Retreat
Gay Cuban Refugees

Earthquakes and MCC Buildings 165
Quaking in Los Angeles
Where Do We Go From Here?
Devastation in Haiti
MCC's National Cathedral for a Day
Novenas on Santa Monica Boulevard
Rearranging the Furniture

Sexuality, the Vatican, and
Other Ecumenical Adventures 181
Rage, Obscenity and The King James Bible
Sexuality Seminar — World Council of Churches in Brazil
The Future Pope and I
The Women of Bucharest
Calvin Was Not Smiling! Adventures in Catholic Seminary
Charismatic Renewal and Sexual Healing
God, Grace, Sex and Porn Stars
The Dance of Healing
What Would Jesus Do?
Lesbians on the Yang Tse River

White House Encounters 199
Bullet-proof Vests, 1976
Jimmy Carter's White House
The Clinton White House — on His Right and His Left
From the Easter Prayer Breakfast to the March for Tolerance
A Kiss from our President
The Inaugural Prayer Service, January 2013

Conclusion 213

I love this book! We lived these stories together with so many brave and joyous souls who ventured out like the first apostles to see who was hiding in closets in need of the good news. Oh my! They came to worship and to believe finally that God is the author of all that is good — including us. What a fitting reflection on your decades of service as an out lesbian who was willing to risk your life to be a sign of hope and joy for so many people. Nancy Wilson (including your Rev. Elder Dr.) well done, thou good and faithful servant.

Rev. Elder Troy Perry,
Founder, Metropolitan Community Churches

If anyone ever doubted there was a reason for MCC to continue to exist, they need to read Rev. Elder Dr. Nancy Wilson's book, *I Love to Tell the Story*. This collection of stories is really a collection of lives that have been saved, changed, and found because of the ministry of MCC, and Nancy Wilson in particular. What is compelling about these stories is that they serve as a reminder that there are still people like this in our world and within the reach of MCC who need our love, our care, and our message of God's inclusive love. Storytelling is a very powerful way to honor where we have been and to inspire where we are going. It is also, as Wilson demonstrates, a powerful way to finish conversations, make apologies, and ask questions when stories seem incomplete or have been interrupted.

Rev. Elder Mona West, PhD
Director, Office of Formation and Leadership
Development for Metropolitan Community Churches and
contributing editor of The Queer Bible Commentary

In our current society where religion is so often viewed as dry, legalistic and even divisive, Nancy Wilson's delightful *100 Stories* of her personal experiences as a leader in a new growing faith movement will bring tears at times, laughter at times, and throughout, a greater awareness of a loving and dynamic God who truly reaches out to all us where we are.

Stan C. Kimer,
Past President, North Carolina Council of Churches

What a great feeling this book left with me. It felt like a long late-night talk with a group of old familiar friends going over favorite stories and moving miracles through which so many of us have lived. It felt like a book of treasures. I found myself wanting to share this one story with my kids, and that one with my wife, and another one with a friend on Facebook. I'm so grateful that Nancy took the time to put these in print so that we can continue to share them as the stepping stones which are already worn with the footsteps of the sometimes worn and ragged saints who have made a way for all of us.

Marsha Stevens-Pino,
Singer-Songwriter, Author

REV. DR. NANCY WILSON

Introduction

So many stories have lived in me, some of them for more than four decades of activism and ministry in Metropolitan Community Churches. When I have shared them, in sermons, or lectures or conversation, they have brought laughter, tears, insight, and hope. They have touched hearts and funny bones, and occasionally inspired action.

These are not stories for a memoir: that is another project. And, they are not all about me, or even things in which I participated. Many stories of people who have profoundly shaped my life are not included. Some of my dearest friends and most valued colleagues do not make an appearance. Those persons who are woven into my life may very well appear in another volume, but not in this one.

For those who feel like you have known me forever, be assured that some stories have never been told before.

Nor is this a comprehensive story compendium. It is not a history of a movement., but that movement is the context for all of it. It is the movement for radical inclusion, for civil and human rights, for the dignity and worth of all people, including LGBTQ people; this is the context.

Some of the best stories I was tempted to include were just too personal, too intimate, or not as interesting to people outside of a smaller circle of friends and colleagues. Some I did not have permission to tell. Some may have to be told after I am gone!

These stories, rather, are meant to stand on their own, as accounts of an amazing time in history.

Some of them are more than four decades old, and they chronicle a sea-change in social attitudes and human rights. Others are poignant portraits of people who no one else would ever remember, but whose story is valuable in itself as a testimony of some value: love, courage, redemption, or healing. Many are inherently intersectional, mirroring our complex realities.

Whether funny, heroic, or sweet, some are full of faith, and others bypass faith altogether.

It is possible, in these stories, to infer a lot about my own theology, my faith practice, and my values, though this is not a thorough explication of these aspects of who I am. I used to say to churches where I served as pastor that you could tell a lot about what I believed by what I did not preach. That may be true here as well.

As a preacher all my adult life, it is not possible for these stories not to preach now and then. You may have heard them more than once but I trust you will still find meaning in them.

Stories about justice do not have a separate category, because, most of them, in one way or another, are about the struggle for justice, about its victories and defeats; about justice delayed and denied, justice realized here or there, on a personal, social and global level. That moral arc of the Universe will hopefully bend at last, in the direction of justice.

As these stories are read, silently or aloud, I hope they bless the reader as much as they have blessed me in the telling of them.

I offer them, with thanksgiving, for all the amazing people whose diverse paths I have been privileged to cross: pastors, porn stars, Presidents and persons with AIDS, robbers and felons, couples and kids, queer and common, celebrities and geniuses. What a gift!

For the reader, I hope you see yourself in these stories, and those you have loved. Or that it pushes you to open yourself and your heart to risk love.

Finally, I hope that others in our movement may be inspired to tell the thousands and thousands of stories, just like these, that weave a spiritual story for the ages, a tale of empowerment and redemption.

Clockwise, above: Rev. Dr. Nancy Wilson (front row, behind banner) and MCC friends carry the banner at LA Pride in 1996. *Top left:* Nancy Wilson and Paula Schoenwether celebrate their first holy union in Detroit, Michigan, in 1978. *Top right:* Bill Leavens and David Krumroy walk down the steps of the chancel at the end of their holy union in 1977. Rev. Wilson presided. *Middle right:* Connie and Eva, 1973. *Bottom right:* David Manor.

Weddings, Love and Marriage Equality

The story of same-sex marriage equality is certainly the most dramatic and visible story of LGBTQ civil rights of the last decade.

What is also true is that the struggle for marriage equality, in a public way, in the US and around the world, is many decades old. The first public wedding of a same-sex couple was performed by Rev. Troy Perry, and chronicled by *The Advocate* and in the June 8, 1969, *Time* magazine.

MCC churches, from the beginning, were committed to the ideal of full equality, which seemed like a far-off fantasy. Most of us who are over fifty never thought marriage for same-gender couples would happen anywhere in the world, in our lifetime.

Still, we are very aware that marriage equality is not the only civil or human right that matters. For so many around the world, basic safety from violence or harassment, the de-criminalization of homosexuality, the de-pathologizing of transgender people, are desperate social and human rights needs.

At the same time, those of us in our inclusive faith movement, in MCC and beyond, have had a lot of experience with all kinds of weddings, same-sex and straight, for a variety of reasons. We have learned that the church, and society, discriminates against many kinds of love. Practicing radical inclusion has meant saying "yes," beyond our own narrow expectations.

The Judge and Her Wife

When I became the new pastor of Metropolitan Community Church of Detroit in late 1975, we met at the Methodist Church on Woodward Ave, in Highland Park. People often dropped by, looking for the Methodist pastor, who was part-time and not always there. Once in a while, they were actually looking for me, the lesbian pastor of the MCC church.

One afternoon, mid-week, a very tall, well-dressed woman appeared at the door, with another, shorter, attractive woman. I invited them into my office. The taller woman told me she was a federal judge, and, as I might imagine, could not be "open." She then told me that she and her partner were very much in love and wanted to be married.

I could see that they were in love, by how they looked at each other, and touched hands.

The judge, more than most, understood this ceremony could not be legal.

She hesitated a little and then asked, could I do the ceremony, then and there, without knowing their last names?

It was so moving to witness the courage of these women to seek me out in those very early days of our church, and in very different times for LGBTQ people.

How painful, it must be, in one way, to not have the dignity of being able to even use one's whole name. They couldn't risk telling me much about themselves. I had to just go on my young instincts.

Of course I would marry them. As a 25-year-old clergy in MCC, I had no problem breaking or bending rules. Anyway, there was no manual. We were all making this up as we went along.

God knew their last names, and everything else about them. All I could do was to be a witness to their profound love and commitment to each other.

Who could forget the love and devotion on their faces, the unmasked joy as we celebrated their wedding in the sanctuary? They didn't want what we then called a "Holy Union" certificate, or anything to be recorded.

I never saw them again and never tried to find out who this federal judge might have been.

I didn't even know where they were from, if they were local or not. But that day, I felt privileged to be a witness as people who had been taught to be ashamed and guilty for their deepest love and passion, claimed the goodness of their love before God.

To this day, I think of them and hope their lives were happy, and that the fear of exposure or punishment never diminished their joy.

The Wedding Cake

Sometime in the early 1990s, my wife Paula started volunteering at the Los Angeles Zoo in the chimpanzee exhibit. It was a great source of joy to her. Paula loves every creature great and small. When a baby giraffe broke out of the exhibit, her quick response saved the day!

The poor baby giraffe was all straddle legs and crying for her mama. Paula was able to coax the baby back to her mama to the great relief of visitors and zookeepers alike.

One zookeeper followed up with the giraffe whisperer and learned that Paula's partner was an MCC pastor. It wasn't long before she asked Paula to put her in touch with me to do her wedding.

The zookeeper and her partner were very much in love and had been together for several years. They had a ranch outside of Los Angeles and were country people. The zookeeper had a large extended family, and everyone was pretty cool with her being a lesbian — except her Mom. Mom lived on the ranch with them in a separate house. She barely acknowledged the partner, and this was the only source of strain or unhappiness between them.

The zookeeper decided she wanted a down-home country wedding on her ranch, right out there by the horse corral, with her family and everyone they loved in attendance, with lots of food and barbeque.

She told her Mom, who was upset and horrified. But, this time, she did not give in to her Mom. She set the date. This was a huge step in the dance between them.

Two days before, Mom called and said, "So what kind of cake do you want?"

The zookeeper said, "Thanks Mom!" and told her what they would like. Then they promptly canceled the cake they had already ordered! The partner was a little worried about whether they would really have a cake, but it seemed worth the risk.

When I arrived, things were in full swing, everyone in their cowboy best, looking smart. We had a brief rehearsal, and somewhere in the process, the 5-year-old nephew-ring-bearer-cowboy lost one of the rings in the haystack. We spent about twenty minutes looking for the ring, and a cheer went up when we finally found it.

As we breathed a sigh of relief about the ring, Mom proudly arrived with a huge smile and an enormous cake with both names inside of a big heart. People rushed to help her carry it to its place of honor on the special table. There was not a dry eye among any of the cowboys or cowgirls.

The wedding finally commenced. The wedding party wore matching bandanas, including the zookeeper's best friend, a big, golden retriever. Mom beamed in the front row. No child of hers was going to be married without one of her special cakes!

Our Many Weddings: Let Me Count The Ways

The first time Paula and I got married was in 1978. We had been going together for a year, which, in those days, was a long-term relationship! I was 27 and Paula was 30. Just before we left the house, all dressed in our outfits, Paula looked at us and said, "Wait, I think you are too tall for me!" It took me a long time to discern when she was kidding.

Though I asked her to marry me right away, Paula was skeptical and did not commit right away. She wanted to make sure we had the same values. She was trying to protect herself from being hurt again. And she finally relented.

We got married November 18, but Paula did not invite or even tell her family. She was still a closeted schoolteacher in suburban Detroit and sodomy laws were still on the books in Michigan. Initially, Paula did not want her last name to be on the invitation. Since this was a public wedding, I told her that we would not get married until she was ready to do that.

So, she put her name on the invitation, probably before she was ready. A few months after the ceremony, she was outed at school. Even with all the precautions we took, a student worked at the photo lab where our wedding pictures were developed. Oops.

And, since I was a public figure, one of the few out people in all of Michigan, there was an article about us in the *Detroit Free Press*! In that article, Paula used an alias, and it was only her back that showed in the photo. From the photo angle, I looked like I was marrying Phil, my friend who was my best man. Paula's friend Jackie, her best person, also a schoolteacher, said she could never wear that jacket again (although only her ear and the back of the jacket were showing!).

By the end of that tough school year, Paula resigned, and we moved to California. Only later would she learn that news of her wedding had been forwarded to the Detroit school board, and would have been a huge battle if we had stayed.

On the day of our wedding, a big surprise was that my Uncle Bob, my mother's older brother, came. He came just for the day, helped blow up balloons and welcomed Paula into the family.

We moved to Los Angeles, and Paula was determined never to be in the closet again. She taught as a substitute teacher, got her counseling license and doctoral degree. She re-invented herself. I worked for MCC at our headquarters in Hollywood, and then became pastor of MCC Los Angeles. Paula began a spiritual journey, explored her Jewish roots, and then converted to Judaism.

Eleven years after our marriage in Detroit, we decided to renew our vows after we had been through some difficult times. With insights coming from work with a wonderful couples counselor, we were ready for whatever came next. We were surrounded by friends, including Jackie, who had been at the Detroit service, and brought her daughter Taylor.

A few years later, Rev. Troy Perry, then Moderator of MCC, went national with marriage equality, and did "The Wedding," in front of the IRS building in Washington DC, just prior to the big March on Washington in 1993. Paula stayed home for that one. My cell phone died sometime just before the ceremony started, but I borrowed Rev. Elder Darlene Garner's phone (she was officiating with Troy). Paula was in the rose garden in the backyard of our home in LA, and I was in a crowd of thousands in Washington DC. We listened to the ceremony together and said our vows across 3,000 miles. It was our first long distance wedding!

When Vermont permitted the first civil unions in 2000, we were headed for my family reunion and took a side trip to Vermont. Paula's mother, Marian, joined us for our vows that time.

The most moving part was when we went to the clerk's office. They greeted us so warmly and made us read the new law that permitted same-sex unions in Vermont. Though it didn't count in Florida, where we lived, we still wanted to participate in history.

For decades, along with most LGBTQ people, we said that we didn't need or want a civil union or marriage. That it was "just a piece of paper," and it was our own ceremonies, our own moral commitment, that mattered. We claimed that things that were not available or accessible to us were not important — a defense mechanism we used to cover up the gaping hole in full equality.

Let me be clear — not everyone wants to be married, and I do not believe marriage should be compulsory. Marriage is not the only way to be in right relationship or to be sexual. Freedom is as important as acknowledging difference and diversity in our relational choices.

But in MCC, from the earliest days, we valued marriage and believed that someday marriage would be legal for same sex couples. When Troy Perry founded MCC, it was a "full service church." We did weddings, baptisms, funerals, all of it. That was his original vision of equality.

We now understand that more than 1,000 legal rights accrue automatically to couples who legally marry in the United States. Other countries have different laws but respect goes with marriage in every corner of the planet.

In the early days of MCC, we just lived with the fact that we couldn't be covered by the other person's insurance, or be guaranteed hospital visitation rights, immigration rights, rights of survivorship, rights to adopt each other's children, or even keep custody of our own children. We lived with inequality so long that we accepted that hurt as the price we paid for being out.

Then in 2004, we went to Provincetown, Massachusetts, and were legally married by Rev. Elder Diane Fisher. Paula and I were married very near the exact place the Pilgrims first landed, before they went to Plymouth Rock. As a descendant of one of those Pilgrims, I took great pleasure in celebrating marriage equality there.

This time, Jackie's son, Colin, played the violin for us. For the first time, we called each other "wife," which took some getting used to. Neither of us had ever wanted to be a "wife," but, Paula in particular, insisted that that was the word that was utterly clear when you said it. In the ten years since then, that has proven to be true.

When we returned to Florida, along with ten other couples, we sued the State of Florida and the U.S. Attorney General to recognize our marriage. The case was thrown out at the time, but since then, victory came for marriage equality in the United States and many other countries.

Our five weddings were all important, marking monumental social change. Paula likes to say she did it for the jewelry, but I know better.

One Love in Jamaica

Marriage was not even on the radar in Jamaica when we began a journey in 2005, of reaching out to brothers and sisters there, who were experiencing lethal homophobia, and who needed the spiritual richness of MCC and our mutual commitment to justice.

After a couple years of conversations, Paula and I went to Mandeville, Jamaica, in 2007. Mandeville was the site where an historic funeral had taken place for our local MCC music director who had been brutally murdered just weeks before we arrived.

Our first stop was at the Church of God to thank the pastor for his Christian kindness in doing the funeral. He had risked violence towards himself and his church because he welcomed the mourners. He stood up for decency as our community mourned. He preached the funeral for someone who was "the least of these."

I quickly realized just by stopping by, we might be endangering him. He was not alone and could not speak frankly at all. We invited him to the pastor's gathering we were having in Kingston that week, to help pastors deal with homophobia and violence, but he did not come. He seemed glad to be invited, but grateful we didn't stay long.

Later that evening, Paula and I met with about 25 young gay men at an out of the way place where the MCC group held weekly meetings. We had security with us, but it was sobering to be in a place where so much violence had happened. We marveled at the courage of people to gather as MCC. Every time we heard a car in the driveway, we flinched.

They wanted me to talk about love, they said. So, I talked about the love of God in the Bible.

They had all grown up with the Bible and were very fluent. But, really, they wanted to talk about romantic love: dating, falling in love, recovering from heartbreak, and all the normal things teenagers and young adults cared about. They laughed and giggled. They were embarrassed, and cried. How desperate they were, asking the advice of two, middle-aged white lesbians struggling to remember what dating was like.

We did our best. Then, the conversation switched to loving our enemies. After a few moments of being able to act just like any normal person of their age, now, they had to talk about the violence.

It is hard to describe the depth, maturity, and power of their testimonies about loving their very real enemies, especially the ones in their families and churches. Resurrection and hope were in the house that night.

Later that week, we met with a large group of lesbian couples. Throughout the meeting, people were looking over their shoulders, looking to see if a strange, unfamiliar car came near the building.

They were all young women, and none had been in a relationship for more than two years. They were astonished at how long we had been together — our relationship was older than many of them! They were hungry to talk about in-laws, children, jealousy, and commitment, like any group of couples or lesbian couples.

Though most of the publicity about the horrific violence has been about gay men in Jamaica, we also saw so much suffering from sexism when lesbians were forced to marry heterosexually. Lesbians who were victims of "corrective rape," and in general, lived with fewer options because they were women.

We are still working toward the day when sexual minorities in Jamaica will be treated with respect so that our family there can move beyond survival to a movement of out, proud people.

Wedding Diversities

Frank and Irene were the first heterosexual couple whose wedding I did, in Detroit, in 1976.

One morning, they appeared at the front door of The Methodist Church. Frank was African-American, and Irene was Polish. They said, "We want to get married," and I felt awkward, because I realized they didn't know I was the MCC pastor, not the Methodist pastor.

Then, I felt even more awkward, because I realized they thought my hesitancy was because they were an interracial couple!

I invited them in and said something like, "Apologies, my hesitation was not because you are an interracial couple, but because you are a man and a woman!" More awkwardness.

Then I explained that I was the MCC pastor; that we had a ministry to LGBTQ persons, and all people, of course, but maybe they were looking for the Methodist minister.

"But can you marry us?" they asked.

"Yes, of course," I said.

Then, I asked the question I asked every same-sex couple I counseled for marriage, "How long have you been living together?" More awkward silence.

I realized I had assumed they had been living together, and they might think that their answer would preclude marrying them. I assured them that it was no barrier to being married if they had already been living together, so they quickly said, "Three years."

I responded with, "Why do you want to get married?" Again, silence. This would be a question I would probably ask any couple, but in their world, the heterosexual world, marriage was the assumption. Of course you would want to marry.

They relaxed and said they felt sure they wanted to be together for life and have a family, and both of them had always wanted to be married. Frank had been married before but not Irene. They talked about their families and about how hard this was for them. They knew having biracial children was still a challenge. But they felt strong enough to face whatever would come.

I liked them both and was delighted to perform their wedding. We held it in the chapel, where a huge banner proclaimed, "The Lord is My Shepherd and He Knows I'm Gay!" I didn't even think about taking it down for the occasion, and Frank and Irene did not seem to care.

I did notice some of Frank's family staring at the banner quizzically. Was someone wondering, "Does this mean Frank and Irene are gay?"

I don't think any of Irene's family came. What a shame. The service went beautifully. Frank's family greeted her warmly and even warmed up to me a little bit, gay banners notwithstanding.

For more than 20 years, every year, Irene wrote to me and thanked me for doing their wedding. She wrote about how happy they were and what a great family they were raising. At some point, we lost contact, but I thank God for the opportunity they gave me to participate in their journey.

Maybe *They* Won't Turn Us Down!

Russ and Mary had lived together for 25 years and had not married. Both of them had been married previously, in the Catholic Church. They were both divorced but did not marry. People who met them after they moved to Sarasota just assumed they were married. In some ways, it was their secret.

Mary then got a very serious diagnosis of cancer. She and Russ decided that they should get married, so things would be easier legally. They knew they could not get married in the Catholic Church, but they thought they'd try a couple of other churches in the area.

That morning and early afternoon, they tried three churches, and were turned down by all of them, even after they knew the circumstances! One declined because they were not members of the church; the other two, because they had been living together for 25 years "in sin."

As they were returning home and were about to pass Church of the Trinity MCC, Russ turned suddenly into our driveway.

Mary asked, "Do you know where you are going? And what kind of church this is?"

Russ said, "Yes, and maybe they won't turn us down!"

They came into the office, and when Paul, our administrative assistant, greeted them, he could tell they were agitated and a little upset. That always made Paul a little nervous. So, he quickly knocked on my door, and I welcomed them into my office.

They poured out their hearts and told me their story. I assured them that they had come to the right place, if not the expected place, and that I would be honored to marry them. I understood completely why they had not married, and why they wanted to be married now. No judgment.

We scheduled the wedding for a week later. Russ surprised Mary by inviting her three sons. They were big guys, very heterosexual, and a little confused or amused, I guess, by their choice of a church and a pastor to do the wedding. Mary was delighted they were there but admonished them to reign in their homophobia or any hint of rudeness.

When I met them, they were models of civility and very quiet and respectful, even a little meek.

The church was beautifully decorated for Christmas. Someone from MCC took photos for them. We provided a couple of witnesses, and with the sons, it was a beautiful and emotional wedding.

I kept in touch with Russ and Mary for almost a year, and then Mary died. Russ came to Wednesday night dinners for a few months. It was a place he could get some home cooking and be around people. He was not a church person, but he felt support just being around us.

Church members helped him clean out Mary's closet and found a place to donate her clothes. Eventually, he moved away to be closer to his daughter.

I will always be grateful that Russ turned into our driveway that day and took a chance on us.

Cruising Towards Marriage Equality 2004

Just after our wedding in Provincetown, Massachusetts, in 2004, we hopped on a ship with over a thousand lesbians on an Olivia tour. Originally, hundreds of couples were expecting to be married before the ship sailed, but there was some legal controversy over whether out-of-state weddings could be performed. Olivia's management decided to be cautious about it, and many were disappointed as we set sail.

They decided to have an onboard commitment ceremony anyway, without legal marriage. The director of the tour found out I was on the cruise, and asked me to perform the mass ceremony. I was introduced as the "Pope" of the LGBTQ community, as leader of the Metropolitan Community Church.

The tour leaders were nervous. Many lesbians on the cruise would not identify as religious, certainly not as Christian, and they were not convinced I would be sensitive to that even with reassurances.

All their fears were allayed as the service unfolded. I followed Rev. Perry's model from 1993, wore a clerical collar, but did a totally non-denominational, inter-faith service. I spoke of our act of marrying each other as an act of resistance, there, on the high seas, where laws did not apply. I asked them to say their vows to each other which was so moving to watch.

The cruise directors had not thought to issue a certificate of any kind, but everyone got a simple sheet of paper with the invitation to the wedding on it. Women rushed to the stage and asked me to sign it after the ceremony.

They had to set up a separate room, and I sat there for over an hour, as hundreds of people waited in line. I wrote both names on the piece of paper, dated it, and signed my name. Very sophisticated women, mostly not religious, were teary and thrilled that Olivia had asked "a real clergyperson" to do the wedding. That made me chuckle to think about how many times my legitimacy as a "real clergyperson" had been questioned. Many couples were eager to tell me the story of how they met and how long they had been together.

I took my time with each couple, taking it as seriously as they did. It was a huge moment for many of them, and I felt like I had the privilege of redeeming the disappointment for the time being. The intensity of the hunger for marriage equality, and for some kind of spiritual sanction, some kind of elevating of the experience, was palpable and ran deep — even among people who would not be caught in church!

The Wedding Whisperer

Joan was referred to me by someone who attended MCC Los Angeles. She had a long tale of marital woes including divorce, and being left at the altar several times. Now, she wanted to marry her best friend, a bisexual man, who had asked her to marry him before, but for one reason or another, over the years, they had both chickened out.

I was probably in my late 30s, and they were in their 50s. Don's previous relationships with men and women hadn't been particularly happy or successful.

We talked together for several months. Over that time, I became convinced that, in a certain way, they were made for each other and could offer a life that would give them both happiness.

I never met people who had more wedding jitters, but they made it. They had a beautiful wedding in their home in the Hollywood Hills with family on both sides attending.

Joan called me about a year later, and I worried what it might be about. She said her sister loved the wedding so much she wanted me to do hers. She also had a tale of woe but felt like this man "was the one." And, she was sure no priest or minister other than one from MCC would take a chance on her next wedding.

I married her to her third husband.

A year later, another call came from Joan, this time for her other sister!

I had become the "Wedding Whisperer" for their family. So, delighted, I met this couple as well who also had their stories of woe and complications. Charmed by them, I did their wedding also.

In the decades since then, besides family weddings, most of the heterosexual weddings I did included special circumstances, multiple divorces, interracial, interfaith, and other complications. For people who still wanted a spiritual presence, a clergyperson to do their wedding, I was often the safe choice, referred by an MCC member or a gay friend.

David and Bill's Wedding

At the 40th anniversary party for MCC Detroit, someone showed me a picture from the early days of MCC and of the out LGBTQ community in Detroit. I had a shock of joy and grief in seeing it, and have spent some time thinking about why.

The picture is taken at the end of the holy union (wedding) service for David Krumroy and Bill Leavens. I'm behind them, in clerical robes, smiling. They had a big wedding, lots of family and friends from both sides — unusual for 1977.

It was the third week of November. I remember it, because, my wife Paula and I had just met a month or so before, and this was our first public date, a wedding I was doing for friends and members of the church. I even asked Paula to marry me after this inspiring event. She said, "Don't be silly, I hardly know you!" She was so sensible, unlike other lesbians of the U-Haul generation. When we found someone to love, renting a U-Haul and moving happened in lieu of a second date!

Paula's careful consideration made me want to marry her all the more!

I love this picture because of how happy David and Bill look. David appears triumphant, in fact, like he could break out in song or speech! He was proud, and so grateful. I love their matching tuxes with colorful piping which still reminds me it was the 70s! I love the big bow ties. Bill was grasping David's hand, shyly smiling, while carefully negotiating the steps of the chancel. I love how they are both frozen in time, and yet in motion, moving into a new level of commitment. A metaphor for how we were all feeling about our young, vibrant, courageous movement. It is a moment of joy, and maybe a little relief, as the ceremony ends and the party begins.

David had been radicalized the year before. He was arrested in a sting operation, in a series of arrests and entrapments by the Detroit police. They had apprehended scores of men in Hines Park for soliciting. It was very public, and it ruined lives back in 1976. And, it was farcical at times.

One case involved a man who was deaf and mute, and the officer insisted that he speak to him! There were suicides and suicide attempts; people lost jobs and family and were publicly humiliated. Humiliation was David's first response to being outed in this way, but then he got angry, very angry.

And, then he got political.

He started a newspaper, *Metro Gay News*. He became a powerful, respected editor and influencer and became even more political when he founded a statewide LGBTQ rights organization, MOHR (Michigan Organization for Human Rights).

As a member of MCC Detroit, David was a friend, confidante, and fellow-activist during a difficult and challenging couple of years. I depended on him, and, I think, he on me. We were very young leaders in our 20s, and aspiring grown-ups in a community that needed both.

He met Bill, a quiet, handsome man, at church. They fell in love, and I had the joy of marrying them, just as I was also finding the love of my life.

Paula and I moved to Los Angeles, and David and Bill to Chicago. We kept in touch over the years. David and Bill eventually both tested positive for HIV. David died in early 1989, and I had the honor of celebrating his memorial service. Bill was not well and asked me if I would do his service as well. This was in a time before protease inhibitors, when AIDS was a death sentence.

I was at MCC's General Conference in Minneapolis in the summer of 1989, when I got word that Bill had died. We tried but could not find a date when I could come to Chicago to do the service which also worked for the family. I always regretted that we could not make it work. That was the nature of things in those days — we went from funeral to funeral, hospital room to hospital room, and sometimes ran out of time, energy or options.

I can recall, painfully, how exhausted I was, how conflicted about saying no. Someone else, I have no idea who, presided at Bill's memorial. In seeing this picture, I am moved to ask his forgiveness, all these years later. I wish it had been me, to complete the circle.

I love this picture because I have a visceral memory of being that young and, yet, feeling a sense of destiny about what we were up to together.

Finally, I love this picture, because it was a special, hallowed time, a time of great liberation, coming out, of hope. It was before we were overwhelmed and challenged, in every way, by AIDS. Sometimes it is hard to remember that there was such a time. We believed we could change the world, and we did.

David and Bill would have been thrilled about marriage equality, and all the amazing progress we have made. David would still be angry that marriage equality was not the reality everywhere in the world, I am sure. Bill would have been quietly supporting his brave, activist husband.

As Paula and I celebrate many decades of married life, I think about their lives and marriage cut short, and how fortunate we are.

May their memory be for a blessing!

A Ukrainian Wedding: We Want It!

Rev. Jim Mulcahy was a Jesuit priest who, as a young man, served in the Middle East and Eastern Europe. In his later years, he came out as a gay man and became a minister in MCC.

He was interested in our work in Eastern Europe. He lived and worked in Ukraine with Orthodox priests who were coming out, some of whom sought to become MCC clergy, leading communities of faith.

Jim said he was just called to love people wherever he went. He sought orders in the Orthodox Church and received them. To this day, he brings his Jesuit, MCC, and Orthodox vocation to the people he serves. Jim offers Orthodox confession to those who have not felt like they could safely confess for years, something so essential in their religious culture.

He counsels, listens, prays and teaches, and leads retreats.

In addition, he is an activist in his own right, though most of the work is behind the scenes.

One year, Jim attended a Pride celebration in a city in Ukraine, and it turned violent. After the event, he performed the wedding for two lesbians. About sixty people showed up at the wedding. Many of them were traumatized by the violence at the pride event, but also excited to participate in a lesbian wedding conducted by a priest!

Jim longed to offer communion, an inclusive MCC communion to all those attending the wedding, but he did not want to offend those who were from an Orthodox background. So, he explained the idea of an open communion, and said, "But you only have to receive it if you want to."

From the back of the hall came the voice of a woman, "We want it! We want it!" Then, everyone started chanting, "We want it. We want it!"

There was hardly a dry eye as Jim said the familiar words of consecration, and everyone streamed forward to receive that amazing gift of being included in the Body of Christ.

My Cousin's Catholic Wedding

I grew up with dozens of first cousins, but one of my closest cousins was Peg who was four years older than me. I was the maid of honor at her wedding. She married a man with two sons, and then had a third son with him. Later, her middle son came out as gay. Peg, a lawyer and an active lay leader in the United Church of Christ, accepted him.

Her youngest son, Joe, fell in love with a woman from New Hampshire who was from a large, French Canadian, Catholic family. When they decided to get married, they asked her two Catholic priest brothers to officiate. And, then they asked me to officiate with them, as well. Joe wanted the minister in his family to be a part of this important day in their lives.

This was a first for me. I grew up in a Catholic neighborhood before Vatican II. We were very segregated, and as a Protestant, even showing up at a Catholic service was frowned upon from all sides. When my mother's youngest brother married a Catholic woman, they had to do the wedding on the "floor," not up on the chancel near the altar. He had to agree to raise his kids Catholic. They later all became Episcopalians.

At the wedding rehearsal, I met the first brother, a very tall, handsome man who looked much better in his robes than I did in mine! He was so hospitable and easy going. He suggested that I do the blessing of the rings, with the altar boy assisting, and that I give the benediction. He and his brother would divide up the other parts.

When it came to communion, he wanted me to stand with them at the table, and told me I was welcome to receive communion. He knew that it might upset some of the older folks in the church, but it was my choice. I told him I did not need to take communion, and that I did not want to do anything to upset anyone (although, truthfully, just having a clergywoman on the altar, helping do the wedding might seem upsetting enough!).

At the actual wedding, he introduced me said I was the leader of Metropolitan Community Churches. Now, I am sure most did not know what that was, but still, I thought it was very generous.

I sang the benediction, and Joe and Denise were very touched. My family was thrilled that I was participating. I had to pinch myself to even take in that local Catholic churches and priests were this open.

Both of Denise's brothers eventually left the priesthood, a great loss for the Catholic Church. I hope the openness we experienced does not leave with men like them.

I thought of them, years later, when my administrative assistant, and friend, Connie, lost her partner. The service was held in the Catholic Church to which Hilde was deeply committed. At the memorial mass, the priest acknowledged Connie as her partner, and had her do a blessing of the ashes reserved for husbands and wives, ordinarily. He talked about Hilde's support of Connie and her work with MCC. He acknowledged my presence. It was remarkable.

These encouraging occurrences were more and more frequent, which was why the Vatican's new efforts at changing their tone about LGBTQ people were long overdue and welcomed in many Catholic parishes. People were hungry for generosity and inclusion. Younger people like Joe and Denise expected it.

Thanksgiving for Forty Years

Connie and Eva met at Marlene Dietrich's lesbian bar in 1932 in Berlin. Connie, an African American, was a student at Columbia University, and was in Europe studying in the early 1930s. Eva was fifteen years her senior and had been the lover of a baroness who had been fifteen years older than her.

Together, they traveled by train to Russia and fell in love.

They came to me on Thanksgiving in 1972, forty years after they first met, and wanted to talk to me. The Thanksgiving Day service was a little later, so I took the time to meet with them.

Eva told me she had lived a very privileged life, including gambling at Monte Carlo. Somehow, they both ended up in Berlin that fateful night in 1932 and fell in love. Germany was quickly coming under the thrall of Nazi Socialism whose minions not only killed millions of Jews but untold numbers of lesbians and gay men, disabled people, gypsies, and resistors.

When the war started, Connie had to return to the United States without Eva, and they were separated for nine years.

As I listened to their story of separation, they told me that they were both completely faithful to each other the whole time and winked. As a 22- year-old, very new to gay life, much less gay life in the 1930s, I remember being quite shocked by their humor and candor.

Finally, Eva was able to emigrate to the U.S. They bought a house together in conservative Woburn, Massachusetts, where they lived as "Mrs. Eva Winne and her maid Connie," through the 1950s and 60s.

I asked them how they found MCC on Thanksgiving Day? It turned out that they read a little article, probably by me, in the Daughters of Bilitis magazine (an early lesbian publication). The article was about Metropolitan Community Church starting in Boston and about our Thanksgiving service and dinner.

The service started not long after our long conversation. Although they did not marry that day, for the first time, they knelt at the altar together and took communion as the lovers and friends they had been for 40 years.

As I got to know them, Eva expressed worries about fascism in the United States and homophobia. She confided that she was an agnostic, but came to church for Connie who was a person of faith.

When they were asked how they had stayed together so long, they had many different answers. Really, I am not sure they knew, except they said it was not easy. They usually had a twinkle in their eyes which contained many secrets and stories, most of which we will never know.

I am not sure what they would have thought of marriage equality; it may have seemed too bourgeois for them or too unimaginable — or both.

They were messengers to us, in 1972, of an earlier era over 80 years ago, during which the openness of the German society to sexual minorities blossomed and then quickly shut down. A reminder to be vigilant in the struggle for human rights and to not take anything for granted.

For me, they were a gift. I can see them, kneeling there in all their differences, holding hands in that small chapel, out and proud, and giving thanks.

Breaking into the Wedding Chapel at New York City Hall (thanks to Mel Bryant)

For decades, MCC members around the world joined Rev. Troy Perry in Valentine's Day Actions. We would go to the local Clerk or Justice of the Peace, as same-sex couples, dramatically ask for a marriage license, and just as dramatically be turned down. Sometimes we would also take action on April 15, U.S. tax-filing deadline day. We were tax-payers, we have rights! The press was always invited, and if it was a slow news day, they would show up, film us being turned down, and film our picket lines. It was a good local story.

One very, very cold Valentine's Day in 2005, same-sex couples from MCC New York made their way to the New York City Clerk's office in Manhattan, once again, to request a marriage license. They knew they would be denied — AGAIN!

Very few people then had any idea that marriage equality was just around the corner. Some press was there, and they respectfully asked if they could follow the marriage petitioners. Mel and Bradley went first. After requesting an application for the license, the clerk handed them a prepared statement while she read it. Basically, it said that in the State of New York, they could not be legally wed. Not a surprise, but always infuriating to hear.

In other words, they were second-class citizens. Their lives and loves did not matter. The more than 1,000 protections afforded to heterosexual couples were not afforded to them. Other same-sex couples, mostly from MCC New York, were lined up to ask for a license. Then an opportunity came. Someone noticed that the armed guard protecting the chapel at City Hall was not there, and the door was wide open! Mary Jane Gibney, Rev. Pat Bumgardner's spouse, had been prepared for this moment. Earlier, Rev. Pat had told her, that if they got the chance, they would storm the chapel at City Hall. As the County Clerk's assistant droned on, the chapel suddenly seemed unguarded. Mary Jane seized the moment and shouted, "Let's Go Queers!" They took the chapel and locked the door behind them.

Everyone was a little stunned. Just then, Rev. Pat shed her black cape and underneath she was wearing full clergy vestments! With all eyes locked on her, Rev. Pat powered through the first set of vows as fast as she could. They all wondered what would be next. Arrest? Jail? Our folks kept letting people into the chapel, and locking the door. They heard a commotion behind them, but Rev. Pat kept going, never stopping and never looking away from the couple she was marrying.

As it turned out, the guard and staff had to search for the keys which gave Rev. Pat time to perform two ceremonies: one for Bradley and Mel, and one for Gerard and Angel. Someone finally got in and said "You shouldn't be here!" They shouted, "The Clerk is on his way!"

But when the Clerk arrived, he said that we were to be left alone to finish.

With a nod towards Rev. Pat, he said to one of the MCC members, "She sure is persistent, that one." That kind of lightened up the atmosphere as fears of jail or arrest subsided. Persistence was the word of the day. The dam broke, and many same-sex couples, without a license, had their vows blessed by Rev. Pat that Valentine's Day in the City Hall chapel. What no one realized then was that it was the first time any ordained clergy performed a marriage ceremony in that space, gay or straight! Rules and traditions were broken that day. It was part of our MCC vocation.

The very day marriage equality came at last to New York State, Rev. Pat performed legal marriages for Mel and Bradley; and for Gerard and Angel who were married, once more, but this time in the middle of Times Square!

Funny Wedding Stories

Not all MCC stories about weddings are dramatic, serious, or poignant; some are also just funny and sweet.

In the days before Viagra commercials were on prime time television, even before *Will and Grace,* information about heterosexual sex, gay sex, or any kind of safe sex was not very visible or available. Those were the days in which, early in the AIDS crisis, young men who had never married did not think they needed to know about condoms. They had to be taught to use one. MCC pastors had to be sex educators and then HIV prevention experts.

As a life-long lesbian, I had little use for such information. But, as a pastor to gay men, I had to learn. I actually went to a workshop where I learned to roll a condom onto a banana. Then I had to make sure I had fresh bananas and condoms in my office, so I could help the guys who were too young or too shy to ask.

I routinely asked them if they were practicing safe sex, told them not to lie to me, and asked them if they knew how to use a condom. Most of the time they had no idea what I was talking about. I would demonstrate on the banana, and then hand them a bunch of condoms.

Then, there was Greg, who was developmentally disabled and sexually active at age nineteen. After my demonstration, he kept looking at me and the banana. He was hungry, it turned out. Sure, have the banana, without the condom.

Sometime in the late 1980s, two very young, very effeminate Latino men (boys, really, maybe in their late teens) came to see me to get married.

For them, as for many people just coming out, there was still a lot of misunderstanding and mystery about LGBTQ sexuality, gender, and roles. The LGBTQ lexicon was early in its development, as we moved beyond code words such as "are you a friend of Dorothy?"

The more vocal of the two was very feminine in presentation and said he was troubled by one thing: he was afraid he was bisexual.

Hmmm. Bisexual? I had my doubts. But, as I would come to learn, anything was possible.

So, I asked, "What do you mean by bisexual?"

Since he did not have the words, he made a gesture, and put his hands together, flatly, and turned them one way, and then another. Amazingly, I got it.

"You mean that you and your beloved exchange roles? Sometimes one is on top, other times, you are on top. Is that what you mean?" cutting to the chase.

"Yes! That's what I mean!" he said.

"Well, that's not what bisexual means," I said, and proceeded to explain.

When he realized what bisexual meant, he used both of those same hands to cover his mouth in horror.

"Oh no, Reverend, I am most surely not that!"

Not surprised.

The first month I started serving as pastor at MCC Detroit, my predecessor told me about a couple he was counseling for a holy union. They had one more counseling session scheduled before their ceremony. They hoped to get married in the next month, so I called and met with them for their final session. I made sure everything was prepared.

The day came for the wedding, and the man who had been the primary contact showed up with a different man to marry! Like I wouldn't notice! Not so fast! We went back to the drawing board.

Pastoring the Lost and Found

As a pastor, my role in leading a church is to help create a place where people who are lost can find themselves. A place where they can find peace, identity, strength, and courage to come out. Over the years I have heard myriad coming out stories emerging from the diversity of people's lives.

While MCC churches, as part of a larger movement, are about shaking up the status quo, fighting for justice and human rights, we are also about welcoming the outcast. We see this as a matter of justice as well. We are a church full of prodigals; people who never thought they would ever again belong or become part of a church community.

People in these stories were lost physically, emotionally, and spiritually. They found sanctuary and healing in a place that was also a force for radical change in the world.

And A Little Dog Will Lead Them

For decades, MCC Los Angeles had moved from place to place. In the early days, bigotry caused the fledgling church to move every couple of weeks. They moved from Rev. Perry's home, to a women's club, to a theater, and many other places.

Then, a fire destroyed the first building, and they were on the move again.

When I was pastor, we sold an old, huge theater in downtown LA, next to a porno theater. The neighborhood was challenging; we couldn't hold events at night for fear of cars being stolen. It needed earthquake proofing for millions of dollars. And, it was no longer in proximity to gay-friendly neighborhoods.

We moved into Culver City, more or less on the west side of LA, into a building that had been a chicken restaurant, a roller rink, and a furniture store.

When we moved there, we moved very close to where Pam lived. Pam was a lesbian but very closeted. She was a person of many lives and secrets who struggled to live spiritually whole and free. She heard that MCC had moved into her neighborhood and was curious. She walked her dog by the church, and when they got near the parking lot, the dog just sat down.

She tried to get him to move, but he would not. Becky, a lay person, saw Pam and rushed over to her, introducing herself, while Pam was pulling on the dog's leash, desperately trying to move on.

The dog decided to lay down. Becky rushed to my office and got me to come out to the parking lot. She introduced me to Pam as well.

"Hi, I am Rev. Nancy. Do you live around here?"

"Yeah, I was walking Misty when he just stopped moving. His real name is Artemus, but I call him Misty."

Pam was sweating and occasionally pulling on her dog's leash. By this time Misty was napping on the sidewalk and wouldn't budge.

"We would like you come to our church."

She looked panicked and stammered something.

At last, Misty dog got up. Pam seemed to be in agony and I learned later that she felt like she had just promised a preacher she would show up at church, and she didn't want to lie to a preacher!

She kept her promise, reluctantly, and came to church. A whole new chapter began for her, as she opened her life to community, love, hope, and healing.

Pam got involved right away in ushering.

Early on, a tall, man with a greying beard would come in just before church started at 9AM. As Pam handed him a bulletin one Sunday, she asked him if he was new. He just smiled and said, "No." Two weeks later, while taking the membership class and watching a film on the history of MCC, she suddenly realized that the man was none other than the Rev. Troy Perry, Founder of MCC.

Praise Jesus!

Stuart Bermudez was a petite, bleach-blonde gay man who came to MCC with a couple of close friends and lovers. When he came, he was probably already ill with HIV, but he did not make a big deal about it.

He had a campy sense of humor.

"Oh my God! (Sorry pastor!) I have the worst time keeping my roots dyed. Blonds do NOT have more fun! We have to work at it!"

Stuart came to church almost every Sunday, but he didn't come to other church activities.

I am not even sure how he supported himself. He did not seem to have any money, means, or a job. He may have already been on Social Security. As he became sick, it seemed to me that some of his friends just disappeared.

He had AIDS Dementia, something that was common at that time. We just incorporated dementia into our community life and consciousness in those days.

Stuart came to the Thanksgiving Interfaith Service that year, and sat in the front row. The Rabbi of one of the gay-friendly synagogues was preaching, and Stuart, oblivious to interfaith etiquette, really loved the sermon and frequently shouted, "Praise Jesus!"

Thankfully, no one minded, including the Rabbi, who knew what was going on. There were congregants at his synagogue struggling with the same issues.

Several months later, we noticed that we had not seen Stuart in a couple of weeks, and efforts to contact him at home failed. In fact, he was no longer there at all. I spent time calling hospitals and the hospice facility, to no avail.

One day, while visiting County Hospital in downtown LA, a huge, cavernous, teaching hospital with lots of HIV/AIDS patients, I thought that it just might be possible that he was lost in that place. My last stop was the pulmonary ward, and there he was in an intensive care kind of place, in a room with lots of nurses and doctors. He was dripping with fever, flushed, and struggling for breath.

I walked into the room. He saw me and began to flail and get very agitated. The nurses tried to throw me out, but I said, "NO! He is just happy to see me," and I pushed passed them and touched him.

He instantly calmed down, tears streaming down his face. He immediately began to breathe better, which made the medical staff happier with my presence. I just stood there, stroking his face and touching his hand, so grateful to see him, alive and fighting for his life.

Stuart lived long enough to get out of the hospital and into a good hospice, where he was often the one who made people laugh.

When he died, the hospice called me, and let me know that Stuart had generously left his church family about $600, whatever was in his account. That money helped us pay the mortgage that month, and we would have been hard-pressed without it. I am amazed he even had $600.

Mostly, when I remember him, I remember that powerful moment of connection, of recognition in that awful moment when he could not breathe, and when no one on earth knew where he was.

Words fail to describe what it meant to me to find him, and for him to be found.

It May as Well Have Been a Million

Frank was a homeless man who lived in and around MCC Los Angeles when we were in Culver City, in the late 1980s and early 1990s. He panhandled, but in the most humble and unobtrusive ways. He became our unofficial night watchman at the church for years, letting us know if a window was broken, or a door was ajar, or if someone was hanging around who was up to no good. This was his territory, and he guarded it, including the church.

Once I took him for a meal at the McDonald's across the street. It was too much for him, I realized. He wasn't used to lunchtime conversation and was humoring me, for sure. He did tell me, though, that he had been a churchgoer, as a younger person. He was from Texas. That was about it. That was all he was giving up that day.

When the Culver City church building collapsed in the earthquake of 1994, it not only impacted our church family but also those in our neighborhood.

Hundreds of people went in and out of that church every week. They depended on the gas station across the street, restaurants, and other vendors. Many others came by, as well, looking to us for help, for community, for food, for prayer.

Frank was one of those. When we all came back to say goodbye to the sanctuary, before they tore it down completely, I didn't see him at first. I was praying an opening prayer and felt a hand on my shoulder. When I turned around, it was him. It was the first and only time he had ever touched me.

I had been keeping it together just fine — until that moment. I felt his loss, and then I felt mine. His gesture made the moment even more poignant and overwhelming. Those were tough days of frequent loss from HIV/AIDS; other losses on top of that were really hard to feel and absorb.

As it turned out, we stayed on the property a while longer. We worshipped elsewhere, but since we were still paying a mortgage on that property, and still trying to decide whether to rebuild, we put up a trailer in the parking lot and used it as our offices and small meeting/classrooms.

One night, I was locking up after a very difficult day. I am not even sure what made it so awful — there were so many things. We were having a hard time financially. I am not sure how we really survived it. Every day, I had to look out from the trailer and see the flattened remains of the building we had lovingly built. On top of that, our leadership — every one of us — was stressed to the max. Something challenging, unexpected, and often discouraging happened every day.

In the long night of the Reagan and Bush presidencies, civil rights seemed to be stalled. Marriage equality was a far off dream.

Clergy have days like this, times like this, just like everyone else. It feels like you are up against the impossible. God seems silent, inaccessible, or, frankly, irreverently, just a tad useless.

As I was locking up, I saw Frank approaching me. And, I have to say, my first internal response was not good or generous. I felt irritated, that he might be coming over to ask me for money. It was not that I did not have a few dollars. The truth was I had nothing to give emotionally or morally at that moment and resented even the anticipation of being asked to give when I felt like I could not.

Just as I was about to say something, he stopped me. He smiled a really big smile. I had never seen him smile like this.

He said, "Um, I really had a great day today, I wanted you to know that. And, I also wanted to share this with you and the church."

He handed me five dollars. My jaw kind of dropped, and I took the bill from him. It may as well have been a million dollars. I was humbled, embarrassed, and touched, all at once. I thanked him profusely. Whether it was or not, it felt like a sign from a good God that all would be well, despite my exhaustion, fear, and despair.

I didn't ask him for any details about his really good day. Sometimes I wish I had. The church moved shortly after that, for good, and I never saw Frank again.

Sometimes, though, in times of discouragement, I can still feel his hand on my shoulder or see that smile and the five dollar bill in his hand.

You Made My Christmas

For many years, our HIV/AIDS visitation team would meet after morning services on Sunday and split up into groups to visit various hospices. We visited some of our own members, and those we did not know, many of whom had no other visitors.

We also did this on holidays, especially Christmas Eve and Christmas Day. One Christmas Day, we visited several hospices, and had some particularly intense encounters and conversations. One person died while we were there. We spent time with another person's family.

No other church group visited many of these places at all, much less on Christmas. When priests and pastors refused to show up for last rights or final prayers, we were there, as soon as we could get there. More than any other place, we knew we were needed.

We all met up afterwards at the restaurant that was a community favorite in West Hollywood. There were times I spent all day there meeting with people. It was a church joke that if you needed to see someone or to get in touch with them, just hang out at that restaurant for 48 hours, and you would find them!

We were tired, but it felt good to share our experiences and stories, laugh, and let off some steam about what we had been able to do that day. Some of our team had Christmas plans for later; for others, this was their Christmas plan.

As we were nearing the end of our meal, a man came up to us and said, "I don't know who you people are, or what you have been doing today, but I was so touched by the way you were enjoying each other. I have been alone today, but just being near you made me feel much less alone. Really, you made my Christmas, and I want you to know I have paid for your meal."

We were stunned. One of us, I am not sure who, followed him out the door to thank him again, explain a little, and even invite him to church. But I am not sure I ever saw him there. It made us feel good that day, about our ministry, our witness, even to people who didn't know why we had the joy we had. Who would have thought, as giddy as we were, that we had spent a day in a place that few wanted to visit.

Garret, a deacon in the church, who was there that day, used this story as he consecrated communion several weeks later. He said that Jesus, like the man we met, had already paid for our communion meal, and that we had the great privilege, if we would only say yes, to really make God's day.

Tie a Yellow Ribbon

I am writing this story about Jim Harris, because no one else will.

Jim came into MCC in the early 1970s. He had a Southern Baptist background and had grown up in Texas or thereabouts. He had been a truck driver, among other things, before coming out and into MCC ministry.

Jim had a big personality, and his ego seemed unchecked. When I served on his ordination interview team in 1976, I expressed some doubts and mentioned that he was controversial.

That was actually a euphemism. He had a reputation in Dallas for bar fights and a bad temper. He was not very tolerant of feminists like me. In response to my comment that he was controversial, he said, "So was Jesus Christ!"

Did I mention he was humble, as well?

Jim easily fit in the 1970s frontier-style, anything-goes MCC clergy stereotype that was sometimes well-earned. He was a cowboy who did manage to grow the church in Dallas, as he said himself, one drag show at a time, one spaghetti dinner at a time. And, apparently, one bar room brawl at a time!

No surprise, Jim was authoritarian in his management style. There was some kind of blow up in Dallas, and he ended up in MCC in St. Louis for a while.

Then, Jim dropped out and got lost, as the 1980s progressed. I lost track of him. Homeless and jobless, he came to live with friends in Los Angeles.

Then, the story takes a weird, awful turn. Jim robbed a bank.

It was such a cowboy thing to do, and he was really bad at it. He apparently either left his checkbook on the counter, and/or the exploding dye pack in the money blew up all over him and his car. He was arrested almost immediately.

He did not have a gun, but faked having a gun. Of course, this could have gotten him or others killed.

His friends said he was despondent, could not find work, including a pastorate. He had a bad drinking problem. So robbing a bank seemed to make sense to him. It sounded like the kind of macho stunt Jim would try to pull. My judgmentalism was in full swing.

Jim pled guilty, and went to federal prison.

There he was diagnosed with AIDS. His health was deteriorating, and he was a broken, beaten man, only in his 50s.

At the time, I worked fulltime for MCC at our headquarters in Los Angeles, as the Clerk of MCC with administrative duties. The budget did not include a secretary for me. In a time before computers, we just used typewriters, reel-to-reel answering machines, and filing cabinets. I had not had any office help for five years, and really didn't think that would ever happen.

One day, Troy came into my office and told me he had mostly good news — I was going to get a secretary!

What? Wow, I was already thinking of the kind of person I would hire. Then, I realized, oops, there had to be a catch.

There was.

Troy had been speaking to the chaplain at the federal prison. They did not think Jim would survive in prison, but if he had a job guarantee, they did not think he really posed a threat to anyone. Really?

Would I mind if Jim came to work for me? Oh brother!

I knew Troy was right about Jim not surviving. I was just not sure I could survive being his supervisor and babysitter.

Could Jim type? I doubt it.

A week later, Jim Harris came to my office for his first day. This time he was really humbled, looking old, and beaten. No swagger.

Something about the sight of him, the change in him, touched me. I had worked a lot with men and women in prison. In our country, prison is the lowest of the low. Many people never recover from being in prison. They die there or die sooner when they get out.

AIDS was still a death sentence then. I felt a compassion I was not really prepared to feel. I was doing this because Troy asked me. But now, confronted with someone in Jim's shoes, I looked at him and told him I was glad to see him and hoped we could work together.

Jim teared up and thanked me, and said he would do his best to help me. We both started crying. And, something odd happened. All of the past just sort of dissolved. Something, a friendship, an understanding, was born.

Later, Jim would quip and say that when they offered him the choice of staying in federal prison and working for Nancy Wilson, he asked if he could have a day to think about it!! He had his views about me to overcome as well.

Jim came to work every day and did my filing. He didn't type; he didn't really even have a desk. He was very helpful in a lot of ways. He made himself surprisingly useful. He was grateful, and caused no trouble. And, I was grateful, too. We got to know each other.

A month later, my goddaughter who was four, whose mother was in prison, ended up living with us for a while, and I had no daycare. She took a shine to Jim, and he would take her to MacDonald's for me and help me keep her entertained at my office. I would look at them, walking down the street, this child of a felon, walking hand in hand with this big truck driver-minister-ex-felon with a bald head, bushy mustache, earring, baseball cap, faded jeans and cowboy boots and shake my head.

Six months later, I became pastor of MCC Los Angeles, and Jim told me he wanted to come with me as a volunteer staff pastor. Now, that may sound incredible, but Jim had only received a suspension of his credentials, and they got restored. That would never happen today to someone convicted of a felony, but these were different times. We were still an outlaw church to some degree. We didn't follow all the rules of risk management that we follow today, sometimes for better, sometimes for worse, believe me.

Jim found a day job and volunteered for me for several years at MCC Los Angeles.

Jim had skills I needed in that very broken church. We were meeting in a building in downtown Los Angeles located in a very challenging neighborhood. He could still sport the cowboy/truckdriver "don't f___ with me" image.

And, they didn't. Jim was very good with the crowd of younger men who attended the church and lived in downtown area hotels, many of whom were disabled and indigent. They came to the church for food and company and had lots of issues — issues that Jim understood.

Jim still drank, but I never saw him drunk. I could call him any hour, day or night, and he would rescue someone, or be there when the cops showed up. He could sound reasonable and competent. He could handle weddings and funerals. He cleaned up well enough to do that in his collar and vestments.

He would preach for me sometimes, when I was away on MCC denominational business. He preached simple, Baptist sermons, Jesus saves, with a good story or two. I could count on one or two letters from people who would think he had crossed a line somewhere, but nothing horrible. He could run the service competently, and people minded him.

He would consecrate communion using that schmaltzy song "Tie A Yellow Ribbon." He talked about having been in prison and being welcomed home, how all are welcome. There wasn't a dry eye.

Jim eventually ran an adult group home for men with severe developmental disabilities. How the hell the state of California allowed a convicted felon to do that is beyond me. I guess they were as desperate as I was!

He was kind to those very vulnerable men. On Sundays he would bring as many as he could fit in a van to church. One of the men played hymns on the piano and sometimes played during communion. Jim would be proud, and, in tears, say, "Those boys need Jesus too!" In those days, in downtown Los Angeles, where attendance was a challenge, I didn't mind him filling up a back row.

Jim said that he taught me to curse, and I taught him to love Jesus. That is untrue on both counts. I already knew how to curse, and he knew Jesus well before he knew me, before I was born. He just got a kick out of saying stuff like that, burnishing his tough-guy image.

He won over my wife Paula in a few ways. He lived not too far from us, and every once in a while, he would knock on our door and leave a peach cobbler, still warm, on the doorstep. He never wanted to intrude. He could be so gentlemanly, even courtly, at times. Paula also knew that I could count on him, in many ways that others might not easily understand.

When Paula's mother, Marian, started coming to Los Angeles in the mid-1980s, after Paula's Dad died, Jim would sometimes provide transportation. He was very kind to her, but also a little mischievous. He loved telling the story that he brought her to her first gay bar, "Mr. Mike's," in our neighborhood.

It was late afternoon, and there were not enough folks in the bar for her to know that it was gay, but he loved teasing her about it. I remember her asking, "Is Mr. Mike's really a gay bar?" Yes, a very boring one, but, yes.

Truthfully, Jim was easy to work with, to have on staff. But, he started to get sick, and really didn't want me to know. He said that now that he was doing better, and was able to function. He wanted to pastor a church. I thought that was a terrible idea. I knew that he would need us when he got really sick. I really didn't think that he could do that on his own, with all the stresses of being a solo pastor in a smaller church, which was the only kind of church to which he would be called.

But, he went to MCC in Shreveport, Louisiana, over the objections of many. I never saw him again.

His time there was not good — he became very ill, and ultimately could not pastor. His behavior deteriorated, and his mental state was poor. A few people in the church continued to help him, as his condition worsened, and he died. His was not an easy death. And it did not have a good impact on the church, either.

Jim's pride would not allow him to stay in Los Angeles where we could care for him. I am still mad at him about that. Damn cowboy, truck-driver, ex-felon, clergy pride.

Whenever Paula and I see or smell peach cobbler, we think of him. When I remember him, I thank God who uses us even in our brokenness, and that my one-dimensional stereotypes about Jim Harris got challenged and healed.

Fat Lady or Angel?

Lou was already a member of MCC Los Angeles for a very long time when I became pastor. There were lots of stories about her, and I collected a few of my own.

Lou was a hard-living person who grew up too soon, and she grew old before her time. When I met her, she was using a cane, and sometimes a wheelchair. Her accent was a blend. I could hear Tennessee sometimes, Southern Texas, or even Louisiana.

She was already diminished in some ways, size for one, but she was still a tall tale. Legend had it that she had been — among many things in her long, lesbian life — a fat lady in a circus.

Not until I was in MCC had I met people who actually ran away with the circus as young teens, but MCC is full of them. In another era, I am sure it was what LGBTQ kids and abused kids did to get away from abuse and bullying. Thank God for the circus, I guess.

Another claim to fame was that she had beat Minnesota Fats at a game of pool. I have no way to verify that, but the story had staying power.

Lou was starting to lose it, more and more. She lived at the appalling St. Francis Hotel, that, thank God, someone finally had the good sense and common decency to tear down. It had been her home for decades, so when she had to leave, it was awful. As long as I live I will never get the smell of that hotel out of my memory.

She desperately wanted to be independent and found that she could ride the buses that were specially equipped to take on wheelchairs. However, when coming to church, she would get off at the wrong stop and then end up spinning in the middle of the street. More than one MCC person, on their way to church, would see Lou and try to help orient her or get her on the right bus again.

At church, the ushers had a bright idea to help Lou feel like she was contributing. She whined a lot about wanting to help, so they found something. When the offering was collected, Lou put the plates in her lap and wheeled down the aisle and gave them to the pastor or worship leader who lifted the plates and prayed.

During those years, I am sure children growing up in MCC LA believed that it was some kind of rule or tradition that only a person in a wheelchair could process the offering!

That was all good until Lou started losing more dexterity. Plates crashed, cash and checks fell all over the floor. Crying emanated from the back of the sanctuary which is never a good thing!

The head usher came to me and begged me to deal with this problem. I reminded them, I had not created the situation. Their intentions were good, but evidently I got paid the big bucks to handle problems so I did the bait and switch thing.

I told Lou that I needed her to do a different job on Sunday mornings. I said that people thought I needed to smile more during my sermons, and I needed help. I asked her to sit in the front row and just smile at me from time to time.

Well, that worked for a while. Seeing her grinning did make me smile, just not in the right places. After a while she took it so seriously, it wore her out, so she ended up half-smiling, half-grimacing much of the time.

And then, Lou began to miss Sunday services.

One weekday morning, quite unexpectedly, she showed up at church. I was praying in the sanctuary, and I could hear her very squeaky wheelchair (it was unmistakable) coming down the aisle. When she got near me, she burst into tears.

"Rev. Wilson, I went to the doctor yesterday, and he told me I have cancer. I don't have long!" Her sobs broke my heart.

I tried to calm her down, fixed her a sandwich, and got her a drink. I went upstairs to my office and called Marcel who was her caregiver. He was furious!

"What is she doing there? I have been looking all over for her! She needs to take her meds!"

I said, "Well, she is here. She's very upset because she saw the doctor, and she has cancer."

"She does not have cancer! I took her to the doctor yesterday, she was afraid she had cancer, but she just has a bladder infection, and needs to take her meds!"

Back down to the first floor I go. I sit next to Lou who is chewing on her sandwich, and say, "Lou, I just talked to Marcel. He is worried about you, you are supposed to be home. And, he says you don't have cancer."

"Thank God! Thank God!!!" she says, as if she had not heard this before, and if I am somehow the source of her healing.

Truthfully, her service to MCC Los Angeles was a hoot. So many people had great, funny, poignant or outrageous stories about her. What a life she had led. What a larger than life presence she was until the end!

Lou did eventually die, but not of cancer. She died during the hectic season of our 30th anniversary. We held a memorial service. We were her family and we supported her as best we could. Perhaps we were her final circus!

Staff pastor Lori and I inherited her ashes. We kept Lou's ashes in the church office for several weeks. Finally, we took them with us on one of our walks along the Thompson Trail near Mount Baldy.

We found a low area and scattered the ashes with a prayer. Just as we finished, an enormous golden eagle swooped down near us, landed briefly, and before we could catch our breath, took flight again.

Lori and I were speechless, as we had never seen a golden eagle up close like that in all the years we'd walked that trail.

Who was that woman, really? We both thought it, and then said it out loud and laughed. Our Lou, an angel we had entertained, unawares.

CHIRP: Coming back to life

MCC Los Angeles had a powerful role during a very amazing period in our LGBTQ and HIV/AIDS history: the time when protease inhibitors began to actually work in the mid 1990s. Suddenly, people who knew they were going to die were going to live. They started to get well. It was a miracle, the end of the automatic death sentence.

Gay men and others who had lost everything — their homes, their friends, their jobs or careers, their savings if they had them — had lifetimes stretch out, generously and mysteriously before them.

Many walked out of hospices and hospitals with improved prospects for their health, and no prospects for recovering a life like one they might have remembered with jobs, family, friends, a social life, luxuries, and vacations. For other people, who had lived in the margins, who were addicts or used to very hard living, there was the terrifying prospect of a different kind of life. Their health had improved in the hospice, with a safe place to live, decent food, and for some, counseling.

All of them were now dependent on a complicated regime of pills and the necessity to comply.

Some people didn't make it through that strange time. Some took their own lives; others succumbed to the ravages of other illnesses or addictions. Some could not face this brave new world. For others, the helpful drugs came too late. Or they didn't work. Or compliance was just too hard.

But many did survive. In West Hollywood, where our church was located, there were "AIDS hotels," Section 8 housing for those who had survived, but who were still HIV positive for life, with no life to which they could return.

I saw them all over town, hanging out in the gay restaurants, nursing a third cup of coffee at Starbucks. Some attended one of the 14 twelve-step groups housed at the church. Many had the look of combat fatigue, of PTSD.

They made me think of Lazarus with the grave clothes still clinging to them. Loss, despair, unresolved grief. As if life was now a speeding train they would never catch.

They bore the guilt of surviving what so many did not survive and wondering, "Why me?" Overpowering loneliness and dark questions abounded. Many were too fatigued to try to make friends or build community on their own which was why church was important.

One such person was Paul Gronberg. Paul had been involved in MCC decades prior in San Francisco. He had been the lover of an MCC clergyperson who died from AIDS. In his day, Paul was a gorgeous man who could have been a model. He had sexy, ice blue eyes, full lips, and lots of energy. He had tried all the recreational drugs, the party circuits, and had lived a reckless life. The mystery was that he had survived at all.

He came to MCC LA after moving into one of those Section 8 housing units. He was battling lots of psychological problems and did not always take his medication.

On his first Sunday at church, I recognized him from years earlier which pleased him no end. So many he knew were gone or did not remember him fondly or at all. We met, and he told me more of his whole story, very sobering to say the least.

But what he really wanted was something to do. He was bored out of his mind. I wasn't sure what he could do, so we experimented. Paul was a lone wolf, in a way, and not great as a team player. Yet, our part-time and volunteer staff, all with wounds of their own, welcomed him. He helped the janitor scrub floors and painted the building inside and out. As he worked, and accomplished simple projects, I watched him heal.

There were days he could not leave his house. Or, got into a fight and couldn't come to work. But, more often than not, he managed to get there.

He could play the piano, though he did not like to do that at church services. He did it for himself and for me. I loved to hear him play while I worked.

Sometimes he answered the phones, which was always risky, but we were desperate at times, and he filled in. On some occasions, we had to clean things up afterwards.

And, he could sing. He had a beautiful bass voice. We formed an a cappella quartet, which sang at the 9AM services. We sang old hymns and songs in four part harmony. That was an experience of pure joy for me.

Paul became a church mouse, someone who was there almost every time the church opened. He also had his dark and difficult times. He still had anger issues and even got thrown out of his residence on occasion. Paul struggled with getting on and staying on the right meds. He couldn't drive and didn't have a car, so he usually took the bus. Sometimes, that was a problem, and I had to pick him up for his volunteer job. In Los Angeles, people who had good jobs could not volunteer during the day, when we most needed volunteer staff. I was glad to fetch people like Paul who worked hard and for free!

In all this, I felt a deep, pastoral affection for him. He had a wicked sense of humor and a strong sense of irony. Mostly, he was very respectful of my time and privacy. That is more than I can so for many who were healthier than he was at the time.

One Valentine's Day, Paula and I went to the West Hollywood Clerk of the Court to request a marriage license, along with a whole group, and were of course, turned down. This was an event orchestrated by MCC, throughout the United States and several other countries. We were on local television like celebrities for the day in West Hollywood. As we were driving back to the church, Paul was walking down the street and saw us. He leaped in the air, high-fiving us and grinning from ear to ear. In that moment, I saw the healing his new-found love for his community had produced in him.

It was the next year or so that Paul also started two other projects. He rode his bike in the AIDS Ride from San Francisco to Los Angeles, which he did for many years, and he started volunteering as a supporter for The Tribe, our young adults group.

In the AIDS Ride, Paul was reclaiming himself as a long term survivor who was strong enough to do this rigorous ride, and who had the support of his community as he did it. He was riding for a cure, and for prevention, and for all those who did not live to ride.

In his ministry, Paul was able to pass on his own wisdom and support to young adults. They respected him as one who had a very difficult young adulthood, and who endured abuse and exploitation.

When I left MCC Los Angeles as pastor, it meant leaving people like Paul, who I had seen rise up, quite literally, from death beds and despair. From time to time, Paul would leave me a message which always started or ended with "CHIRP." He knew I was a bird-watcher, which he found amusing for some reason.

In July of 2007, I heard the news that Paul died but not in a way anyone expected. On a Saturday church outing to Laguna Beach with members of The Tribe, Paul was hit by a huge wave which broke some ribs, one of which punctured his heart, and he died. Ironically, after all that HIV/AIDS struggle, he died suddenly in the very happiest time of his life.

I can still see him, that Valentine's Day, on Santa Monica Blvd., leaping in the air for joy, for liberation, for hope. CHIRP.

Dumped on the Lawn

In my opinion, the best story of how someone got to MCC is Dave's story.

In the mid 1970s, Dave was in the Navy, closeted as a gay man and suffering. He was drinking too much, causing pain to those who loved him. Finally, in desperation, Dave's friends tied him up, still in his Navy uniform, put him in the trunk of a car, and drove him to MCC San Diego. They dumped him on the front lawn and said, "Grow up!"

It just so happened that the pastor of MCC San Diego, Rev. David Farrell, was himself a recovering alcoholic. He had been a Catholic brother, and the assistant to the Bishop of San Diego as a closeted gay man and a hopeless drunk. Finding MCC healed him, as it was his pathway to AA and sobriety. Rev. David not only recovered, but he became MCC clergy and the pastor of the church that saved his life.

Dave found help and home at MCC San Diego, and then at MCC Los Angeles when he moved there to pursue his private catering and party business.

He was on the board of directors of MCC Los Angeles when I became pastor. He was originally from the South from a very poor background with little formal education, and became a brilliant entrepreneur and business person.

But, sometimes, the gaps in his education showed. When we formed an "ad hoc" committee to find a new building, Dave was a little lost, not having ever heard the phrase "ad hoc." Someone who knew him well said, "Dave, that was, 'ad hoc,' not 'Ham Hoc!'" Mostly, he covered the gaps in his own education.

Dave was a consistent, generous tither and someone a pastor could always count on to come through in a crunch. And, there were lots of crunches, believe me.

When we moved to Culver City, Dave was interested in the design of the new building and volunteered to chair that committee. He was perfectly qualified for it.

Meanwhile, without telling anyone, he had tested positive for HIV, and in fact, had full blown AIDS. For whatever complex reasons, Dave was one of those persons, and there were many, who had enormous shame about contracting AIDS. It was internalized homophobia. Somehow, it was okay to be gay, as long as no one thought you were having sex, or certain kinds of sex.

Dave was sort of out to his family, but it was more like a "don't ask, don't tell" situation. There was a powerful denial myth afloat that if you were white, successful, and could pass for straight, AIDS would not really touch you or kill you. It was a disease of poor gay people, barflies, drag queens, men of color, Haitians — not people like him.

I do not know for certain that this was Dave's issue, because he would never talk about it. Maybe he just did not want to break his mother's heart. He wouldn't talk about being sick or having AIDS with anyone. It was as if he thought that if he acknowledged it, he would die. For a while, it seemed like his strategy might work. He was cheery and seemed to be coping okay.

But, then, he started losing ground. He was thin as a rail, going blind, and didn't want to admit it. If you tried to bring it up with him, he would push you away.

The problem was that we needed someone to drive the building project, and Dave could not do that any longer. As a pastor, I knew this would be add insult to injury.

I picked him up at his house (he was no longer driving, thank God), and we met at the church. I gently told him that we still wanted him on the committee, but we needed someone new to lead the process of renovation of our new place. Dave was furious. He got up, left my office, and started walking home. Blind — and in a rage.

I asked my assistant pastor to follow him in the car, and to offer him a ride, if possible. Danny followed Dave for the three miles to his home. Dave walked the whole way without allowing Danny to assist him.

Dave died of AIDS on MCC's anniversary in 1989, while I was fasting to hold onto our new building and the home for Caring for Babies with AIDS.

Even though he was mad at me, he continued to let MCC Los Angeles be his home and family through the end.

I prayed that in letting go in death, Dave would be able to forgive me, forgive us, and cheer us on, so that we might continue to offer the life-saving help he received as a young man. I prayed that he could receive in his heart and soul the truth that he impacted so many people through his gifts and service to MCC.

I am not sure if Dave got dumped on the lawn of heaven, but if he did, I hope he laughed this time.

Welcome to MCC: "She's An Idiot"

Now and then, pastors are entitled to do or say something outrageous, out of character, and get a free pass for it.

My time came one of the Sundays after the earthquake forced MCC Los Angeles to move into a junior high school auditorium for our worship services.

Our head usher had just quit and a woman who I really did not want to have the role moved herself right into it. With so much going on, I let it slide (always the wrong thing to do), but kept one eye on her.

This particular Sunday, she had positioned herself as the guide and gatekeeper at the front of the sanctuary. As people were coming forward for communion she directed them to the next station. She did this as if she were a field marshal, mind you, and I was a little worried.

Then I saw a young man in tears, who I did not know, come forward. Just as he was about to come to me, she yanked him to make him wait for someone else, who she thought should go next.

I signaled to this man to come to me anyway, and he did. Then, I looked him square in the face, as God is my witness, and said, "I am so sorry, she's an idiot." And for once, I didn't care who heard me.

That broke the ice. He burst into laughter, and then into tears as I held him. It turned out this was his first time at MCC, and he got there through his participation in our grief group. All through his journey in becoming a member, then even a board member at the church, we never forgot the strange circumstances of our first encounter!

I was so grateful that he appreciated my intemperate response to truly idiotic behavior. The truth is, when we try to love and include everyone, we allow and enable an awful lot of that kind of behavior in churches.

There, I've said it.

Charles Manson and Susan Atkins

While Charles Manson had the right at age 80, in prison, to marry a 26-year-old, many of us did not have marriage equality. What a strange world we live in!

Prisons are just strange, but we worked hard to keep our humanity and to support the humanity of the women we met at a prison called the California Institute for Women in Norco, California. We met all kinds of people, all races, backgrounds, and sexual orientations.

Some women came to our worship services just to be somewhere for an hour and break the boredom; some came to see their friends, some for the message, and I am sure there were other reasons.

For a while we met in the chapel, where we were greeted by women who had been appointed as "chaplain assistants." They were there to provide staff support for some of the worship services of the many groups that met in the chapel. They were women deemed responsible enough to represent the chaplain and sensitive to the needs of the diverse groups that met there.

One night, probably in the late 1980s, the chaplain's assistant was none other than Susan Atkins, who was in prison for life for her part in the LaBianca-Tate murders as a member of the Charles Manson gang.

I met Susan very briefly that first night. She was slight, not unattractive, and still a young woman. She stayed in the back of the sanctuary, listening to the message. At communion, she came forward with the others, and came to me to receive.

I was so conflicted in that moment. She was as vulnerable looking as any of those women. She was quiet, and I think, genuinely moved by the message. She seemed emotional as she came forward. But, fear seized me. When I saw her, I cannot say in that instant that I saw a child of God. I saw the monster she had been in those terrible times.

Susan's eyes were closed, but my eyes, in a reflex I do not think I could have controlled if I had tried, would not take a chance to close in the presence of someone who could suddenly go into a savage rage.

I felt ashamed after that — and a bit silly. As I look back in compassion, I can see how hard it was, as a young pastor, to be in the presence of a legendary criminal and maintain my own center.

Later, I had conversations with Susan, and she offered her own testimony at MCC services. She spoke about how she had become a person of faith and had accepted God's forgiveness. She spoke about her long, difficult road of trying to accept that forgiveness. She shared how much she loved the message of MCC, and how welcome she felt, even as a heterosexual who had her share of lesbian affairs in prison.

I was impressed with her articulate, measured, and genuine speeches and conversations. She had won over the trust of the chaplain (not easy, really), the women who attended MCC, many of the other highly respected lifers, and even the guards.

Susan made attempts to achieve parole, but no one, except possibly her, thought it was ever going to happen. No one who had committed those unspeakable things, or followed Charles Manson, was eligible for mercy in our judicial system.

Eventually she died of cancer in that same prison. I said a prayer for her and left her in the hands of God. Rest in peace.

To God Be the Glory: Ken Martin's story

At the 1974 MCC General Conference in San Francisco, a handsome young man testified and sang with barely contained emotion, "To God Be the Glory," by Bill Gaither. It was Ken Martin from Chicago. The story of how he got to that early MCC conference is one of my favorites.

Ken grew up Southern Baptist, in Mississippi, with all the attendant homophobia, shame, and guilt. Since childhood, Ken yearned for the warring within him, over his sexuality and spirituality, to cease. But it did not.

He pastored small Southern Baptist Churches, and then went to seminary in Louisville, Kentucky. In 1974, his last year in seminary, he was the assistant pastor of a large UCC church in southern Indiana, where he was called to serve after a student field placement.

At that time, Ken was 30-years-old, and married with a 4-year-old son. As he likes to tell it, he was preaching grace for everyone but himself. He had taken the marriage cure, which was not working.

Ken was losing the war inside of himself, hatching, instead, a plan to take his own life. He imagined driving his car into the Ohio River and make it look like an accident. God forbid that anyone would have known he was unhappy or in pain. Or bring shame upon his family.

One Thursday morning, as this plan became more and more real, Ken followed his usual routine, driving from New Albany, Indiana, to the seminary in Louisville, to give an exam. Ken was a Garrett Fellow, and this was part of his responsibility. He stopped in the restaurant he always stopped in and slid into the same booth to have breakfast.

There, next to him on the red faux leather seat, was a book, face down. Ken loved books and reflexively turned it over. It was the paperback edition of Rev. Troy Perry's *The Lord is My Shepherd and He Knows I'm Gay*.

In shock, Ken skimmed through the book, realized what it was, and called the other Garrett Fellow to substitute for him that morning. He left there quickly, hiding the book, so no one would see him with what must have seemed like contraband!

Ken drove to a park on that same Ohio River, the one in his suicide plan, and sat and read all day through the whole, amazing book.

On the back cover, it said there were 12 MCC churches (there were actually about twice as many by that time), and the closest one was in Chicago. There was actually one in Indianapolis, much closer, but Ken had no way of knowing that.

It was hard to wait until Sunday. Ken made arrangements to cover his duties at church, rose at 3 AM and drove straight through to Chicago, hoping to get there for morning services. He stopped at a gas station and phone booth, and found an address for Metropolitan Community Church on the South side of Chicago, and a map of the city.

Ken got there on time and watched heterosexual African-American families entering the church. He sat in the car, confused. Finally, he went to a phone booth and called the church, and a woman answered. He said, "Is this Metropolitan Community Church?"

"Yes," she replied. After a long silence, she said, kindly, "Honey, are you looking for Rev. Perry's church?"

"Yes, ma'am!" he answered.

So she gave him the Wellington Street address on the North side of Chicago, the address of the United Church of Christ in which MCC met.

Ken got back in his Volkswagen Bug and found the church on the north side. It was 11:30, and church was halfway through the service. He sat down in the back and saw a church full of white, heterosexual families.

"This is not right, either," he thought. He walked outside and saw the small print of "Good Shepherd Metropolitan Community Church," below the larger United Church of Christ sign.

Desperate, but still hopeful, he walked around the church, went in the back door, and heard a man speaking with a pronounced effeminate sound. Maybe I am in the right place, he thought. But, the man was teaching a children's Sunday school class.

Ken checked into a hotel, and prayed again, "God, if you want me to find this church, you have to help me!"

He remembered the woman at the first church had given him a phone number. Trembling, he found it in his wallet and called.

The church service was at 7PM in the evening!

When Ken bounded up the steps just before 7PM, that Sunday evening in March, 1974, Bruce Beasley, the man teaching Sunday school earlier in the day, greeted Ken. Bruce attended the UCC and the MCC, was an usher, and showed Ken to his seat at his first MCC service.

After testifying at the General Conference a few months later, Ken was elected pastor of Good Shepherd Parish MCC in Chicago. In 1975, Ken started dating Tom Cole, who has since been his partner for more than 40 years. Ken went on to pastor MCC churches in North Hollywood, California, and Austin, Texas. He also served as a full time Elder in MCC.

Sadly, for eighteen years, Ken did not see his son Beck. Ken's ex-wife had remarried, to George, a man who was deeply opposed to Beck seeing his father.

George, who had been a Lutheran all his life, had a conversion experience in a little Southern Baptist Church in South Carolina. Immediately afterwards, he had a serious heart attack. In the process of those two experiences, George repented of his attitude towards Ken and urged his wife C.J., and their son Beck, to find Ken and reconcile.

In 1995, Ken met his grownup son at Purdue University, where he was graduating with a doctoral degree. By that time Beck was married to Julie.

Before long, C.J. and George moved to the Austin area, and on Thanksgiving, Beck, Julie, C.J. and George celebrated a family dinner at Ken and Tom's home.

As if that were not miracle enough, C.J. and George joined the MCC church in Austin where Ken was the pastor. In time, C.J. became a deacon, and George served as an usher.

Ken says that Rev. Perry's book showing up on the seat next to him was the only really supernatural experience he ever had in his life and ministry.

But, it turns out, one was enough.

In those early, tumultuous days of coming out, losing family, facing the rigors and challenges of pastoring an MCC church, dealing with AIDS, coming through times of doubt — that singular miracle was a rock, a touchstone, for

Ken. It was enough to remind him of God's providence. That one miracle led to so many others through the decades.

Beck Taylor, who is now the President of Whitworth University in Spokane, Washington, invited his mom, and all three of his dads, to his installation, and introduced them with pride.

George has gone to be with his Maker, the One who taught him to open his heart. Beck and Julie still love to bring their three children to visit grandpas Ken and Tom. To God be the glory.

Funerals, Death and Grieving

When I became a pastor in MCC, I did not aspire to become an expert at officiating funerals or counseling the dying and their loved ones. But, that is what happened.

I have AIDS to thank for that. Even before AIDS, people in our communities died tragically of hate crimes, of suicide, of alcoholism and drug addiction, of homophobia and transphobia, of broken hearts, bodies and spirits. AIDS just speeded up the learning curve.

The special lessons of managing multiple losses became part of my daily survival strategy. Lessons about how to help a community survive and even thrive in the midst of a holocaust that the wider culture denied and trivialized.

Death can be messy, costly, and brutal. The biggest impact is on those who are not dying. Our illusion of immortality is shaken, for a while at least, when we see someone die. What has happened to them will most certainly happen to us.

I learned that there are worse things than dying, and that dying well, surrounded with love, community, comfort, and decent medical help is achievable.

Also, I came to understand that though people often die the way they lived, sometimes, they can die even better than they lived. For some, the true meaning of their lives becomes clear in the days, months, or years before death.

A sudden death limits the dying person's pain, and people often say, "I want to go quick." But when a death is not sudden, friends, family, and faith gain meaning. Being a pastor is like being a spiritual mid-wife to those who are dying. In the midst of terrible loss, something can be born: mercy, love, and deep connection. In that spirit I offer these stories.

Race, Culture, and Funerals

I have learned so much from my African-American friends, colleagues, and church members about funerals in the Black Church tradition. For me, it was, at times, a steep learning curve as I learned to be a good pastor to church members from cultures and backgrounds other than my own.

Black funerals have a cultural reality that is so different from the funerals I grew up with in my very white, suburban context.

"Papa Jimmi" Irving, the gospel choir leader and song leader at MCC Los Angeles for many decades, loved to go to funerals. He would dress in his church whites from his First Church of Deliverance background and stay through the many hours of the long service. Was it cathartic? Did it provide reassurance in the face of so much death? I am not sure.

Jimmi was the first person I ever met who loved to go to funerals. He sought them out and went to funerals of people he hardly knew. He was happiest when he was going to a funeral. It was a social event, a chance to see people in his vast network of connections. It didn't matter if the deceased was gay or straight.

Funerals often had great music, fiery preaching, moving testimonies, and great food. He would come back from the funerals beaming, satisfied, all aglow, and, of course, sad for the deceased.

This was nothing like the funerals in the very white world where I came of age. Our funerals were muted, quiet affairs, grim, sometimes to be dreaded. We were all pleased when the mourners "held up," stoically, and did not break down too much. We didn't like to witness sobbing and carrying on. Funerals were to be endured, suffered, and avoided, if possible.

I learned the hard way that Black preachers often visited the family and prayed with them before heading to the funeral home or church. I had to apologize to the family of an African-American staff member for not showing up at their home in advance of the service. It was awkward and regrettable.

The last thing the white people in my family and neighborhood wanted, before going to a funeral, was to have the priest or pastor at their home.

I was dismayed that I could work with people for years and not know these very key things. The racial and cultural segregation of the more intimate parts of our lives were often evident, and that could be costly.

When an African-American staff member's mother died, I conducted the grave side service. After the interment, we went back to the house, where a wonderful feast — the best fried chicken you can imagine — had been prepared.

Rev. Barbara Haynes had accompanied me, and had that plaintive look on her face, hoping I was not going to do what I often did, and rush off and leave all that food.

When I said, "Are you kidding? We are going to eat first!" she let out such a loud "Thank you Jesus!" that the people turned and looked at us! Barbara enjoyed her funeral food, and I had learned to enjoy it as well.

MCC churches are often a blend of cultures and religious backgrounds. Because of AIDS, we ended up doing a lot of funerals. I am so grateful for the African American, Latino/a, Pentecostal, and Holiness (White or Black) influences in MCC that make funerals and memorials more meaningful, more interesting, more real, more personal, more transformative than anything I had witnessed in my childhood.

Death Drama/Trauma

For some reason, at MCC Los Angeles, it seemed as though we always had a lot of drama in and around our anniversaries.

On our 25th anniversary, my assistant pastor, Danny Mahoney, was dying of AIDS and had run out of morphine. I went to a pharmacy in the neighborhood, where I knew the pharmacist and begged him for morphine. Danny simply could not endure going all the way to the VA emergency room, and he had not yet been admitted to hospice. He was home with his partner, in very bad shape, and needed pain relief. To my utter shock, the pharmacist, not saying a word, gave me the drugs. We never spoke about it.

That next day, I learned that a woman in our church had read her partner's secret journal in which she fantasized about having a relationship with me. I did not know about this journal, and the partner, who had an alcohol problem, decided to bring her gun to church.

People who knew her well intercepted, and we did not have to call the police, but, oh my. The woman who wrote the journal was actually having an affair with someone else in the church, on and on and on.

Drama with a capital "D" can happen in church!

On our 30th anniversary, October 6, 1998, Matthew Shepherd was attacked in Laramie, Wyoming, which became national news. We had experienced several recent deaths in the church, and grief and anger was just below the surface.

One of those deaths was the co-chair of the Anniversary committee. Apparently, he had serious depression issues that we did not know about.

Without clearing it with anyone, weeks before, he wallpapered the welcome center with a design no one liked. He did not have the gay male gene for interior decorating.

As the pastor, I had to be the one to tell him, "We have to paint over it; we are very sorry," and try uselessly to cover my discomfort. He was shocked and devastated far out of proportion to the situation — which should have been a clue.

He flew back east on a business trip, wrote a long, horrible, irrational letter blaming his partner, me, lots of other people, and killed himself. That meant his partner had to arranged to have the remains shipped back to Los Angeles, deal with the coroner's office in New Jersey, etc. I might have just left him there.

We hastily put together his service with his partner. The day of the funeral, as we were about to start the procession, the partner said to me, "Pastor, please don't mention that Bob killed himself, his employees and co-workers are here, and they don't know."

It used to be that we covered up HIV (they died of pneumonia, cancer, blah blah blah). Now we had to cover up suicide, for other people's comfort.

I looked at him and said, "Too late."

We just don't have time for dishonesty, not at funerals. Not anymore.

First of all, his death was very traumatic for the church, including a couple of people who worked for him. I was planned to deal with his suicide in my sermon. When one pastors a church with lots of former Catholics, one had to address suicide. We did not need one more elephant in the room.

Secondly, the partner had approved our MCC practice of people getting up and speaking about the deceased, and I knew I could not control what was about to happen.

People were sad, the music was great, and I think I did okay with the sermon, but it was obvious that Bob's death was a suicide.

At one point, the co-chair of the Anniversary Committee, a very self-possessed, elegant woman who was a therapist, got up and said, "I am just so f – – king pissed at you Bob!" A dam burst in that room! All the suppressed anger at AIDS, violence, bullying, you name it, just let loose. Others got up and were less angry, but still emotional. It was like a raw group therapy. I could see the folks from Bob's company with looks of shock on their face, but, like I said, it was too late.

In some ways, in his tragic and regrettable suicide, Bob gave us the gift of catharsis. I just wish we hadn't needed it that much. Ultimately, his partner seemed quite moved by the service, and seemed forgiving of us for letting the the secret out and for all the raw emotions and swearing as well.

Sometimes, with all of the losses and the political helplessness, we just had to lose it now and then, even at a funeral.

We Don't Do Funerals For Strangers

Sometime in the early 1990s I got a distressing call from an excitable man, Marc, whose dear friend had just died of AIDS. He and his friend David called a church in West Hollywood to ask about holding their friend's funeral. They thought they were talking to the minister of an MCC church, but they were not.

The church had a similar telephone number so it was confusing. A church official told them since they were not members, they should know that the church did not do funerals for strangers. Imagine that, a church of Jesus Christ turning away people who needed a funeral for a friend.

Doing funerals for strangers was a huge part of our lives in the 1980s and 90s, and even today. It is hard to imagine a church that would not open its doors to a hurting community and offer safe space and support. But, many churches turned people away.

Our church, which saw so many deaths from AIDS, is thriving today. That other church in West Hollywood died, because they lost touch with their mission. Whatever reasons they may have given for closing the doors, I feel certain that the truth was more about losing touch with their community and their neighborhood.

Strangers are the lifeblood of every living church.

I assured Marc and David that they were welcome to hold the service at our church in Culver City. They cried on the phone and were deeply grateful and relieved. The man whose life they were celebrating had been David's partner many years before. They had been family to one another, and the loss was devastating.

I attended the service, which they put together. Members of our church and staff also came, to offer hospitality and support — to strangers! Marc and David were so moved and comforted by our willingness to be there for them.

We stayed in touch, and they came to church occasionally. Eventually, David became ill and died, and we did David's service, as well. Multiple losses like that were so common. Some people lost all their close friends. Others just stopped going to funerals. We had to keep doing them; we felt like it was our sacred calling in that moment in time.

A few years later, when Marc met Steve, the new love of his life, one of my Rabbi friends, Lisa Edwards, officiated the wedding with me. They were both survivors of so much loss and took the risk to love again.

Thank God for strangers.

Signs of Hope

When I met Skip Chasey, he was a preppie-looking, very successful financial executive in the "industry" (the only one in Los Angeles — film). He had grown up Southern Baptist and knew from early childhood that he was not only gay, but attracted to leather sexuality.

And, he wanted very badly to be a very good boy.

As an adult, Skip avoided church and got on with his gay life, and more covertly, his leather identity and practice.

He came to MCC Los Angeles when his partner, Victor, died of AIDS. Skip was completely unprepared to face this kind of loss, with only a child-like, failed Baptist faith. He crept into our Sunday night church service, sat in the back, and then made an appointment with me.

Skip was very low-key; I thought he might be depressed. He told me that Victor was Catholic and alienated from his faith as well.

It turns out that Skip was embarrassed to tell me that he wanted a sign that Victor was okay. Was he was safe in the arms of a God who loved him? Or burning in a punishing hell, or banished to a cold nothingness? He was embarrassed because he was well-educated, sophisticated, and shouldn't need such a sign. He thought he was beyond or above all that.

Yet, he did need that sign. He felt tormented not knowing where Victor was.

I took a leap, one that I do not always take.

Without hesitating, I told Skip that I believed he could have that sign. That Victor's alienation from church, and his as well, was not alienation from God. That God was greater than that painful separation. Rejection of church teachings that denigrated you actually pleased God! God did not want our souls to be damaged and destroyed by religion that was wrong about who we are. If the church was not worthy of us, God was still with us.

The caveat, I said in all this, is that when you experience the sign, you must accept it. You cannot ask for another, and then another. That will not help or satisfy. Stay open, and when it comes, accept it. Don't second guess your own experience.

We prayed, and Skip left, and started coming to church. We did not speak about the sign again.

Then, several weeks later, as people were leaving church Sunday morning, Skip pressed my hands, and with tears in his eyes, said, "I got it, today, I got my sign."

I never knew what it was. I did not need to know any details, only to know that it happened.

Skip later came to me, offering to pay for his own training to learn how to run a grief group at the church. Just that week, a woman whose partner of many years had just died, called me to see if we had such a group. I called her back, but had to tell her we didn't. Not yet.

Eileen came to church anyway, and when she did, I introduced her to Skip. They both trained and started a group that ran for decades at MCC Los Angeles, helping hundreds of people heal through their grief. It is not possible to overstate the importance, the ripple effect of that grief group in the life of our church, in the lives of all who were touched by it. This gift of a grief group emanated from Skip's desire to have a sign.

Today, Skip is much more open about his leather life and the spiritual and sexual practices and teachings he offers around the world. As a "priest in black leather," he is an ambassador between leather/kink/fetish communities and various religious and spiritual communities, including MCC. He teaches, preaches, and models healthy integration of radical sexuality and spirituality.

Skip taught me so much about the incredible diversity, complexity, and interconnectedness of spirituality and sexuality, without shame. I also learned to trust the nudge from the Spirit that tells me a sign may be on the way.

I Have Everything I Need

Norm would do just about anything I asked him to do and drove everyone else crazy.

Norm Mason and I had been on a journey since about 1989, and it was about to end in October 2001, not long after the attacks on the World Trade Center.

When MCC Los Angeles was struggling to get into our building in Culver City, I decided to fast in order to raise the money to save the property. Not only was my fast to save the church building, it was to save the first AIDS Hospice for babies, which we housed.

Norm, on the other hand, decided to drive north; he was running away — again.

He had been in church on Sunday morning. Afterwards, he drove north as far as Mt. Shasta, California, where he had a revelation of some kind that propelled him back to Los Angeles. The next day he started, single-handedly, finishing the new sanctuary, even as I moved into the unfinished church building to complete my fast and to call attention to our need for a decent loan.

In that sanctuary, built by Norm, was a memorial wall. He bought a large plaque for "Ernesto," one of the loves of his life, who he would not talk about, that said, "Save a place for me nearby." The wall graced the sanctuary in an alcove on the left side. We remembered families, friends, and every church member who died. When we lost ten people we were visiting at hospice, we secured a large plaque with all their names on it. It was granite and marble, elegant and cherished by all of us. For a while, it helped us express and contain the immensity of our grief and the beauty of our memories.

Norm volunteered for the church or worked for us for about a decade, off and on. He was a graphic artist, who, in the midst of some of the most tumultuous times in the church, made us and me, look good, quite literally. We didn't have a building or proper offices, much of the time, but by God, our Sunday bulletin and newsletter, our publications, our Pride T-Shirts, were first class! He had a way of taking the message and making it so compelling, week after week, image after image.

He was someone who compartmentalized. He had lots of stuff in his background that he never shared. He was a Vietnam Vet with myriad family issues. He had started many businesses, some of which were successful for a while, never made much money and was always moving and starting over.

No one worked harder than he did. He was not what you would call a team player and was not an easy fit for a church staff member.

I knew he loved my preaching, and it touched something in him, some hopeful place in him. I have always loved artists, and he was a brilliant one.

He had the gift of healing and participated in a healing group for a woman in our church who was battling cancer. As much as he could piss people off, he would also do many sweet and thoughtful things without wanting it to be noticed.

Men were always falling in love with him and getting disappointed.

Norm and I hurt and disappointed each other in many ways, as well. And we forgave and started over again. He was brilliant and struggled with so many issues.

He moved to Kansas City when he was starting to get sick from HIV. I think he did it to get away from people who cared about him, sort of like putting himself on an ice floe. No one was happy about Norm's decision to leave Los Angeles.

Norm was energized by fresh starts, what Alcoholics Anonymous called, "the geographic cure." He always felt unfulfilled in his deepest ambitions. He wanted to do something new, somewhere new, with someone new.

Eventually, he became too sick to take care of himself. After one hospitalization, his sister Shirley took him to her home in Lubbock, Texas.

By that time, I was living and pastoring in Sarasota, Florida. I was just about to go see him, in 2001, when 9/11 happened and air travel stopped in the United States.

I had to wait a couple of weeks, but I finally booked one of the first flights going from Tampa to Lubbock through a major hub. It was a weird flight. Security was tight. We were all edgy and quiet. The airport lounges were eerily somber. There were no children on the flights. We were all rare models of cooperation and politeness.

I was there for only a couple of days. I stayed with Norm while his sister ran errands. He seemed glad to see me. We talked a lot, about friends, his health, and how he was really doing.

Truthfully, he seemed pretty good, reconciled, even comfortable at his sister's home. She fussed over him too much, which was to be expected, and he would get really, really tired. One evening when she went out, we shared some ice cream, which tasted particularly good to him.

One afternoon, while he was half awake, half dozing, I sang to him and prayed. I know he took it in, that I was there and that I loved him.

When Shirley left on another errand, she asked him if she could get him anything, and he said, emphatically, "No! Really, Shirl, I have everything I need." His words just hung in the air, and he turned and looked at me, and even smiled with a rare twinkle in his eye. I knew his statement, so emphatic, was about more than going to the grocery store. He had accepted his death and was letting go.

It was hard to say good-bye, but we did. Norm thanked me in a very grown up way for coming to see him. He stood to hug me good-bye. Two days later, they took him in an ambulance to the nearest VA hospital, and he died in route. He never stayed still very long, he was always on his way somewhere.

Norm was buried in Iowa, near his family. He was far from any MCC church, and I don't think I was invited to do something in the way of a memorial, or if I was, I could not manage it. The closure we had those last days was more important than any memorial.

In death, he left me a toy from the 1940s, a tin wind-up boy on a bike, saying, "If you ever need me, I am ready to go!" It is a treasured reminder of a gifted, wounded friend, and healer.

New Year's Eve on a Plane

When I fly, I like my space. I read, nap, or work. I do not like to be trapped into deep conversation. But I have learned that it is not always up to me.

One New Year's Eve, I flew from Los Angeles to Washington DC, for the funeral of a friend and colleague, three weeks after my father died and two weeks after my assistant pastor died. I was knee-deep in grief and loss, and HIV/AIDS. The plane was not crowded, but there were two of us in my row.

The older man sitting next to me started to chit chat. He asked me why I was flying on New Year's Eve. "Most people would be with a loved one or family," he said.

A little reluctantly I told him that I was a clergyperson on my way to a funeral. Pause. I struggled with my own indifference and avoidance.

I asked him, "So, why are you flying on New Year's Eve?"

Pause. He choked up and said his wife had died several years ago, and now on holidays, he just gets on a plane to somewhere, anywhere — as if being 30,000 feet up relieved him of the pain of the loss. That took my breath away. He looked at me, imploringly, and asked the question he had been longing to ask someone. "Do you know where she is?" he said.

There was no passing this one by.

I told him that his wife was in the gentle arms of the One who created her, where he would also be someday, and me as well. I shared that while there were a lot of things I did not know, I knew that. As the years passed, I knew less and less about heaven, but I was very sure we will not be disappointed.

He nodded and that was it. As we left, I wished him well. Today, I still wonder if he is alive, and whether he still gets on planes to nowhere in particular. I wonder whether what I said helped at all, if he has peace, or if he has received his reward. And, the answer to that question once and for all.

REV. DR. NANCY WILSON

A Funeral To Remember

The first person I ordained, after being elected an Elder in MCC in 1976, was Rev. Larry Uhrig. The son of a disgraced evangelist, Larry became one of the most amazing, powerful, and effective preachers in MCC. He grew the church in Washington DC, and was their pastor from 1976 until his death in 1993.

Larry and I were close in age. We loved each other and fought like brother and sister, or sometimes, like cats and dogs. More than once I told him not to make me regret the day I laid hands on him. Larry was loved by a diversity of people, men and women, of all races. And yet, a streak of sexism permeated his leadership. He could be sensitive and engaging one minute, and the next minute, he was an ... well, never mind.

For some reason, the older he got, Larry became more and more conservative. Inclusive language for God sent him over the edge. Still, he could be progressive in so many ways. He took leadership in the HIV/AIDS struggle and was the first MCC person to preach at the National Cathedral in the United States capital at a World AIDS Day Service.

As time went on, he ceased inviting me to preach at his church. We found ourselves on opposite sides of issues. We had a connection and yet we pushed each other away. Underneath it all, we still had an everlasting affection and acted like we would always have time enough to work it out.

But Larry was diagnosed with AIDS. As his church and our whole denomination grieved, Larry grieved, too. He was too young to die; he had more to do. He lived just long enough to see the gorgeous new building completed for his church, MCC Washington DC. He preached there Christmas Eve and died few days later. He did not see the new year.

Rev. Troy Perry would have done his funeral, but he was in Australia and could not get home in time. Rev. Arlene Ackerman, a long-time friend of Larry and the church, preached. As the Vice Moderator of MCC at the time, I participated in the funeral.

It was an enormous event with a huge gospel choir and many dignitaries.

They asked me to read the Gospel, John 14: 1-4, which has more "Fathers" in it than any other passage in the New Testament. I am not sure if that was Larry's idea, but I would not have put it past him.

I was handed Larry's Bible and I was told, "Read it right out of this!" which meant, "And don't use inclusive language."

As far as I was concerned, Larry was dead, I was alive, and I would read it the way I believe the Spirit would have me read it. Did they think I could not read it inclusively right out of Larry's King James Bible?

I did have to strategize some. The MCC DC gospel choir was sitting right behind me when I rose to read. I took a deep breath and read it as if I were Rev. Barbara Haynes, beloved friend and African-Americanstaff member at MCC Los Angeles. I channeled her with all my might, and read it, inclusively and as dramatically as I could muster. As I did, the choir began to sway, and moan, and then shout!! If they noticed the reading was more inclusive, they didn't act like they did, or that it mattered. Mostly, they were responding to my genuine passion for the good news in this passage.

I could see a few people who were furious with me, and they may have never forgiven me having the last word.

My actions were not meant to be disrespectful. It gave Arlene courage to be as inclusive as she wanted in her sermon. Rev. Delores Berry shifted from "We Shall Behold Him" to "We Shall Behold Them," the way she wanted to, because I had already broken the house rules.

Larry invited all these women to lead the service for him, and yet, he struggled so hard with issues that impact us. It was a paradox, for sure. All of us have our contradictions. He was not alone.

It was an amazing funeral, a fitting tribute to Larry, dressed in his robes and red shoes in his casket. He didn't roll over. I hope he enjoyed all the drama and special attention. He was one of a kind and helped change the world.

Hate, Violence and Hate Crimes

Transforming hate is a powerful vocation, one that is so needed in our century. Religion can be a force for fueling hatred and intolerance, for inspiring sectarian violence; or, it can be a force for justice, love, compassion, and understanding. Religious leaders and institutions have inspired many wars, or at times have lacked the courage to risk their lives or reputations for peace. Religious leaders or leaders who are people of faith have also been at the forefront of civil and human rights.

The Church of Jesus Christ, in particular, has come very lately, if at all, to call for mercy or justice for LGBTQ people, our allies, and families. Those of us who hang onto our faith, nevertheless, have had to organize outside of the traditional churches. This is not a new strategy in history but one that is familiar.

In the 1970s, we saw bumper stickers that "good Christians" actually put on their cars: "Kill a Queer for Christ." While we might not see those bumper stickers as often today, in our country, kids are bullied at school for being different, LGBTQ, or gender queer. Right wing preachers export the hate that gets less traction here to Uganda, Jamaica, or other fertile ground.

President Bill Clinton was the first to call for national hearings about hate crimes and used language that included LGBTQ-related crimes. MCC participated in those 1997 congressional hearings by offering our testimony.

It took forty-years to hear a word after the 1973 fire in New Orleans in a gay bar, The Upstairs Lounge. Thirty-two people were killed, including MCC's pastor, Rev. Bill Larsen, and other MCC members. The Roman Catholic Archdiocese apology was covered in an article in *Time Magazine* (June 2013) for their failure to respond with human decency and compassion at the time. They were not alone. Rev. Perry would always say it was the thing that most disappointed him — not the police or the politicians, but the churches.

Today, the transgender community is most at risk in our country and around the world for violence. Laws are changing here and there, but in most countries, to be a transgender human being is to be pathologized, stigmatized, and victimized.

Recently, I marched in the Trans* Pride parade in Toronto, Canada. It reminded me of Gay Pride 40 years ago — chaotic, disorganized, a touch of anarchy and rage, a little nudity, and a lot of people bent on being transgressive and shocking. I felt right at home. Feeling discomfort and on the edge is a home for many of us.

Learning to tolerate and embrace our own discomfort is the way to heal our fear, which, more than anything, breeds the hate that kills.

We Never Called It a Hate Crime

In the mid to late 1970s, MCC Detroit was a leader during a very vibrant time in the story of the LGBTQ movement in the US and of our denomination's movement.

When I came to Detroit as a pastor, I was eager to have our church be in coalition with progressive groups who were dealing with racism and similar challenges in the Motor City.

One such opportunity came when a Nazi bookstore opened its doors in Detroit with "White Power" plastered all over the front. People in Nazi uniforms staffed the counter. It was surreal and horrifying to see the swastika on the windows and arm bands.

A few of us from MCC Detroit brought our signs to the rally, such as "Gay People Against Facism," only to be told they did not want us to join the protest! We would evidently tarnish their reputation and subvert their purpose. We were bringing another agenda to the protest that they had not pre-approved, apparently. We were kicked out of an anti-Nazi protest, a first for me.

We were polite, but firmly refused to get off the picket line which infuriated the organizers who screamed at us.

One of our MCC members, Rose, (a descendant of German Nazis or at least their sympathizers) was not going to let history repeat itself here. Fueled by her passion, she was not going to be thrown off that picket line! No Nazi was going to be allowed to set up shop in *her* city.

We were bold enough to believe that progressives ought to include us, whether they thought so or not. This was a frequent challenge for the early gay liberation movement. We were too far out there for the lefties that day.

We knew Nazis were haters, but we were less willing to call what happened to us hate crimes. It was as if we were not sure what had happened to us was hate, or a crime.

The next story of a hate crime, committed around the same time as the Nazi bookstore protest. This is a story that I have written as an act of penance.

John was a young man, in his mid-thirties who attended MCC Detroit. Like almost every LGBTQ person in Detroit in the mid to late 1970s he was in the closet, especially to his family.

John was murdered one night after leaving the Iron Hinge, a gay bar in a seedy part of downtown Detroit. Leather and drag mixed there. I had been there many times to attend drag show benefits for the church. It was a dive, but it was also one of the few *community-minded* businesses that supported the church.

There were only a few emerging, suburban gay bars then. People who lived and even worked in the suburbs went downtown to be gay, trying to keep divided lives divided. That was just the way it was.

John was attacked as he left the Iron Hinge that night. He was viciously beaten, and then dragged by a car for several blocks through the streets.

The biggest worry his friends had was that John's parents might find out he was gay. So, with the police, who thought they were being kind, they "de-gayed" John's apartment and removed any literature, photos, posters, or hints of anything gay. When they finished, it looked like any straight, single man lived there.

His parents were devastated, of course. I was 26-years-old and had only a few years of pastoral experience. I accompanied his parents to the morgue and listened to the mother, in particular, agonize about what could have happened. Why did this happen to John? What was he doing downtown anyway? I think the father suspected the reason, but could not ask a question, or articulate his feelings or thoughts. I don't remember whether John had any siblings.

I felt so conflicted and ashamed to participate in the charade, to lie to them and to cover it up. We told ourselves we did it because that's what John would have wanted, and why add to the parents' grief by telling them he was gay?

John was the victim of a hate crime, which was not a phrase we used at all then. In those days, gay bashing and murder were just the price you might pay for daring to go to a gay place. We were just grateful if no one outed us in death. The shame trumped the pain. It is hard to believe we all colluded that way. But we did.

Not only that, but I am sure the police also covered it up. As far as I know, they did next to nothing to find the perpetrators and never told John's parents the whole story. To the police, John was the wrong kind of person, in the wrong kind of place at the wrong time. His death was not worthy of investigating. End of story. Case closed. Thank God his parents didn't find out he was gay. That's what really mattered.

John, I am sorry I did not make a big deal of this hate crime with police and politicians. I am sorry that I did not find a way to tell your parents and help them in their agony. They deserved the truth and should not have to wonder what happened to their beloved son. You did nothing wrong. You did not deserve to be murdered for being a gay man who happened to leave a gay bar one night, when haters were on the prowl.

And your parents did not deserve a lifetime of haunting questions. I am so sorry.

Jamaican Newspapers, Hate and Homophobia

One of the things I noticed when I landed in Jamaica the first time was the proliferation of newspapers, and how much they sensationalized homosexuality.

It was 2007, and on the day we landed, one paper shouted on the front page, "GAYS GET OUT!" At first I wondered if we should take it personally, but the story was about a lesbian couple being driven out of their home and community by their neighbors, who threatened to kill them. The newspaper reported this as rational behavior.

I worried when I was interviewed by the press in Jamaica, whether an article about a white American lesbian reinforced the idea that homosexuality was not natural or native to Jamaica but exported by Americans and Europeans. This is a view of many who are against de-criminalization of homosexuality and against civil or human rights for LGBTQ people. Don't encourage the "criminals."

Jamaican LGBTQ leaders reminded me they could not have their faces in the newspapers or on television. "At the end of the day, you are what we have!" I accepted that and did a lot of media while I visited.

For years, even when I was in Florida, Jamaican radio and television interviewed me about LGBTQ people, the Bible, church, and human rights. They were glad to have an openly LGBTQ religious person to interview. Sometimes I knew the interviews boosted ratings through sensationalism, but I always hoped that LGBTQ people and their families, if they were listening, would be encouraged.

After one visit, the newspaper did a front page story about MCC coming to Jamaica, and about same-sex marriage. It was a very sensationalist article with a photo of Paula and me, but they quoted me accurately throughout. I told them I was there because LGBTQ Jamaicans invited me, and LGBTQ Christians needed support as they struggled for human rights and spiritual freedom.

The interview reported that we met with 35 pastors and church leaders, many of whom were uncertain how best to minister to LGBTQ people in their churches. These clergy struggled because LGBTQ people were so vilified in the culture and were terrified to come out to their families and communities. Even if the churches and leaders did not approve of homosexuality, didn't they have to stand up against the violence?

We had met in a local restaurant. The meeting began very soberly, as the clergy confessed how terrifying it was to even attend such a seminar, organized by a mainstream seminary.

A couple of days later, a prominent, conservative, Pentecostal Jamaican pastor wrote an awful letter to the editor, he called me a liar and said I could not possibly have met with church leaders in Jamaica. No *real* Christian pastor or leader would have met with me and that what I was saying was disgusting.

I waited, one, two, three days. Still, not one of those Christian leaders present at the meeting came to my defense.

Finally, on the fourth day, an Anglican Bishop in Jamaica spoke up, and admitted he had been there. He wrote an op-ed for that paper and said that although he was not sure he agreed with me on my interpretation of scripture, he did agree that we had to speak up against this terrible violence. He asked why someone from outside of Jamaica had to come here to tell us that our children and families are hurting because of this violence and homophobia? Don't we already know that? What can we do to stop it?

I am so grateful for that Bishop's courage and honesty and told him so. There were no more letters to the editor — at least for a little while.

Nate Phelps Helps Heal Hate in Topeka

The first time I heard of Fred Phelps and his Westboro Baptist Church was when Matthew Shepherd was murdered in 1998, and they protested at the funeral.

Many MCC churches have been the target of Phelps' wrath, none though as much as MCC Topeka. There were periods of time when protestors were outside of the church once every three weeks or so.

One day, I got a call from Phil Griffin, a long time lay leader at MCC Topeka. He said they were leading a coalition of groups that were sponsoring a speaking event in Topeka for Nate Phelps, Fred's son. He wanted me to come to Topeka that weekend, attend a press conference with Nate, introduce him at the event, and preach at the church on Sunday. I was delighted to say yes.

Nate and I met at the press conference. He is a big guy, very ordinary in some ways, and not a polished speaker. He was clear, at the press conference, that he had come back to Topeka, for the first time since he was 18-years-old, to work on reconciliation. He wanted to apologize to as many groups as possible for his father's actions and to work on reconciliation with at least some of his family.

Nate was on a tour, sharing his story with groups around the country and in Canada, where he now resides. Nate identifies as an agnostic and was clear about that. The coalition that brought him to Topeka included MCC, the Unitarians, the local secular LGBTQ group, and a local Atheist league. Quite a diverse coalition!

No one knew if the Westboro Baptist Church would show up to protest. The atmosphere was electric.

As I came to understand it, Phelps' church had bullied Topeka for decades. That is the only word I can use for it. His church is not a church, in my opinion, except in a legal sense. It is Fred's family, held together by his brutal bullying. No one outside of his family is a part. They do not evangelize; they do not want outsiders in their church. Sociologically, that makes it a cult, not a church — a cult of a very disturbed, mentally ill bully who misuses religion to control his family and others.

The City of Topeka had tried in many ways to shut Fred and his church down, but Fred and his daughters are brilliant lawyers who almost always win. In fact, they won a case before the Supreme Court about their right to protest in very ugly fashion at the funerals of soldiers.

Across the country, churches and LGBTQ groups are told by people who have dealt with Phelps to never touch any of the Phelps people. You will be charged with assault and lawsuits with damages attached will soon follow. They fund all of their travel around the country through lawsuit settlements.

Many Topeka citizens were (and still are) exasperated that their city has been identified with the hateful rhetoric and actions of the Westboro Baptist Church. Like victims of bullying they felt helpless, frustrated, and even traumatized.

More than 800 people showed up for the lecture by Nate Phelps, and the Westboro Baptist never showed up to protest. I introduced Nate, thanked him for his courage and marveled at the common values held by such diverse community groups that made this event happen.

Nate spoke for about an hour. Everyone was at the edge of their seat the entire time. He painted a disturbing picture of a tyrannical, abusive father who made the lives of his children miserable. He said aloud what many had assumed. How tragic it was that no civic or legal force ever was able to stop the abuse, which everyone suspected. Using the cloak of religious freedom, Phelps mentally, emotionally, spiritually, and even physically abused his family. And, no one stopped him.

After describing all that he, his mother, and siblings endured, he told the riveting story of how he planned and executed his escape from the compound at age eighteen. As he shared the poignant story of his process of recovery and healing, I was deeply moved.

In the question and answer period, when pushed by the atheist group to just condemn all religion, he hesitated and said, "If all churches were like MCC, I might not be an agnostic. I don't know, but there are a lot of people of faith who do a lot of good. I know my father was not typical." He also spoke about not wanting to raise his children with traditional Christian ideas about the fear of hell.

At the end, he spoke very poignantly about his father, and about forgiveness, what could and could not be forgiven. Nate, who grew up having to memorize so much scripture told us to take comfort in the scripture that says, "for it is appointed for all men(sic) to die." Sometimes it is only death that will stop some people, some kinds of depravity.

Fred Phelps died in 2013, apparently alone, rejected by the family he bullied for so long. For us, his death was not a time for rejoicing, but for really understanding the power of hate and hate speech, and the power of love to overcome it — if not now, then in the long run.

After the event, members of the atheist organization were very warm to me, and invited me to their barbeque with Nate and his wife. I had a plane to catch, but I was very touched by their hospitality. I know there is tremendous prejudice in our country towards people who do not embrace God or religion. Bless the Nate Phelps of the world who try to build bridges among all of us whom his father so maligned.

Terror at a Funeral

One of the worst incidents of violence towards LGBTQ people in Jamaica occurred in early 2007, at the funeral of the young, gay man who had led music for our new MCC church.

The young man was from Mandeville, where we also had a weekly Bible study group. A Church of God pastor in Mandeville had the courage to host the funeral. Many LGBTQ people and allies from all over the Island came to the funeral, full of anger and pain.

In the middle of the service, hundreds of local people descended on the church with machetes, interrupting the service and terrorizing the mourners. The police stood by and did nothing until some of the mourners, in a Stonewall moment of their own, got machetes out of their cars and moved toward the mob instead of running way. Only then did the police spring into action to disperse the crowd.

Miraculously, no one was killed, though some were injured.

The pastor and funeral director abruptly ended the service and during all the chaos, they quickly buried the young man in an unmarked grave.

Several months later, when I was in Jamaica as a part of a special vigil, some of us went to that unmarked grave to complete the service and to lay a memorial wreath. I will never forget the brave Jamaicans who stood by me as we said that prayer, who were looking over their shoulders, concerned that someone would see us, attack us, or return to desecrate the grave of this beloved young man.

I tell this incident not only because it is so egregious, but because it is emblematic of what goes on week after week for gay people in Jamaica. It is not hyperbole to say that LGBTQ people are being crucified daily in Jamaica, and in many other places around the world.

Healing the Hate: Virgil Scott's Murder

Virgil Scott was an MCC minister who was brutally murdered in 1986, in Stockton, California.

I knew Virgil when he was in Orange County, and in the early 1980s, I preached at his church on a rainy Christmas Eve. The MCC church in Orange County met in a funeral home chapel, and I remember that the organ that night seemed to have only one speed, funereally slow.

Virgil was earnest and devoted to MCC. In response to a need for a church, he moved to Stockton, California, to be the pastor. Stockton was not a hotbed of liberalism, then or now. It is a working class, poor community on the I-5 corridor in central California. It was a headquarters of right wing groups like the Ku Klux Klan. This was not an easy place to grow an MCC, though the need was great.

Like many MCC pastors, Virgil did not have an office. He worked out of his home, and met people for counseling in coffee shops.

One night, late, Virgil got a call from someone who needed something. He got in his car and went to a coffee shop.

A few days later, he was found in the trunk of his car, stabbed dozens of times, murdered in what was clearly a hate crime.

At that time, I was an Elder and the pastor of MCC LA. It was the mid-1980s and I was vacationing with Paula and her mother in San Diego, when I received a call from Rev. Perry about Virgil. I can see the place even today and remember the call.

Virgil was a slight, small, quiet man. He was not flashy or charismatic. He was faithful and compassionate with a servant's heart. He did not have a violent bone in his body.

I was so anguished by this news, I remember going outside of the hotel room to get some air, just to be by myself.

And, then I had a vision. I could see Virgil getting to heaven, still horribly traumatized by the last, frightening, violent minutes of his life. That was no way to enter Paradise, bloody and in terrible pain, alone and scared!

The vision continued. The Spirit of God took time with Virgil, to heal every wound, to heal his soul, body, and mind. God took time to restore him, to erase the trauma, to let it all go. I had the strange awareness that this would take about a week, which makes no sense spiritually, but it felt like there needed to be respect, and real time, human time, devoted to reversing a human act of rage and violence. I have no real explanation. It was an all-absorbing sensation, and I accepted it as a gift in that moment.

I still cling to that vision as an insight I was given, however crude or imperfect, as to how God heals people after death, traumatic or not. Some things cannot be healed in this life, and when death comes so traumatically, it seems so grossly unfair that the last thing someone like Virgil would sense was so horrifying. Maybe it is my own sense of justice that God would take the time to heal Virgil before receiving him into heaven. The joy of entering eternity may require some preparation first.

Some things just take time. Fortunately, Eternity has all the time that is needed.

Matthew Shepard: The Hate Crime that Impacted a Nation

It was during MCC Los Angeles' 30th Anniversary celebration, October 6, 1998, that we got word of a terrible hate crime in Laramie, Wyoming, and first heard the name, Matthew Shepard.

We had a wild, very active young adult group at the church. Rev. Dawn and the group stayed up all night, borrowed a large blue tarp we had used on the roof when we had an awful leak, and made a gigantic poster that said, "Pray for Matthew." They threw it over the roof so it lay flat against the huge side of the building that faced Santa Monica Blvd. About 100,000 cars passed by every day, and for two days, people saw that stark prayer request plastered on our building.

Then he died. It was on a Monday morning, and I was invited to two press conferences, one at the Lesbian and Gay Center, and one at the AIDS Healthcare Foundation, the two largest organizations in our community. I found myself as angry and articulate as I have ever been and called what happened a "lynching."

The details that came out about Matthew's death were horrifying and cruel.

Just in front of the blank wall where we had thrown the tarp was a shorter boxy building with a flat roof. It occurred to us that the roof of that "box" was a perfect stage, and the wall behind it, a perfect screen.

So, we organized a vigil and memorial for Matthew outside, in front of our church in West Hollywood. We got dozens of city officials, politicians, community leaders, and other clergy to come. We projected visuals, music, and words onto the wall that was a screen.

Our AV team was really high tech for the times. We had a ladder that went from the street to the roof and prayed that the roof was sturdy enough to hold those of us who climbed up there. Church members helped women in heels, transgender women, and others climb the ladder to our makeshift outdoor stage. We obtained permission to use the street, but that night, people had to park as far away as the Beverly Center to get near the church. As far as you could see, in every direction, were people, with candles, angry, and mourning.

We resolved, at MCC LA, that from that point on, every time there was a hate crime, we would march, and we did, for most of that year and in years to come.

Later that week, Jesse Jackson asked if he could come to the church, stop by and say a few words. On a Tuesday afternoon, the place was packed out into the streets.

Rev. Jackson wove a tapestry of hope out of the pain of persecuted lives. It had only been a few months before when James Byrd, Jr. had been walking beside the road in Texas and three white men gave him a ride. Before it was over, he was severely beaten, then dragged behind the truck to his death by decapitation. After torturing and murdering him, they dumped Mr. Byrd's remains on the lawn of a Black church — yet one more act of racist terrorism.

All of this was on the hearts of MCC founder, Rev. Troy Perry, and Rev. Dawn Wilder, a pastor from our LA church, as they flew to Laramie, Wyoming, for the funeral. Fred Phelps and his church folks were there with their placards, while volunteers protected the mourners from having to see them as they entered the church. For Troy and Dawn, it was a sad and overwhelming service.

Matthew's murder radicalized his mom, Judy Shepard, who worked tirelessly on hate crimes legislation. Eventually it passed and bears the names of Matthew Shepard and James Byrd, Jr. They will not be forgotten.

We were reminded of MCC's responsibility to be a public, safe place that can also be an open spiritual place, a place of healing, justice, and resolve for an entire community.

Early Hate: Slapped at the Altar

Sometime in early 1973, our new congregation had outgrown the Arlington Street Unitarian Universalist Church chapel, and we moved to Old West Methodist Church near Government Circle in Boston. That Methodist church had a history of rebelliousness and of fighting homophobia. Providing a welcoming church home to MCC Boston for our Sunday evening service was a part of that legacy.

In those early years, odd things happened at our services. We attracted people who were disturbed, for many reasons, and plagued with homophobia and internalized homophobia.

One young man came to church, sat down, took out a thin, tough, wire, and began to strangle himself. People around him had to grab him and the wire, they talked with him outside and arranged a ride to the hospital.

Another middle-aged man, who was reasonably good looking, smart, and a seminary graduate, would pick up young men at church, take them home, have sex with them, and then force them to pray and beg God to forgive them! He would then throw them out, call their place of employment and out them, which often cost them their jobs.

We were not trained well enough to recognize the signs of certain kinds of mental illness. Over and over again we tried to talk with him and warned every young man who came to church. Finally we had to ask for a restraining order to prevent him from coming to church — a tough thing for a church that says we are radically inclusive.

In another case, it was one of the first Sundays at the Old West location, when Larry and I began to consecrate communion. Suddenly, a young man sitting a few rows from the front rushed the altar, slapped me hard in the face and knocked over all the communion elements. He said nothing and ran out of the church before anyone could stop him.

I staggered, and Larry caught me. Then, in the way that he always did, he said quietly, "Calm down everyone, take a deep breath." They did. He slowly and deliberately righted the altar ware, poured juice back in the cup, re-set the paten and wafers, and consecrated the elements.

Communion took on another meaning for us that night. It was our solidarity in the face of violence. The young man may have been disturbed by a woman celebrating communion, or maybe because a lesbian and a gay man were taking the elements into our own hands.

That was a whole year or so before the Episcopal women, the eleven, would be irregularly ordained in Philadelphia, in an act of courage and disobedience. Many of those women also endured violence and harassment.

We never learned who that man was and why he did what he did. We also learned that we had to train our ushers to double as security — watching the doors, noticing who was coming in and out, tracking anything unusual and making a plan if needed.

I have always been grateful that young man did not have a gun or any weapon but his fists.

A month or so later, we were worshipping in the same location, and a family showed up late, kids and all, and sat in the back of the church. Larry and I could see them, and that they were glaring at us. We had eye contact with the ushers who were worried too.

At the end of the sermon, they rushed forward to the middle of the sanctuary and began cursing us and screaming ugly, vile homophobic epithets—even the children. Everyone was stunned again. They rushed out, and Larry gathered us in the middle of the aisle this time. We held on to each other. Some were crying, but he asked us just to say the Lord's Prayer, slowly, calmly. We did, and then went back to our seats and resumed the service.

Meanwhile, the ushers had called the police. Amazingly, the visitors returned, this time because someone had parked behind them, and they could not get their car out! The usher found the person, who took his time, so that the police could get there. The police only reprimanded the hateful intruders. In those days, we were lucky they even did that. We never found out who these people were, and why they chose to violently disrupt our worship.

Because these kinds of things happened so often in that first decade or so of MCC's life, Rev. Perry and others made a vow that we would never disrupt worship in another church or house of prayer. We could peacefully protest at events, do everything to make our opinion known, but we would not interrupt worship. In later years, ACT UP and other AIDS activists disrupted church services, and we understood why, but we never felt like we could participate in that kind of action.

Bomb Threat at 1974 MCC General Conference in San Francisco

The second MCC General Conference that I attended was in San Francisco, California, in August 1974. It was my first time in San Francisco, and in the middle of our conference, Richard Nixon resigned as President.

I have several memories of that early MCC Conference. My interview to be re-licensed as MCC clergy took place in a building that had been torched recently. It had been the church at which MCC San Francisco had been meeting and had no roof!

Having our buildings destroyed by arson and vandals was a common occurrence in the 1970s, and having our interviews there was a powerful, if unintended, object lesson for all of us: this is what you may be in for! Every one of us was aware every day that our lives could be at risk. MCC clergy collars, with the little white tab in the center, could be a target. Our churches and homes were vandalized, and people were beaten and killed. Many of those stories are already fading in our corporate memory, but it was on our minds all the time then.

Later that week, on Friday night of General Conference, as a 24-year-old MCC clergyperson with two years experience, I was invited to do the benediction.

That was exciting for me. It was only my second General Conference.

I sat up on the chancel of the Presbyterian church we were borrowing. The sanctuary was on the second floor, and we were all crammed in there that evening. At about five minutes before eight, Rev. Perry came to the mic and said that the police had barricaded the streets below, because there was a bomb threat. There was no time to safely evacuate, so he asked us first to all check beneath our seats for a bomb, and when none was found, he prayed. He prayed for us all to be safe, but that if we were to die tonight, what a sight it would be at the gates of heaven! He laughed when he said, "Can't you see the look on St. Peter's face to see all these MCCers coming in!"

He prayed with serenity and joy that night. We sat down, and eight o'clock came and went. Then, "Papa" Rev. Paul Van Heck sang, "The King is Coming," and brought down the house.

Paul was probably in the early stages of Alzheimer's. When he preached, he sometimes forgot that he was in MCC and that it was okay to be gay. So mostly at Conferences they had him sing and not preach. He was a dear soul who loved God and loved MCC, when he could remember that's where he was.

Someone preached, I can't remember who, and at the end of the service, I was very honored and excited to do the benediction after all!

Another part of the story that I cannot verify is that one young man was late for the service, and the police did not want him to cross the barricade. Just before eight o'clock, a light surrounded the whole building, and everyone on the street saw it together. The man came into the building as the service was ending, and told the story.

Bomb Threats at 1976 MCC General Conference in DC

In the 1970s, MCC held our General Conference every year until 1978. We also had two or three District Conferences every year. So much was happening, and in the absence of the Internet or a virtual world, we were hungry to see each other as often as possible. We had no money, none at all. We conferenced in borrowed churches, slept on the floors of those churches, or in each other's homes, crammed into vans and cars, took trains, and rarely flew. We ate church potluck food, or fast food, or skipped meals, vowing never to miss another conference.

In 1975, we had the conference at a hotel for the first time, in Dallas, Texas. Most of us stayed elsewhere. I stayed with Rev. Rob Shivers, an early MCC pioneer, along with about six other women. We slept on mattresses or sleeping bags on floors, wherever. There was one car, so we went as early as the first meeting any of us had to attend, and stayed until the last one was done — which meant about four hours of sleep a night. But, we were young!

People would come to conferences having only a one-way ticket, and would have to rely on some special conference offering to get home. We were always merciful and helpful. Anyone who came to the conference on faith, added to our numbers and were welcome. We would find them a way home. There were no scholarships then; we just did what we had to do in the moment.

In 1976, we used a conference hotel in Washington DC, and had all our meetings at the First Congregational Church, where MCC DC met for many years.

By that time, we had developed a strange practice. If we got a bomb threat during a business meeting, we did our best to evacuate. If the bomb threat happened during worship, we just stayed put and trusted God. As if God would protect us a little more in the worship service. I am not sure who decided this, but we all went along with it, so it quickly became our tradition.

That year we had a series of bomb threats, all of them during the day, during our already endless business meetings. Our business meetings went on and on, as we had to discuss and debate everything to death. We were testing ourselves, one another, our leaders and their patience, our processes, our group ethic and style. Egos were fragile, and there were a lot of wounded people who were vying for attention, for recognition. We were creating a denomination in the midst of a ferocious first wave of a civil rights movement that few outside our number embraced. Stress was a constant companion.

At those tumultuous business meetings, there were always the voices of calm and reason among us that called us back to our purposes.

For several days in August 1976, several times a day, our meetings were interrupted with news that there had been a bomb threat, and the police were asking us to evacuate.

I remember standing outside in the warm Washington DC, weather. We would joke and carry on, and continue our discussions while waiting for the room to be cleared.

One time, the evacuation occurred while Rev. Elder Freda Smith was in the restroom. When she came out, it was so eerie that no one was there! The evacuations were not the first thing to come to her mind, and she wondered if the Rapture had come and she was left behind! Moments like that made me glad I did not grow up with such theologies or concepts.

Over time, our conferences became less of a target.

Paying the Price in Jamaica

I became Moderator of MCC in October 2005. A month or so later, I was in Birmingham, Alabama, on a church mission. That morning, I was distressed to read an editorial in the New York Times about violence against LGBTQ activists in Jamaica. Its source was the publication, *Hated to Death*, by Human Rights Watch which documented the lethal homophobia raging in Jamaica. They reported the death of gay rights leader, Brian Williamson.

As the new Moderator, I thought, what could MCC do? So, I called Human Rights Watch, knowing that they, and most human rights groups are naturally suspicious of religious groups, even queer-friendly ones. At first, the woman on the phone tried to put me off. When I persisted, she let out that Brian's roommate was coming to Miami over Christmas week and might appreciate connecting with the MCC community while he was there. I gave her my phone number, and said I would drive to Miami to meet him if he was open to that.

Gareth Henry called me a couple of days after Christmas. I drove to Miami and found him at the apartment of his friend. We drove forever looking for a place to eat lunch and found a Denny's that was crappy even for a Denny's. We ate and talked and drank coffee for about four hours. Gareth was 26 or so at the time, an unintended activist who wanted to be a social worker. Several of his friends had been gay bashed or killed. He had been bashed and harassed. And, now he was the de-facto leader of JFLAG, the Jamaica LGBTQ organization.

During our talk people were texting or calling Gareth. In the middle of the afternoon, he broke down during one call. In Montego Bay, a young man who people suspected of being gay, was pushed by a mob into the ocean, and drowned. Gareth was furious but tried to console his colleagues and friends. Just in those hours, I began to learn that Gareth was well-connected to the community in Jamaica and was becoming a leader in his own right.

He cried quite a bit that day. He told me that his best friend, Brian, and he, had a gay choir, and they would sing at funerals of people who were killed. They visited people in hospitals and acted like a church without a preacher or a building. He wanted to know immediately if MCC could come to Jamaica. He told me, "More than anything we need a spiritual community."

I prayed for him in the car before dropping him off and promised to keep praying, to be in touch, to work with him, to stay connected, and to think about how we might collaborate. And, we did. We eventually started church groups in Jamaica, which I visited a couple of times. The killings and bashings and mob violence continued

One Valentine's Day, Gareth and a couple of others were surrounded by a mob and had to barricade themselves inside a pharmacy. The police almost threw them to the crowd, but Gareth insisted they take them out a back way and in a police car to safety, which they finally did. That insistence saved lives that day.

In our trips to Jamaica, we educated clergy, spoke to political leaders, police, and others. I was on television and radio a great deal, and in the newspapers. No Jamaican could be seen on television yet, as calls for murder of "battyboys," gay men, in particular, were routine.

We did workshops, preached, and met with groups. I was always so amazed at the courage and brilliance of the leaders. Over the last ten years, many of those leaders have had to seek asylum elsewhere. Others died and some disappeared. The constant leadership drain negatively impacted the sustainability of the local LGBTQ rights organization and MCC.

Gareth was targeted so often, that he eventually had to seek asylum in Canada. The adjustment to such a different climate and culture, the loneliness, was very difficult for the first five years. We stayed in touch. A group of us in MCC offered him support through that time.

Today, Gareth is the Director of an HIV/AIDS organization and a leader of a group of Jamaican exiles in Toronto, Ontario. Homosexuality is still criminalized in Jamaica, and the violence continues.

Hate, and Human Rights in the Ecumenical Movements

One of the best features of the WCC meeting in Porto Alegre, Brazil, in 2006, was an enormous area outside the assembly hall where many NGOs, human rights and other organizations, had booths and tables with information about their causes. It was a wonderful place of connection and intersectionality.

One day, a group of Palestinian Christian youth (I think they were Quakers), started a dance through the aisles. "Untouchable" Dalits from India joined them as did MCCers. For my friend Ann, an MCC volunteer at the conference, dancing with the Palestinians and the untouchables was a sublime moment. That, and using her native Greek with unsuspecting Orthodox delegates, were her delights.

Having a booth, however, for MCC, also made us sitting ducks, targets for those who found our very presence to be intolerable. Rev. Elder Diane Fisher was spit on by the Russian Orthodox delegates. Rev. Fisher had helped foster MCC's message of inclusion among young LGBTQ activists in Eastern Europe. We spoke to the leaders of the WCC about the incident, but no one was challenged or made to apologize. We were just reminded by someone on staff of how difficult it was for the Russian Orthodox to accept our presence.

So, spitting was an understandable response?

Years before, about 1991, at a WCC meeting in Canberra, Australia, after speaking in the Women's Tent to about 250 women, I exited the tent and I was met by a young man who spit on me because I was a lesbian. I remember having the distinct thought that if I had simply cast out the demon of homophobia from him, he would have fallen to the ground immediately! I am not sure why I did not have the courage to do it in the moment.

There was another conference in the early 1990s, hosted by the US NCCC, with WCC leaders and personnel attending. This was a time well before the Yogyakarta Principles and before any application of the UN Declaration of Human Rights to LGBTQ human rights.

At that conference, I suggested to those who were working in the area of faith and human rights, that LGBTQ people were experiencing terrible human rights violations all over the globe. I remember people looking at me blankly, like, "LGBTQ? Human Rights?" I thought at the time, what is the problem? Is it the word "human" in connection to LGBTQ persons or the word "rights"?

At that time, people felt like religious people had a right to discriminate (they still do), and that sexuality and gender categories were not legitimate categories for human rights. We can contrast that to a time only a few years ago when Secretary of State Hillary Clinton stood before the United Nations and said, "Gay rights are human rights." At last, our long-held conviction was given a global voice.

Someday, all religions will defend human rights for LGBTQ people.

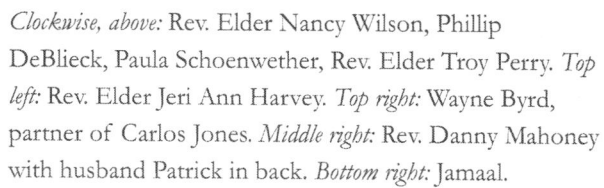

Clockwise, above: Rev. Elder Nancy Wilson, Phillip DeBlieck, Paula Schoenwether, Rev. Elder Troy Perry. *Top left:* Rev. Elder Jeri Ann Harvey. *Top right:* Wayne Byrd, partner of Carlos Jones. *Middle right:* Rev. Danny Mahoney with husband Patrick in back. *Bottom right:* Jamaal.

Laughter is the Best Medicine

When I was a kid, my parents were readers, but we did not own many books. We used the Public Library. This amazing institution in the U.S. had a huge impact on me which made countless worlds accessible to many of us. Bookstores only existed in big cities, and most people did not buy a lot of books. It was in the library that I first read sermons of preachers long gone who inspired me in my secret ambition to preach.

In our house we eventually had an encyclopedia (in the days way before Google), and every month *Reader's Digest* came in the mail.

I rushed to read it when my parents were done. I loved the short stories and "Quotable Quotes." In fact, I clipped them out when everyone was done with the little magazine. I pasted them in a notebook that I kept for years, even before I knew I would need such stories as sermon illustrations! I was queer in more ways than one as a kid.

But even more than the quotes, I loved the *Reader's Digest's* feature, "Laughter is the Best Medicine." I included lots of those little punchlines, jokes, and gags in my quote collection as well.

In the middle ages, every Easter sermon was supposed to begin with a joke, as it was the best time to laugh at the devil (Jesus is Risen, haha, take that, you old devil!). I try to include that in my practice of Easter preaching, when I have the chance.

Today, it is mainstream medicine to acknowledge that laughter, a physiological, emotional, psychological phenomenon, really does contribute to physical and emotional healing. Laughter releases endorphins and lifts us out of ourselves. It humbles us and puts events and our troubles into perspective. And, it is free!

Every recovering alcoholic knows this. The thing you hear most at the best AA meeting with old-timers is roars of laughter. It is the secret weapon of their success. If you want to laugh, go to an AA meeting where people are telling their "drunkalogs."

A member of Church of the Trinity in Sarasota, on our Recovery Sunday one year, told of the event that was her "bottom" (the moment when you realize you need to get help to stop drinking, before you die). She was on a binge in her home, and decided it was a good time to mop the floor. The next morning she woke up with her face stuck to the floor with Mop-And-Glo! It took quite a long time to free herself and for her face to heal. Sobriety was the happy result.

As a child, I loved the comedians the best. In the place deep within, where I was afraid, scared of being different, anxious, or sad, the comedians came to my rescue. They healed me, when I didn't even have a name for what ailed me.

So many times, late at night, around a kitchen table, in a restaurant, even at a campfire, MCC pastors and members have entertained one another with our stories, sometimes laughing harder at our own stories than anyone else's!

When I came out, I learned to love the particular humor of some gay men. To this day, a gay man with a quick wit and a sarcastic, iconoclastic, irreverent sense of humor can save me from my too serious self. I know that other people are funny too, but, really, gay men are the best.

Pants Down!

In the 1980s and 90s, women clergy and lay leaders in Southern California worked together to support an MCC congregation called "Free to Be MCC" within the walls of the California Institute for Women, CIW. Attendance at our services ranged from about 25 and could be as high as 75 or more.

This prison was built to house about 1,500 women, and when we were working with our group there, it housed about 3,000 women. Overpopulation heightened every risk, so outside "do-gooders" were not appreciated — especially a group of queer church people. CIW officials and many of the chaplains from conservative traditions were not thrilled.

Sometimes we would make the 80 mile trek from Los Angeles, only to find that they were on lock-down and could not let us in. Sometimes we wondered if it was even true. We wondered if the women were waiting and thought we decided not to come. Those women loved the services, the contact from us, and it was disappointing to miss. But, through the years, we persevered. Along the way, we were able to help some of the women as they left CIW.

Rev. Don Pederson was our MCC District Coordinator at the time, so the prison church community was technically under his supervision. His job was to appoint the leader, and he was supposed to visit all MCCs in the Southwest District annually, if he could. "Free to Be MCC" inside the walls of CIW was part of his flock.

We made a special provision for him to visit with our team during an anniversary of the congregation. He could preach and get to know a little more about the women and the ministry.

California Institute for Women is in Corona, California, out in the cow pastures, quite literally. There are cattle ranches for miles around and not much else. You can smell that you are getting near the prison, as the manure stench from some of the ranches is eye-watering.

When you arrive for the first time, except for the barbed wire around the perimeter, you might think you were at a school of some kind. They call it a campus, after all. Only after you go through four separate doors, and each one clangs loudly behind you, do you really get it. This is a prison.

I was always struck by the fact that once inside, in the yard, many of the inmates looked like they might be lesbians; many of the guards looked like they were lesbians, and most of us who were visiting were lesbians as well.

On this day, Don came with us, his first time in a women's prison. We knew the drill. We submitted our IDs, took off our shoes, and went through the metal detector. The woman behind the desk was someone we had seen many times. She was friendly enough, knew who we were, knew we were no threat, etc. The guards sometimes joked around, but mostly they were friendly, business-like, and efficient.

Don had grown up in a conservative faith tradition. He is a sweet-tempered pastor. Today, he is a hospital chaplain. Don was very moved by the idea of our church within the walls of CIW and was very proud of our team and all the effort it took to build this ministry over the years.

He was also someone who was deferential to authority as a result of his fundamentalist background. When he went through the metal detector, it buzzed. So, he had to take his jacket off. Then came his belt. As he was taking clothing off in front of us, the buzzer kept going off and Don's face kept turning beet red.

Then, the guard at the desk, in a very stern voice said, "Well, that's it, I guess, you have to drop your drawers!" And, he did.

She was, of course, joking.

And, when he took off his pants, he did it in front of all of our team, and the big plate glass window that opened to the parking lot, and the windows that opened into the waiting room. The guard behind the counter was laughing so hard, she disappeared, bent over on the other side. All of us were horrified, embarrassed, and laughing.

It took Don a couple of seconds, and oh, they were long seconds, to catch on. When he did he pulled his pants up, he was redder than ever. She buzzed him in and we moved onto the next doors and the service.

MCC clergy and leaders have to sacrifice a lot to do what we do, sometimes including our dignity. I will always be grateful that Don cared enough about the women in prison that day to go completely outside his comfort zone, and to be a good sport about it all.

Star Struck and Singing Like Ethel Merman

When I think about AIDS and MCC, it is impossible not to talk about Rev. Steve Pieters. Steve came into MCC in the early 1970s, when Rev. Elder Ken Martin was pastor of Good Shepherd MCC in Chicago. Steve went to McCormick Seminary, where he had a family connection, and pastored MCC

Hartford, Connecticut, before moving to Los Angeles. Steve was a bright and rising star in MCC with a great singing voice, and he was a really good preacher.

He was also one of the first in MCC to be diagnosed with AIDS in 1984. By that time he had been ill for two years, when they were still calling it GRID (Gay Related Immune Deficiency). Steve was devastated. He had AIDS in a time when it was a death sentence.

It was right before Easter.

His friend Lucia Chappelle and others gathered around and watched an "I Love Lucy" marathon. Thus came an early lesson: laughter and friends are a key to beating something as lethal as AIDS. That became such an important principle over the years. In MCC, in worship, in our most serious or dramatic moments, laughter was healing — physically and spiritually. God help us if we could not laugh at ourselves.

Steve got sick fast. Rev. Elder Ken Martin offered up his pulpit and asked Steve to preach himself into the Resurrection that Sunday. Steve preached, "God is Greater Than AIDS," which became an MCC rallying cry. Steve became sicker. We did all we could for him, as others also became sick all around us.

In 1985, Steve was chosen to participate in one of the first trials of AIDS drugs, Suramin, which had been used to cure African sleeping sickness.

Steve had always been star-struck, and he was what we affectionately called, "a musical comedy queen." His very gay response to being attached to an IV pole for hours at a time at the hospital was to sing his way through it, one musical after another. One nurse wrote on his chart: "Only side effect of drug: singing like Ethel Merman!"

Steve was the only one who survived after that trial. The drugs blew out his adrenal glands but did not kill him. This brought years of medical ups and downs for Steve, during which he also became a prominent, and one of the first, poster boys for the disease.

The very first Hollywood AIDS benefit was held in September 1985 for the AIDS Project Los Angeles called, "Commitment to Life." Steve was asked to be the first Person with AIDS who would speak at that first glittery Hollywood event.

The event was chaired by the glamorous Elizabeth Taylor, who Steve would come to know over the years. That night she gave the first Commitment to Life Award to First Lady Betty Ford.

The same night, an emotional Burt Lancaster read a moving letter from Rock Hudson, who at that moment lay dying of AIDS in a hospital in Los Angeles.

In the green room, Steve sat with Phil Donahue, Marlo Thomas, Shirley McLane, Carol Burnett, Stevie Wonder, Linda Evans (who had kissed Rock Hudson), and Cher. Steve was in heaven, never mind AIDS! This was something he had only fantasized about all his life.

Before they went on, Steve and the celebrities were thrust into a press room with all kinds of paparazzi. When it came to the TV media, no one asked Steve a question, until Rona Barrett risked it and asked him how he felt about being the poster boy for this disease.

Out of 1,000 attendees, at least 200 were world-renown movie stars and celebrities. The rest, they hoped, were people connected to the industry who had deep pockets.

Shirley McLane introduced Steve and said, "Just speak the truth, Reverend!" And he did. He told them he was living with AIDS, not dying, and that he could still dance (he tap-danced!). He told them that all who were ill or soon to be ill needed their help and needed it now!

This was the first in more than a decade of such benefits and experiences. Shortly before her death, Steve would meet Lucille Ball and thank her for the timeless comedy which saved his life in the early days of HIV/AIDS.

He was a guest on Tammy Faye Baker's "House Party." She cried, complete with mascara streaking, and called him "Rev. Steve, a gay Christian with AIDS," which infuriated the Religious Right. Tammy endured her own fall, but she fell into the arms of the LGBTQ community as a sort of drag icon. Many embraced her with acceptance and love, and she blessed them.

Steve kept on fighting. Paula, my wife, who edited an MCC feature magazine, offered Steve a column to be able to have an outlet (in the days before blogs) for his message of hope. That column did a lot for Steve and for all who eagerly read his messages.

He almost died several times. Along with others, I did laundry for him, brought him food, and kept him company. It took a village, and Steve humbly accepted our help. Another lesson: those who humbly accepted help lived longer.

Steve worked fulltime for MCC for ten years as our HIV/AIDS Field Director, traveling all over the world. He was our ambassador for overcoming HIV/AIDS, as well. He counseled clergy who were afraid to share their diagnosis, helped churches be visible and courageous in the fight in their communities, presided at funerals, represented us in national tables of religious people dealing with HIV/AIDS, and worked celebrity events, of course!

His relentless optimism, compassion, and embodiment of hope continued to be a witness to the Resurrection. And, he kept us honest as we looked for answers to questions like, why do some make it, and most die? What can we do, besides pray for a cure, comfort the dying, and bury the dead?

With the advent of protease inhibitors, Steve is still one of the longest surviving persons with HIV/AIDS, and lives his passion for life, for the miraculous, for healing every day. Laughter is still the best medicine.

IT IS NOW 1 AM!

In the late 1970s and early 80s, as MCC was entering our second decade, before anyone could have imagined AIDS, we were struggling as a new movement with a powerful new message about the meaning of inclusion.

Specifically, women in MCC were coming into our own and were pushing the envelope regarding language about human beings and God that included women and the Divine Feminine. Battle lines were drawn, heated arguments ensued, some churches led the way, and others rebelled. We were wrestling with our identity and our mission and message. Some who understood the connection between feminism and LGBTQ liberation, who understood that homophobia was rooted in misogyny, pushed the edge to expand MCC's self-understanding.

Some of our most powerful women leaders were also from Evangelical traditions and were more conservative about God language or Jesus language. They often felt caught in the middle, between more liberal, feminist women, men friends, and their evangelical colleagues and allies in MCC.

Rev. Jeri Ann Harvey was an evangelist through and through, pastor of MCC LA, which we then called "The Mother Church." She had Baptist roots and leanings. She was looked to by many as holding up the standard, not letting people dilute the message of Jesus. At the same time, she was always drawn to women who were challenging her theology. As a Native American, she had other traditions that expanded and challenged her sense of God and theology. It was all very confusing at times.

Rev. Jean White was born and raised in the Plymouth Brethren Church, a very fundamentalist denomination in England. She had served as a medical missionary for the China Inland Mission, and was captured by the Red Guard. She was a national hero in England until she was outed as a lesbian.

A few years later, she heard Rev. Troy Perry, MCC's founder, speak at Karl Marx Hall in London and fell in love with the message of MCC. She joined MCC London and became their first woman pastor. She treasured her evangelical roots, while growing in her appreciation of so much more.

Jean and Jeri Ann were both elected Elders (spiritual, pastoral leaders) in MCC in 1979.

In 1981, our General Conference was considering proposals from an Inclusive Language Task Force on how churches were to implement inclusive language in worship and in church life.

We were all at a clergy conference early that year, and it had been hard going for Rev. Perry and MCC leaders who were on the hotspot for many issues. There was a lot of drama and trauma. We were investing all of our lives, whatever we had, into this movement. We were also afraid that someone would do something to ruin it. We were so passionate about everything, uncompromising, and so worried that the center would not hold. It almost didn't.

One evening, a couple of younger women clergy sought out Jean and Jeri Ann for counsel about how they might vote at General Conference.

It was a long evening, and Jeri and Jean, who were rooming together, got to bed quite late, and both were still quite agitated.

Suddenly, Jean bolted out of bed and said, "Jeri Ann, it's the Lord! I heard His voice, He said, 'I AM THAT I AM!"

Jeri turned over, looked at the clock, then at Jean and said, "Jean, that's my talking clock saying, "IT IS NOW 1 AM!"

Martina's Right to Bear Arms

It was another March on Washington for LGBTQ equality in 2000, a year before I moved to Florida. Rev. Troy Perry was one of the organizers and leaders of the parade and was on the speaker's roster. He asked me to lead the MCC delegation as I had done in 1993 in New York at Stonewall 25.

It was a gorgeous day, but the politics within the LGBTQ movement on this march were dicey. The Human Rights Campaign and MCC supported the march, but the National Gay and Lesbian Task Force (NGLTF) opposed it. Robin Tyler had been producing it, but was let go part way through. At the end of the parade and events of the day, someone absconded with most of the funds. There was a lot of infighting and ugliness.

In the midst of that, Troy found himself, once again, being bumped lower and lower down the speaker list by people who had not risked themselves for the movement, and who were probably not fans of religion. There were last minute add-ons, including people who had not supported the march at all, like Congressman Barney Frank. It infuriated Troy and stressed him no end. The anti-religion bias always seemed to rule the day.

I had not been invited backstage to wait — there were only a few tickets. But, singer-songwriter Marsha Stevens was performing. She had an extra pass, so Marsha got me in with the politicians, celebrities, and others. This was the "good old girl" connection at work.

Marsha has been called "The Mother of Contemporary Music," by church music historians. Her classic, "For Those Tears I Died," was ripped out of church hymnals when it became known that she had come out a lesbian. People would rip it out, and then mail it to her!

She likes to say that in some hymnals, it was on the other side of Martin Luther's "A Might Fortress Is Our God," so, at least she was in good company!

Just as Martina Navratilova finished speaking, Marsha and I were in the alley way on our way to the tent, when we happily crossed her path. We stopped, gawking, and said "hello!" I was wearing my collar which got Martina's attention for a minute, and she started amplifying her speech to me. As I listened, I did what I might do as a pastor and put my hand on her shoulder and upper arm.

As I did that, I realized this was "the" upper arm and shoulder of the greatest tennis player in the world who happened to be a very attractive lesbian! My hand just froze. I couldn't remove it. I told my hand to just let go, but it would not obey me. Tens of thousands of lesbians would be so thrilled to be doing what I was doing, so innocently. How could I end the moment? I was so concerned about my intrusive hand on her gorgeous arm I could hardly pay attention to what she was saying!

Finally, the moment came. We were done talking, Martina was being moved on by her people, and I watched my hand withdraw reluctantly.

Marsha watched this very amused. We made our way into the tent to wait with Troy and all the others. It was all downhill for me the rest of that day.

With Jerry Falwell on the Ron Reagan Jr. Show

I was on the Ron Reagan, Jr. show in the early 1990s in a studio in Los Angeles. I had been recruited for a show he was doing with the famously homophobic Rev. Jerry Falwell.

We met in the waiting room — me, Falwell, and his son who was accompanying him. It was very awkward. I tried making small talk, not my specialty, and trust me, not his either. Sometimes, with political foes, you can talk casually despite your differences, but religious foes are always way too serious.

At one point I said, "You also travel a lot; do you enjoy it?" he harrumphed something back. I thought, "If I had to be giving your message of doom and gloom everywhere I went, I might not enjoy it either."

We went to make-up, and Ron Reagan was quite cheery and eager for this match-up. He let me know his bias — in my favor.

About 30 MCC people showed up for the taping. Falwell and I were seated next to each other in these very small chairs. He was a big guy, and he was pouring out of his chair into my space. At one point, he kind of touched or patted my knee and about 10 lesbians in the front row suddenly looked like they were going to rush the stage. I glared at them, and they backed off.

I remembered my media training so I used all the questions to focus on getting my message across to the listening audience. Jerry Falwell was not my audience. He would never be convinced of anything. I had to get to those LGBTQ persons, parents, and straight allies who were watching and needed to see me as the more attractive, winsome, and spiritual person. And, a little levity can really unnerve a hater.

At one point I said, "Jerry, the only reason I would want to die before you is so that I could be on the welcome wagon when you got to heaven!" He actually guffawed, in spite of himself. I don't remember a thing he said, but I do remember that he was sweating profusely. And that I was glad to get out of that chair.

The show only went for about 12 episodes, but it played on and on for years. I would run into people all the time who saw that show, and who remembered the laugh line.

The Two Jerrys

This is a story I have heard Rev. Elder Don Eastman tell so well, many times. I asked his permission to include it.

MCC in Des Moines, Iowa, began in 1974. It was started by Rev. Jerry Sloan who was a member of the MCC in Kansas City and an attorney.

In his younger life, Jerry had been a Baptist. He felt called to the ministry. He attended and graduated from the Baptist Bible College in Springfield, Missouri.

As he came to terms with being gay, ministry for Jerry as a Baptist would not happen. When his Pastor learned Jerry was gay, he asked him to leave the Baptist church. For the next decade, Jerry Sloan was an outcast.

MCC in Kansas City changed everything for him. It was a resurrection. It was a new life. He had returned from exile. Jerry Sloan was home again.

Upon his arrival in Des Moines, Jerry arranged to speak with the religion editor of the local newspaper. He told her about MCC and his plans to start a new congregation there. She was fascinated. A church for gay people in Des Moines? This was news!

Her story included Jerry's education at the Baptist Bible College. The Baptists were not amused. Within a few weeks, Jerry received a letter from the college. The letter demanded that Jerry Sloan return his diploma. The last sentence warned, "I pray that you will repent of this evil or that God will remove you from the face of the earth."

Jerry took the letter to the religion editor of the newspaper. Now the story was carried worldwide by Associated Press. He returned to Kansas City and recruited 15 people from the MCC to go with him to Springfield. He contacted the local television stations to let them know he was going to lead a demonstration in front of the Baptist Bible College to inform them that he refused to return his diploma. The school went into nearly total shutdown.

Jerry went from Des Moines to Wichita, Kansas, to start the MCC congregation, and from there to Fort Worth, Texas, where he served as the Pastor of Agape MCC. In Fort Worth, Jerry and his church became the target of a very prominent and highly homophobic television evangelist, James Robinson.

Robinson's national telecast originated weekly from a major network television station in Dallas. Robinson condemned MCC by name on the telecast. So, Jerry Sloan went to the TV station and demanded equal time under the "fairness doctrine" which was a federal regulation at the time.

The following week, Robinson was taken off the air and Jerry Sloan was given his time slot. Jerry had 30 minutes of free national television time to share MCC's message of God's unconditional love and acceptance of gay and lesbian people.

From Fort Worth, Jerry moved to Sacramento, California, where he was a co-founder of the LGBTQ Center. Here's where Jerry's story gets really interesting. When Jerry Sloan was a student back at Baptist Bible College, he had a classmate and friend also named Jerry — Jerry Falwell.

By the early 1980s, Rev. Jerry Falwell was a nationally prominent pastor of a Baptist megachurch and a television evangelist with millions of viewers. He was also the founder and leader of the Moral Majority, a very powerful political arm of the religious right in the United States. Falwell was one of the most homophobic voices in the world.

It was during this same time that our denomination, Metropolitan Community Churches (MCC), was applying for membership in the National Council of Churches in the US By November 1983, after two years of intense dialogue and debate, the controversy over our membership application was so great among the 32 member denominations of the NCC that they voted not to vote.

The next week on his telecast, Jerry Falwell talked about the vote and Metropolitan Community Churches. He called us "brute beasts" and said "this vile and satanic system will one day be utterly annihilated and there'll be a celebration in heaven."

Several months later Falwell came to Sacramento. He was the guest on a local morning television talk show. Jerry Sloan was in the audience. Jerry Sloan stood and faced his former classmate: "Hi Jerry; Hi Jerry." Jerry Sloan then confronted Jerry Falwell with the hateful comments made about MCC. Falwell denied making the statements. Jerry Sloan said he had a tape cassette with the statements. Falwell got agitated and offered Jerry Sloan $5,000 to produce the tape.

Jerry Sloan brought the tape cassette to the television station and on the evening news the reporters played the tape and interviewed him. They all agreed that Falwell had made the statements. So, Jerry Sloan wrote to Jerry Falwell asking for his $5,000. Falwell refused to pay. So Jerry Sloan filed a lawsuit in a California court and won the case.

Jerry Sloan received a check from the Moral Majority. The amount was over $8,000 because of sanctions added by the court against Jerry Falwell. A condition was stated on the back of the check where it was to be endorsed. It provided that Jerry Sloan in accepting the payment "agrees not to gloat." So Jerry Sloan called a press conference to say he was not gloating but just wanted to say how the money would be spent. The Moral Majority was buying new furniture and equipment for the Sacramento Gay & Lesbian Center. He blew up a copy of the check with Falwell's signature as art work for the lobby of the Center!

Don Eastman said, "I will forever be grateful to Jerry Sloan. He inspired me to come out. He created a new community of faith where I could finally be honest with myself and with others. His confidence and courage were contagious."

Jerry Sloan's creativity and boldness in confronting the hate speech and lies of the Religious Right were matchless!

The Palms

Sometimes, pastors have to deal with things that they wish they didn't have to.

At MCC Los Angeles, decades ago, Mary and Jo Ann were church leaders, deacon and treasurer. We had purchased a building in Culver City, California, and it needed some serious renovation and earthquake proofing. In order to do that, we had to find a place to worship for several months while the work got done, so we could have a permit to meet in the building. Our offices were in a small house across the alley from the church building, and we could stay there, but we had to move services.

We finally found a place at Fairfax United Methodist Church. They used the sanctuary at 11AM (with less than 20 people) and invited us to use it at 9AM for our only morning service and at 6PM. We could use it Wednesday nights, as well. That was good enough for me but really challenged those who believed church was properly celebrated at 11AM Sunday mornings. We crammed in at least 150 or more at 9AM, and anywhere from 50 to 100 in the evenings. It was a lovely, wide, old sanctuary.

The first week we held services there was Palm Sunday. In all the rush, transition, and stress, we neglected to order palms for the Palm Sunday service. I apologized that day and hoped that people would understand.

But, Mary and Jo Ann did not understand and were upset. In a time when AIDS was raging and there were no drugs, and not enough hospices, or hours in the day, they felt it was a good use of their time and mine to make a special appointment with me. They came to my office to tell me how upset they were that we had forgotten the palms. Really?

This was something I could not change or fix. Only promise not to forget again, which I had already done, publicly, on Palm Sunday.

I did my best to be kind and pastoral, but underneath, I was seething and incredulous. Being a pastor for a long time by that point, I knew that certain rituals and symbols and traditions were very important, and that it could touch something deep within that had little to do with whatever the presenting issue might be. But, inside, my less understanding side said, "Do these women have any idea of what we are up against every single day? With not enough resources, people getting ill and dying every day, with all the challenges of any church, was this really a good use of my time?"

I said none of this to them and simply apologized again. What else was there to say?

They left my office and returned to their car in the parking lot, only to find it was covered in palm branches from the palm tree in the church parking lot shedding its fronds.

It was several weeks before one of them told me what had happened. They got the joke from nature. It truly made my day. I appreciated that she would have the courage to tell me and to laugh at themselves in the process.

Taking It to the Boom Boom Room

After the earthquake of 1994, MCC Los Angeles struggled desperately to find space for our programs and ministries since we were without a church building. For a while, we rented a double wide trailer and put it up in the parking lot of the building that was destroyed in the earthquake. It was cheap enough to do that, and since we were still paying the mortgage on that space, it seemed okay. It was really not big enough, especially for the choir that suffered when they squeezed in there on weeknights for rehearsals.

So, we rented space on the ground floor of the Lesbian and Gay Center on LaBrea and Santa Monica. We were there until we moved into our new space, but during Lent and Holy Week, we had problems. We needed space for our mid-week Lenten programs, Holy Thursday, and Good Friday services.

One of those years before we settled into West Hollywood, we hatched a special plan for mid-week Lenten services. I had worked for years on an "Outing the Bible" comedy routine that I did at MCC conferences, but rarely elsewhere. I loved playing with the material, making light of Biblical homophobia, and playing with new ways to make the Bible funny and interesting. To be sure, no one thought I should quit my day job, but we had fun anyway.

Someone we knew had a connection to the Comedy Store in West Hollywood, and they had an upstairs room, the "Boom Boom Room," that they were not able to fill on Wednesday nights. They gave it to us, as long as we were open to the public. For seven Wednesday nights in Lent, we put on a comedy routine about the Bible. Several of us worked together to write and create the routines. It was a blast! One night, the comedienne Robin Tyler opened for us. We were in heaven!

Church members, mostly, sat around tables, ordered drinks, and encouraged us in our performance. There was no cover charge which had a side benefit because there was at least a $10 cover charge downstairs, in the main room, where Richard Pryor was playing at least one of the weeks. Tourists who did not want to pay the cover charge came upstairs to see us first and then went to see the main event. Some even liked the performance! Who knew that religious comedy was so avant garde?

Then, we had no where to go for Holy Thursday services, so the Acapulco Restaurant gave us a room, where we had a Mexican dinner followed by our Holy Thursday communion with tortillas! We innovated in a city where renting a place for a busy church was out of sight for us financially. As frustrating and complicated as those times were, I am grateful for the creativity and commitment that took us to such places.

Things In a Pastor's Closet

Pastors have a closet, a room, or a place where they keep the gifts grateful parishioners have given them. Some of those gifts are lovely and have a place in my office or home. They match my style or are reminders of why I am doing this.

But, oh, there are so many others.

Now before I go further, if you have ever given me a gift, I truly am grateful because your heart is in the right place, but by the time you get to the end of this story about my closet, you will see the humor of having a plethora of gifts. People are grateful for the impact of an understanding pastor, and pastors are touched by the gratitude.

There are gifts people give you when you are traveling that you could never fit in your suitcase, and it won't fit on a shelf, or a desk, or on a wall, or even in a separate room if you had one! There are gifts that cost more to mail home than they are worth.

There was the enormous Bible someone made out of tin, with all the members signing it. I am not sure how I got it home. I feel guilty about not displaying it, much less giving it away!

God help the pastor who mentions they have an affinity for frogs, butterflies, birds, tennis shoes — whatever. You will soon have so many of them, you will never want to see it again — ever!

Let's talk about the crosses. How many crosses does a pastor need? I have so many, and I wear only a few.

Then there are the paintings of Jesus. One painting I did keep was of Jesus hugging a young girl, given to me by a woman who I helped heal from abuse. That picture represented her new sense of acceptance. But, oh my, all the others!

How about a solid milk chocolate depiction of Jesus on the Cross, or the Last Supper? Just go ahead, chomp on that!

I have a Bible collection and a hymnal collection, but they keep coming. I give them away and more arrive.

Giant cards signed by whole congregations come to me. It is so touching to see all the names — but where to put it?

I receive things I can't eat and have to give them away so they will not enter my house.

Plaques with sweet, or corny, or meaningful quotes and Bible verses.

Framed pictures of people with me.

I had a member give me his mother's ashes. He had nowhere to put them where he was staying, and he didn't want to think about scattering them. They lived in the trunk of my car for a while. Finally, I had to scatter Juanita's ashes myself in an appropriate place.

One day, after liberating her ashes from my car, I scattered them in the church yard in the rose garden. We had special guests visiting later that day. Eddie, a volunteer, was aware of my new found place to scatter ashes of members or family members. As he showed them around the church and the very lovely rose garden, the woman said, breathlessly, "*What* do you feed your roses?" For once, Eddie was speechless.

People give me things they thought other people might need, that I could distribute, as if I were Goodwill. I brokered food, clothing, furniture, paper goods, kitchen supplies, bedding, condoms, left over morphine and narcotics, on and on. It is not really in the job description, but just kind of understood. The pastor will know what to do with this stuff!

For a while, at MCC Los Angeles, we had a collection of church organs. We could have opened a store. People died and left them to us. How many did they think we needed?

Leftover hymnals piled up. This is from the days when we did not have PowerPoint projection in church. I had a real challenge that any pastor can relate to. We had these "old fogey" hymnals that had really terrible theology. I had the money to get new ones, but the two, beloved men who had donated the original hymnals had died tragically together in a car accident. Their names were inscribed on every one of those hymnals. Talk about sacred cows!

I found a church that was just starting out that had no hymnals and no hope of getting any. I did what I could to assuage my guilt around passing on bad theology.

We boxed them up, placed them in the front of the church one Sunday, laid hands on them, and blessed them as they left to bless another church. We wrote the congregation a special letter mentioning our two beloved deceased donors, whose names were in every single one.

We were without hymnals for a week, so when the new ones arrived, everyone was happy to see them, to hold the new ones in their hands with new names in each cover and much better theology.

Let me mention a few other special gifts:

The bleeding hearts of Jesus or Mary.
Paintings on velvet of Jesus or Mary.
Sculptures of Jesus, or a saint, or some religious theme.
Key chains with crosses, rainbows, or rainbow crosses.
Beaded rainbow key chains, with or without crosses.
Beaded bookmarks, with crosses — with or without rainbow.
Knitted stoles.
Rainbow stoles.
Knitted Rainbow Stoles.
Stoles that were too short.
Homemade chasubles, hand sewn, but not neatly.
The latest bracelet with the latest cause and color. Half a dozen of them — but I only have two wrists.
More crosses.
More Bibles, and Bible covers — knitted Bible covers with rainbows.
And pictures of crosses on velvet.
Crosses on knitted, rainbow stoles.

I am becoming an unwitting hoarder. The closet is no longer big enough. I need to rent a storage unit.

I hope you are laughing and cringing with me — even if you recognize your gift in my lists. To every person and every gift, I say thank you!

Behind every gift is a loving heart.

Ecumenical Humor at MCC Conference in 1999

Dr. Paul Sherry was the President and General Minister of the United Church of Christ in the 1990s. Paul was a courageous, faithful, and consistent ally for MCC, especially at the National and World Council of Churches. I could always count on Paul to stand for justice, to stand for full inclusion of LGBTQ people, and for inclusion of MCC in the ecumenical world.

Paul and his wife Mary attended our 1995 General Conference in Atlanta. He was our keynote speaker. This was a wonderful gesture of friendship.

In 1999, Paul was getting ready to pass the torch of the UCC Presidency to Rev. John Thomas who had served as the Ecumenical Officers for the UCC and was also very supportive. We invited both of them to our General Conference, as we were beginning to talk about a denomination-to-denomination bilateral conversation between the MCC and the UCC.

Because of their schedules, we invited them to attend our opening worship service on Monday evening and to bring greetings from the UCC. For some reason, worship on that Monday night just got out of control. Sometimes, in the effort to be diverse and inclusive, our worship services go long.

This service, apparently as a last minute change, included the flag/liturgical dance team from MCC Long Beach, which was our most charismatic church. They eventually left because MCC was too liberal in its beliefs and practices. This kind of many-colored flag liturgical dance is common in more charismatic churches, and it not everyone's cup of tea. I know the worship organizers wanted to make the folks from MCC Long Beach feel like they were contributing in a significant way.

I have a bias here. I don't like most liturgical dance, because it is often not done well, and I am often sitting in the front row and fear getting injured.

With that disclosure, our guests were in the front row, and this wild, repetitive, flag waving dancing went on for 20 minutes. There was just no stopping it. Some in the congregation were thrilled; others, not so much.

In addition, MCCers who are into leather always pick a night to dress up in their church leathers (no nudity, more modest leather, but, lots of it). The group is called PLAY (People in Leather Among You), and its purpose is meant to make a visible statement of including everyone. Of course, they picked opening night, Monday night, as their night to wear their leather, en mass.

So, the wild flag waving goes on and on, and the place is dripping in leather.

The announcements go on too long, and then, Dr. Sherry and Rev. Thomas, our esteemed guests, are finally introduced!

There they were, in their gray suits, with their grey hair, tall, modest, nice looking, generally quiet, conservative in appearance, if not in theology. No one else in the whole place looked like them, really. Even Rev. Troy Perry was in a dark suit and a collar.

Paul Sherry made some very generous and kind remarks, and got a warm reception. But, when it was John's turn, he just looked out at the congregation, paused, and then said,

"Well, actually, I feel a little underdressed tonight..."

The whole place exploded in laughter. Thank you, John, for saying the obvious, and giving us all a great laugh, and surviving opening night at an MCC General Conference.

Earl's Chest Hairs

Earl was someone who always had woes, problems, and challenges. Every time we had a healing service at MCC Los Angeles, he would be there asking for prayer. I told others not to judge people who were always coming up for prayer. If they needed it every time, who were we to withhold it or judge them?

But, truthfully, I was getting a little irritated with Earl, in spite of myself.

One Sunday night, I was determined to really get to the bottom of things with Earl, to really pray him through in a way that would make a difference.

So, the moment came, the music was going, we were praying, and Earl came forward. Others came up around him as well.

I grabbed the front of Earl's shirt, and began praying in earnest and with a lot of passion. My voice rose, Earl started moaning and crying, and really, really sweating and crying, until it seemed like maybe we were done; we were prayed through.

As we finished, Earl was still sweating a little, and I said, "Earl, are you okay?"

To which he said, "Well, yeah, but when you grabbed my shirt, you also grabbed my chest hairs, and I didn't want to interrupt you, but, boy that really hurt!"

Chest hairs, what does a lesbian preacher know about chest hairs?

I was embarrassed, but Earl seemed to be done with his healing, and didn't come up for prayers for quite a while. It was the chest hairs cure!

Portraits

These stories are more about a person and their impact, and how their story, or the portion I am sharing, impacted me and others.

Reader's Digest had a regular feature, "My Most Unforgettable Character," and perhaps that's what these are. I could write dozens more of these. Part of the wonder of ministry is coming to know people who arrive on your doorstep with a great story already, and then their growing sense of vocation shifts the narrative one more time.

By writing stories of people who are not celebrities, but people of faith who made a contribution, I hope to share the "unforgettableness" of several special human beings.

You Too, Grandma?

I met Barbara Haynes at MCC Los Angeles when I was a candidate to be their pastor. She was a member of the gospel choir who had a preacher's voice when she spoke or prayed.

I first really heard that voice when someone asked me why churches invited guest preachers to spiritual renewals, why couldn't the pastor preach at those events?

Barbara piped up, "You can't always eat your own cooking." I remember turning around to see who that was. Somehow, this woman would be important in my life and in MCC.

I invited her, and a group of people I believed had natural authority and "gravitas" to train to become deacons. She did that, but it was not enough. As the manager of the night time maintenance staff at a local college with special discounts, in her 60s, she completed her degree, and her training to be MCC clergy.

Barbara is also the proud mother of Mike Haynes, a National Football League Hall of Famer.

She and her partner of over 40 years, Evelyn, had quite a story. Barbara came from rural Texas, where her single mother picked cotton to supplement their income. Whole families did that, including Barbara's, just to get along. She tells the story of her mother complaining about her aunt Helen, muttering, "Aunt Helen thinks she's too good to pick cotton." Five year old Barbara thought that over and said, "Mama, I think I favor Aunt Helen, I think I am too good to pick cotton too." She also talked about her mother being very frustrated with her outspokenness. Outspoken black children might be cute, but now, or later, they could end up dead. So, Barbara's mother tried to beat that outspokenness out of her, to no avail.

Barbara tells the story of going to MCC Los Angeles choir rehearsal at the trailer we set up in the parking lot of the building that was destroyed in the earthquake. The choir was singing, and there was a knock at the door. Apparently a little boy in the neighborhood had been charging to take other kids to see the queers in the trailer. No one had come out of the trailer for a while, so he knocked.

Barbara, in her mid to late 60s, answered the door. The little boy said, "is anybody in there gay?" She said, quite calmly, matter of factly, "Honey, I think all of us in here tonight are gay."

"You too, grandma?" he said incredulously. "Me too, honey, for a long time!" And he and the kids ran away. I guess encountering a gay grandma was more than they could take!

Barbara loved to tell that story, saying, "You, too grandma?"

Barbara ministered in many ways in MCC, even while getting a late start. She served as the MCC chaplain to women at the California Institute for Women; she was pastor at Resurrection Beach MCC in Costa Mesa before she retired. Off and on for many years, she served as volunteer staff at MCC Los Angeles. She was preaching, praying, singing, teaching, visiting, loving people who came through the doors of that church.

An Unlikely Friendship

I first met Bishop Paul, a Coptic Orthodox Bishop from Egypt, with responsibilities for youth, for work in Kenya and all over east Africa, at a small Bible study group at the World Council of Churches Assembly in Zimbabwe. This was a very controversial conference, at which there was a lot of talk before and around the conference about LGBTQ Human Rights. The LGBTQ rights group in Zimbabwe, GALZ (Gays and Lesbians of Zimbabwe), had been under vicious attack by President Mugabe and were fighting for their lives and their freedom.

For this reason, hundreds of LGBTQ Christians were at this conference, about a dozen from MCC in the United States and Africa, and many others. We met nightly, strategizing about how to make an impact. We made sure that at every WCC press conference, the issue was raised. Because the WCC would not allow GALZ to have a workshop at the conference itself, MCC rented a local space, invited activists and the press to attend as we told the stories publically.

But, aside from the daily activism, I was one of the only openly LGBTQ persons to have access to the voting body of the WCC. Every morning, members of the WCC and delegated observers and guests (that's where I fit in), had a structured Bible study.

There were eight or nine in my group. I was the only woman. The others were heads of communions or lay leaders, from India, Pakistan, and Germany.

I waited a day or so before coming out. Being a lesbian was only slightly more awkward than being the only woman and the only American.

We were in the Bible study for almost two weeks, and in that time, we saw the WCC consider a proposal for membership for a few African Indigenous religious groups that had been polygamous, but were forswearing it as part of their commitment to be traditionally Christian, and recognized by the WCC. Their only caveat was, for the sake of mercy, to ask that the older members not be asked to "put away" or divorce their additional wives. The WCC membership committee thought this was reasonable, but all hell broke loose on the floor. Especially Africans, and others who were not from the West, were horrified, as though this was opening some kind of Pandora's Box.

The proposal and the severe reaction of total rejection by the WCC made for interesting conversation in my Bible study as we strayed far from the day's topic. It was like a dam bursting, as these church men talked more frankly about sexuality, about monogamy and polygamy in their cultures, and what they really thought. They wondered if monogamy was a "natural" state of being and if that was why there was so much divorce, adultery, and sex outside of marriage in their cultures. No one ever said it exactly, but it was as if they were wondering if the churches trying to get into the WCC by promising new commitment to monogamy were giving away too much. In that context, there was also a little more discussion about homosexuality.

I wondered if the huge blow up on the floor of the WCC was a signal to us in MCC, and the 200 visitors who were LGBTQ, not to hold our breath about inclusion, at least not for a while. The anxiety around the issue of homosexuality, human rights and the WCC got acted out in the polygamy debate — which was not really a debate at all. The churches were not asking to be included with their practice, but only to be allowed the flexibility to move into it without harming those who had practiced it.

In the midst of all of this, Bishop Paul and I ended up walking every morning from our Bible Study to the plenary tent, to worship or some event. During those walks, we had very honest conversations. We talked about homosexuality, which he seemed to understand very little. He thought of it in terms of people who were in prison, and had no "choice." As gently as I could, I helped him understand that the community I belonged to saw our sexuality as normative, as part of the variety of creation.

We talked about the Bible, about marriage, oh my, about so many things. About HIV/AIDS, in which he was very involved already. As we talked, we also laughed, and it felt like a generous conversation all the way around. As time went on, I introduced him to my colleagues, and he spoke of me as "my friend Nancy." He invited me to visit his ministry in East Africa.

I saw Paul again, in 2006 at the Porto Alegre Conference, I could see that he had aged, though he is younger than me. Again, we sought each other out, and walked around the campus together and talked like old friends.

Bishop Paul came to the White House in 2011 at the World AIDS Conference for the faith gathering. It was a struggle for him to walk, so I sat with him, and we held hands. Something spiritual transcended our enormous gulf of difference. His devotion to the health of young people in Africa, especially in his Orthodox community, is powerful and his greatest passion. He inspires me.

I cannot explain the affection and power that flowed from our connection to each other, from that Bible study more than a decade or so ago. I only know it is real and it is a sign of what can happen when we open ourselves up to people who seem to be so different, and even so opposed to us. At the level of dealing with those who are suffering, who have no one else to advocate for them, we are one heart and mind.

I Have One Year Left

I knew Danny Mahoney from the time he was the very young partner of Rev. Charlie Arehart, in Denver, Colorado, in the 1970s.

Danny was from Alabama, originally, and went into the Navy when he was just barely 18. He was petite, smart, with organizational aptitude, and became the "aide de camp" to a Navy Admiral.

In fact, Danny Mahoney was the one who took the call from President Nixon telling the Admiral to evacuate Saigon, ending the Vietnam War.

Danny grew up Baptist. He fell in love with Charlie and with MCC all at the same time. He poured himself into that church, in practical and amazing ways. When he and Charlie ended their relationship, on good terms, Danny worked on his theological education, and was eventually ordained, in about 1990.

Danny knew he had to get out of Denver, to make his own way in ministry. He knew what we had been going through in Los Angeles, moving into a new building, having to leave it to get it earthquake-proofed, moving back in. He knew I did not have enough help and support. He offered to come and work for me and learn from me. He offered to do this for minimal support.

His husband Patrick was able to work, and transfer his job, and Danny was on social security, so he could not earn a lot anyway. He was on SSI because he was HIV positive, and in fact, had AIDS.

By this time, we had had so many deaths, including deaths of clergy on staff, that I hesitated. I knew Danny could feel my hesitation.

He had skills, he was a hard worker, trustworthy, a good man. I knew he would be very helpful, but I knew that to invite him to Los Angeles meant I would also eventually do his funeral.

They came anyway. I am not sure I ever said yes, but they showed up. Danny got right to work managing the office and the facilities. He was truly a God-send to me and had a servant's heart. Patrick, or "Mrs. Danny Mahoney," as he liked to be called, was a wonderful help to him.

Danny was not a great preacher, but he was endearing, sincere, and emotional, and people loved that about him.

When Paula was in a bad car accident, I remember him running out of the office as I pulled up in my car, with accurate information, directions to the hospital, asking me if I needed him to drive. He was my Radar O'Reilly (from the television show "M.A.S.H."). Danny used to say that he was the little guy going behind the circus with the broom, and that I was the circus.

Danny did more than clean up when the Rodney King decision came down. There were riots in Los Angeles, and I was away at a conference. Danny handled the church, gave people space to deal with their anger and fears, and held a forum on Sunday. The National Guard was just blocks from the church, and depending on where you lived, and what color you were, you might have a very different set of thoughts and feelings about all that had happened. For our very diverse congregation, it was important not to have business as usual, but to be a place of prayer, support, unity, and honesty. Danny made that happened. He was not really cut out to be the one in charge, but he could manage it if needed. On that one weekend I was away, he came through with grace and leadership.

Then, I watched him begin to slow down — and to lose weight. I saw him lose his patience, and be overwhelmed. He missed days at work, and then Sundays. I did not want this to be true. He had worked his way into my heart, and damn it, into the hearts of the congregation. Besides, I needed him.

We were doing his annual review, the end of 1992, and he told me, "Boss, (he called me that instead of my name), I have about a year left. I will do my best to serve as much as I can of this year." I was stunned, and wanted to argue. But, he just looked at me, steadily, firmly. He knew.

When he was not in church for three Sundays, and we did not mention it, Rev. Steve Pieters called me on it. He said, "If I didn't already know it, I would not know that this congregation had an assistant pastor who is dying of AIDS." That really hurt. Denial stalked us all the time, seducing us with the notion that if we didn't talk about it, it must not be happening.

We said it out loud, and, I worked with Danny to adjust his work hours, and expectations. He got weaker and weaker. Finally, he just couldn't do it anymore, so, I said we would change his job description. I brought student clergy, staff, and deacons to his home, as he shared with us what it was like to go through this. He was generous in offering his time that way. He pushed me about finishing my book. He wrote lists of reminders, and things that had to be taken care of by someone.

In late 1993, Danny got more and more ill. Patrick, who was also HIV positive and starting to get sick himself, had to leave for work at 6AM. For several weeks, I went to their home every weekday morning, just until the hospice worker could get there. He was in a hospital bed in the living room, and I would be at the foot of the bed, reading. Sometimes he could talk, sometimes he couldn't. Sometimes he would mouth the words, "I love you." Being there, with him, in that condition, meant that I had to be with him for some very painful moments, difficult physical things that no one should have to go through. In times like that, nothing else matters but alleviating pain and being present.

I thought of my hesitation to welcome Danny into our church, into my own heart. I knew in those early mornings, that I had no regrets — none.

Danny continued to decline. When my father died on December 7, my friend Judy Dahl took me to the airport the next morning. On the way, I stopped to say good-bye to Danny, who I knew I would not see again in this life.

The day of my father's funeral, December 13, they admitted Danny to the hospice, and he died five minutes after his head touched the pillow. He was always efficient.

A few days later, Patrick, their friend Linda, and I witnessed Danny's cremation. His memorial service was packed. What a wonderful tribute. I played Danny's favorite version of "All Hail the Power of Jesus' Name" on the piano. Nathan, an MCC deacon who would later be ordained, sang "Danny Boy."

Just a month later, on the morning of January 17, 1994, the Northridge earthquake threw Patrick out of his bed and into the door, very violently. He was very, very banged up. He went to his doctor, and, then, they realized, he had an AIDS-related cancer. I could see that Patrick was not going to survive Danny by much. Two months later, he was admitted to the same hospice in which Danny died. I stopped in the early morning of a March day, on my way to a MCC leadership meeting, and held his hand as he died. I was grateful to have made it in time, for Danny's sake as well.

Mabel O'Dell Moves In

Mabel and Amos O'Dell were from rural Michigan. Their son Rick was a senior in high school when he came out. He left home and moved to Detroit, Michigan, falling in love with a deacon in the church, and eventually moving to Los Angeles, where he worked at MCC Headquarters for several years.

Rick caught the early wave of AIDS. His partner Phil got sick first and died. Rick had psoriatic arthritis, and suffered a great deal. George, from our AIDS Team, visited Rick frequently, kept me updated. Finally, it was clear that Rick was too sick to manage at home, and was dying. George and another woman from the team had to transport him to the hospice in Long Beach, where we had a special connection. Rick's skin disease was so advanced that they had to keep the car windows open all the way, because of the smell.

George opened his home to Mabel, Rick's mother. George had been in touch with her, and let her know how serious things were. Mabel and Amos did not have much money, and a plane ticket to Los Angeles was costly enough. George let her stay with him. She was there for a few weeks, when the cook quit at the hospice. Lee, an early MCC pioneer, who ran the hospice, hired Mabel on the spot to temporarily fill in. That gave her a little income, and she just moved in. George continued to be supportive, to visit, and to be there for Mabel as well.

Amos came when Rick was about to die, and said his last good-bye's.

But, Mabel had news for Amos. She just could not pack up and leave Lee and the patients at the hospice in the lurch. They had grown to love her cooking, and it gave her a sense of purpose.

Amos missed her cooking too. But, he was understanding, and encouraged her.

Mabel O'Dell stayed on about a year, as she managed her grief by offering her gifts to others. She touched them, hugged them, cooked for them, and was a motherly presence in the house that really needed her.

God Works in Mysterious Ways

When we went to the 2006 World Council of Churches meeting in Porto Alegre, Brazil, we were determined to meet delegates from Jamaica. We hoped they would listen to our struggles, and help us as we collaborated with those on the ground in Jamaica who were planting MCC, and also fighting for basic human rights and safety.

There were three delegates from Jamaica, out of over 5,000 people, and it was not easy to find people who were not in leadership, or who did not have a booth. We prayed for a way to find them.

Connie Meadows, my assistant, and her partner Hilde had come to the Council meeting to represent MCC, and to help me, at their own expense. Connie was very passionate about the work of MCC, and our witness in Brazil. She had retired from secular work, and come out of retirement to volunteer at the church where I pastored. Later, she came to work for me when I became Moderator. A very modest person, Connie had organizational management, financial management and entrepreneurial expertise, and spoke five languages.

A few days into the Conference, Connie slipped and twisted her ankle in one of the hallways, where lots of folks passed them by. A woman finally stopped. She bent down and explained that she had been a nurse in another life. Connie noticed her accent, and then her badge, lo and behold! She was from Jamaica!

For a moment, Connie forgot about her ankle and told her the story of our efforts to try to find anyone from Jamaica at the WCC Conference. Not only was this woman from Jamaica, she was the assistant Dean of the Protestant Theological Seminary in Kingston, and very happy to find someone from MCC.

More than that, she was of course, just the person we needed to collaborate with in Jamaica and very supportive of our cause. She, in fact, had faced homophobic violence in her own family, as a gay cousin, a government official, was brutally murdered.

A year later, she and I would co-present at the first somewhat public meeting of clergy in Jamaica who wanted to understand more about how to minister with LGBTQ persons, and how to stand against violence.

Those first conversations in Porto Alegre, Brazil, at the WCC General Assembly, with our first faith ally in Jamaica, were invaluable.

Connie came to MCC late in life. In fact, she was already retired when she visited Church of the Trinity in Sarasota, Florida, and began volunteering. She and her partner Hilde, of many decades, had never really been "out," or involved in LGBTQ friendly organizations. They stuck to the symphony and community projects.

All that was about to change, as Connie got more and more involved in the local MCC. When I became Moderator of MCC, either she informed me, or I invited her, to come with me. Her amazing skills of organization, language and technology were invaluable in the first half of my years as Moderator of MCC globally.

Over the years, Connie and I had many adventures: going to the WCC headquarter in Geneva; to Taize, France; to seminary at the Episcopal Divinity School, (she for her Masters' in Theology, me for my doctorate of ministry). We traveled to a conference in Hawaii, and to meetings at a very rustic dude ranch in Texas.

Connie could be fierce at times. One pastor called, trying to get an appointment with me to talk at the last minute about arranging to pay back assessments, so they could vote at our Conference. Connie knew that this church had made many promises, broken them, and failed to respond when we contacted them. She told him she was not going to interrupt me or waste my time. If they did the right thing, they could vote at the next conference. End of conversation.

I didn't know this had happened until Connie retired.

A year or so later, the pastor called me, complaining about Connie. He also mentioned that they were now complying with their obligations, and would be ready to vote at the next conference. It was not lost on me that her setting that boundary actually had a good effect. I apologized for any "tone" that was distressing, but also acknowledged the new leaf they had turned over. Sometimes Connie's toughness worked better than my accommodations.

In 2009, Connie lost her partner Hilde, to cancer.

A couple of years later, quite unexpectedly, a new love captured Connie's heart, and brought deep healing and joy.

Even in retirement, Connie and her new partner continue to serve MCC and the Moderator's Office, they opened their home and heart to MCC leaders, those who work for human rights and share MCC message in places around the world.

We still marvel at how God could use a sprained ankle to move forward human and religious rights in Jamaica!

Been Coming to MCC all My Life

Carlos Jones and Wayne Byrd were young, African-Americanmen, steeped in the church all their lives, who found MCC in West Hollywood, when I was pastor. Wayne had been Methodist, and Carlos, Baptist. Carlos, in fact, was a Baptist minister, who had lost his ministry when he had come out and was then diagnosed with AIDS.

Carlos was already showing some signs of illness when we first met him. He was a petite, attractive, emotional person. His eyes blazed with passion about the new, inclusive gospel he was embracing.

Carlos was a creative preacher. I remember his sermon, from Genesis, "In the Beginning, God..." He left off the end of the sentence, and did an amazing riff on God, in the beginning, before all things. He was poetic, and colorful in his speech, and could talk on his feet. During Pride one year, we did a radio show together, and he was just amazing.

One time he was testifying in church, and I was doing a question and answer thing, and I said, "Carlos, how long have you been coming to MCC?" He did not hesitate, and said, "Pastor Wilson, I have been coming to MCC ALL MY LIFE!"

I think that was true, he had been on his way to us, all his life, and found his true home.

Wayne and Carlos were married by me, in a time when Carlos was really losing ground. He was almost too ill to really participate in his own wedding. Weeks later, he died.

Wayne went on to become a deacon, and immersed himself in church work. He was deeply sincere, and sometimes it seemed to me, was putting all his grief to work as a way to stay ahead of his profound loss. Wayne also had a wonderful sense of humor, and a sweetness. With all the grief that was all around us in those days, somehow, his was particularly poignant. Young people like Wayne and Carlos could have been the future of MCC, and losing them was losing a part of that future.

I have a stole from my last Sunday as pastor of MCC LA that everyone signed. Wayne signed it from him and from Carlos, who had been gone a while, "May the twins, Grace and Mercy, go with you." And also with you, dear brothers, of blessed memory.

"Just a Minute There, Mr. Schuller!"

In the 1980s, MCC churches were growing, and some in MCC were wanting to learn more about the "Church Growth Movement," which was mostly popular in more conservative, evangelical circles.

One of the places where church growth was touted as a science and an art was at Robert Schuller's Crystal Cathedral in Garden Grove, California. The Schuller Institute was an annual seminar for pastors in how to employ the principles and methods of church growth practitioners. The Cathedral was the model, and Dr. Schuller was the main feature, though, over time, other speakers and successful church growers were invited.

Rev. Don Eastman sought to build a bridge between what was happening in that world, and MCC's need for those resources and encouragement. The annual Schuler Church Leadership Institute was open, and there were group rates, so Don organized a group of pastor of larger MCC churches to go to the conference.

This was during the same time period that MCC was also seeking membership in the National Council of Churches (USA), and we were always looking for ways to test church groups about their inclusivity. Don was surprised that we were accepted to the Schuller Institute. They were eager for registrants, and did not have any kind of litmus test, so MCC pastors went.

The idea was for MCCers to go, and not necessarily make a big deal of going, not to lie about who we were, but not to make that the centerpiece of our participation. We were going to learn how we could apply what they were doing "right" to our churches.

MCC's participation seemed mostly to be a non-event, with several MCC pastors having one-on-one testimonies from encounters that turned out positive. The Institute itself had no comment about our participation.

A few years into this process, I decided to go, and Rev. Robert Pierce, from Church of the Trinity in Sarasota (where I would later be pastor) was in attendance. By this time, the Institute had grown considerably, and the number of MCC pastors in attendance was at an all-time high (maybe 35 or so).

One of the MCC clergy was Robert, a former Catholic brother, who had also served in the Navy. He came out in Hawaii, and became an MCC clergy while studying with Rev. Jim Sandmire, in San Francisco.

Robert, a young, energetic pastor who had a very sharp New England accent, could do a very good imitation of a sharp, sarcastic queen.

On the first evening, Dr. Schuller made a presentation, and, in the process, made a couple of surprisingly homophobic comments. When the time came for questions from the audience, I looked at Robert, who was making his way up to the microphone, and I sensed that he was going to handle this. Well, did he!

Robert started, with "Just a minute there, Mr. Schullah!" pronouncing his name with a heavy New England accent. Robert, angry and articulate, called attention to the fact that there were 35 of us LGBTQ folk there, paying our way, and did not appreciate being spoken about or to as we were that evening.

Schuller for his part was enraged at being spoken to like this and began sputtering and responding in more inappropriate ways, when a staff person came up and just gently guided him off the stage. We never saw Dr. Schuller again at the conference.

I later learned that although Dr. Schuller held certain views, the Cathedral had its own version of a support group for LGBTQ people, and was trying in its own way to foster conversation and openness. It was not coming from the top, but nevertheless, they were trying to become more open.

MCC leaders met with the staff of the Institute while we were there, they apologized, and invited me to con-celebrate communion on the last day, which I was happy to do. There is even a picture (rare one!) of me in a skirt on the chancel.

Robert and I had one other profound encounter. When Rev. Jim Sandmire died, an Elder in MCC and a pioneering force in the first two decades, his memorial service was at Grace Cathedral (Episcopal) in San Francisco, a very gay-friendly, "high" Episcopal Church.

Dianne Feinstein, then the former Mayor of San Francisco, and many other politicians and celebrities were in attendance. Jim was a very well known political leader in San Francisco, as well as an MCC pastor. Robert and I were invited to concelebrate communion, and Rev. Troy Perry preached.

When it came time for communion, the table had already been set by the Episcopalians, I guess. The table was so high, that Robert and I felt dwarfed behind the immense table in the immense Cathedral. I think Robert was already not feeling well, as someone with HIV/AIDS, and seemed a little nervous (who wouldn't be with that crowd.)

We consecrated communion, only to realize at the last minute, that we had consecrated an empty communion cup. Robert's eyes widened, I just touched his hand, and acted like I was pouring extra wine into the cup, as we sometimes did at the end, when in fact, there had been nothing in the cup at all.

It was all we could do not to start giggling. Rev. Sandmire, who could be very grand and theatrical and very down to earth, would have loved it! It was our Zen moment at Grace Cathedral. We had consecrated an empty cup, and just went on with the show.

Life rushed on, and I never had the chance even to debrief that moment with Robert. He died of AIDS in 1991, in his late 30s.

And that is a story too. He took the fledging, second version of MCC in Sarasota to a time of great growth. They bought land, which had an old house and garage. They outgrew the garage, and in 1990, began building a new church building on the grounds. Robert, at age 39, did not live to see the finished building. The first service in the yet unfinished building which only had a floor, a roof, and beams holding the roof up, no walls. That first service was his funeral, conducted in the pouring rain by Rev. Elder Jeri Ann Harvey.

That building today is my church home, and the social hall, the former garage/sanctuary, is named "Pierce Hall" after Robert. When I was the pastor, there, for a few years, I would always feel his presence on the grounds, in that social hall and especially in the sanctuary.

The Vicar of Brixton

I have so many stories about my friend, Rev. Elder Jean White. I first met her when she came to the 1979 General Conference in Los Angeles. She arrived a couple of days early, and slept at our new home in Los Angeles. At that Conference, though Jean was so new to MCC, I knew that her testimony and presence would sweep her into leadership in MCC as an Elder, and it did.

Jean collected people. She loved going to the park to walk the dog, and have a coffee. People would find out she was there, and talk with her, ask her advice, seek comfort, and find encouragement. She had her collection of people who had special needs, she balanced their checkbooks, protected them from abuse.

There were the old people, who she especially loved. She would help them with their health issues, ease their loneliness, and just "come around" to see how they were.

Two such elderly women were Vi and Miss Stocker. These women were her Sunday School teachers as a child. They had lived together for decades, and were lesbians in a time when no one said the word. When Vi died, her relatives came and took everything from Miss Stocker.

Miss Stocker, who was, by then, frail as well, told Jean, "Jean, I would just love to have Vi's watch, to remember her by." Jean found the watch and "nicked it" as she said, and gave it to Miss Stocker. Jean had a profound sense of justice, and a need to right wrongs. She was practical and pastoral, all at the same time.

I remember her multitasking before the word was invented — cooking dinner, talking on the phone, answering letters, counseling someone. One night at dinner, she had to take a call from an elderly, alcoholic Anglican vicar. She was helping him sort out if he was gay, and discussed his fantasies during masturbation, which ought to be a clue, she advised. She was the clinical nurse one minute, and the friend with whom you could share anything the next.

Jean was a nurse mid-wife, and had delivered countless numbers of babies. She loved children. She helped the youngest daughter of our pastor in Nigeria go to school, which was her dream. When she asked Mary, "what do you like about school," Mary volunteered, "They don't talk about Jesus!" which made Jean howl with laughter. Spoken like a true pastor's kid.

Jean, in her travels for MCC had many adventures and misadventures, but she was fearless. She was the first MCCer to go to Indonesia to meet with a group there, and she worked hard learning the language, only to find when she arrived, it was the wrong Indonesian dialect!

She contracted the plague, on one of her trips. She wrote thousands of letters, faithfully, in the days when letters were the main way people kept in touch over long distances.

Her obituary in the London Times said that she learned Chinese from her missionary roommate, Gladys Aylwin, the woman whose life was portrayed by Ingrid Bergman in "Inn of the Sixth Happiness." This was not something Jean liked to talk about — nor her captivity by the Red Guard in China during the Cultural Revolution, as a British missionary.

When a very famous pop artist was deep in his drug addiction, he came to MCC London, smelling bad and looking worse. Jean dressed him down, told him to go home and bathe and take care of himself, for the sake of all the people who looked up to him, if not for his own well-being. She was not into coddling celebrities.

Her student clergy called her, "Mother Ayatolla" with deep affection. She was tough and tender, she was an amazing pioneer of the liberating gospel.

And, she had a great laugh, especially when laughing at herself. She would be so proper and serious, and then, catch herself, and laugh a huge, wonderful laugh that reddened her face. Blessed be.

"Mom" Edith Allen Perry

I had the great privilege, for a time to be Edith Perry's pastor. Edith was the mother of our MCC Founder, the Rev. Troy Perry. Before that, I had known her because I was a leader in MCC, and we had shared some moments, and social times together with her family, especially Troy.

When I became pastor of MCC Los Angeles, in 1986, Edith was a member of the church, and not very well. She struggled with diabetes.

We visited at her home, sometimes sharing a meal. She was always lovely to me and even extended the honor of calling me her "daughter." Edith had five sons, and I think she really enjoyed having a pastor who was a woman. I know that made it easier to talk about some things.

We did talk about a lot of things — about Troy, and their journey together — about her story, how she managed to raise five boys in very tough times, especially after losing her husband in an accident when Troy was only 12.

One of the most insightful things she told me was how much more she enjoyed Troy's preaching after he came into MCC. Troy had gone from being a Southern Baptist (her background) to being Pentecostal, Church of God of Prophecy, very, very conservative. She said, when he was a Pentecostal, he was judgmental in his preaching. She didn't care for it. When he had his spiritual awakening and started MCC, it was like a different spirit, one of mercy and compassion and inclusion flowed through his preaching.

"Mom" Perry was not a prude, she could take a joke, and she could tell one. She loved the people of MCC and was the model of an accepting parent before there was PFLAG. She called everyone, "honey" in that slow, South Alabama drawl. I can hear her voice even now. Her faithfulness, generosity, courage and love will be a part of the MCC story forever.

Promoted to Glory

Dr. Gary McClelland was a gynecologist in private practice in Los Angeles, who grew up in the Salvation Army. As a gay man, he became very alienated from a faith that had been very important to him.

I met Gary in the first few weeks of becoming the Pastor of MCC Los Angeles in 1986. I was impressed with him. The MCC church in Los Angles had lost a lot of its more middle or upper class folks, professional class over the years. In its downtown location, far away from the emerging LGBTQ community in West Hollywood, it was out of the mainstream, away from the heart of the community, and away from some of its stronger supporters.

Part of my vision was to restore MCC Los Angeles' lost leadership role in the wider LGBTQ community, which probably meant we would have to move — and we did. But, at the beginning, I just needed to find some reliable folks who would work with me to revive and reshape our Founding Church.

Gary turned out to be one of those people. He attended the Sunday morning Bible Study that I began, and quickly let me know that he supported my leadership. I asked him to train to be a deacon, which he did. Gary was a natural leader, a good speaker, a person of deep integrity, passion and commitment.

Over the years, Gary offered leadership in many ways. As one of a couple of doctors in the church, he was often there to help people who needed advice or care. He treated homeless people who came to our church, and he was available whenever called upon.

He got involved with our HIV/AIDS ministry, and then, most profoundly, in our theological school, Samaritan, where he became President of the board.

In all this, we had a deep friendship. Gary never withheld his opinions, but even when he disagreed with me, he was supportive.

Gary was diagnosed with HIV/AIDS. He had to give up leadership in many things, including the school, and church leadership roles. He had to give up his medical practice. His health, even mental health, to some degree, deteriorated.

In the process, his brother, Michael, moved in with him to take care of him. Michael's wife was wonderfully supportive during this time.

Gary, with some Salvation Army still in him, worried about Michael's faith. So, as sick as he was, unable to drive, he had Mike bring him to church every Sunday. Mike liked MCC, he told me later, because he didn't have to wear a tie (even though Gary did, most of the time!).

Mike came to love MCC, and to rely on Gary's church friends and family. We were in and out of Gary's house all the time as he got sicker.

Gary, being a doctor, told me early on that when he got too ill, he wanted to take his own life, before he suffered too much, or made it hard on his family. Many doctors I knew with AIDS said this kind of thing, though very few followed through.

The person Gary wanted to help him with this was his colleague, a lesbian who was in his private practice. But she got pancreatic cancer and died.

One day, Gary reminded me about his desire to end it before the end, but told me that as sick as he was, there were good days, and something inside of him just would not let him do it.

Gary got very sick at the end, and suffered a lot. We were with him around the clock, with home hospice care. We were all stressed and grieving. Normal boundaries between pastor, friend, and family dissolved. These were extraordinary times, there were no road maps.

One really bad night, Gary started hemorrhaging from a lesion in his mouth. It was horrifying, and I suddenly became very unsettled. I had been holding his hand, praying, doing whatever I could as a caregiver. His suffering seemed so prolonged and unbearable. We were all exhausted, especially him. I saw the pillow next to him, and thought, for a moment, if I had any real courage, I would just smother him now and end his terrible ordeal.

I thought about what would happen if it was discovered that I had done this. Could I face whatever would come? Would anyone in his family want to bring charges? Would Gary really want me to do this? What would be the consequences for my partner, family, the church?

I knew that a lot of this was my own exhaustion. I was his sister, friend, and I was his pastor. Really, the only accountability that mattered in that moment was to the God we both believed in, imperfectly. I really asked myself if God would forgive this, understand it, or if this was not my choice to make.

The moment passed. I knew I could not do it, even if I really thought it was the right thing, and that it would end his suffering sooner. I was not able to, at least in those circumstances.

I spoke to his hospice nurse, who came early in the morning, and told him how much Gary was suffering. This very young hospice nurse had attended at least twenty-six AIDS patients. I knew he knew what to do. He made me leave the room, and I am sure he increased Gary's morphine, as he had done for many others before him. About an hour later, Gary died, peacefully. No one ever questioned it.

Somehow, as young as he was, I knew this nurse knew what he was doing, and could get away with it without there being any stigma, or mess up, or violence, or any legal consequences. I had no qualms at all about it at the time, though afterwards I wondered if I had just passed the buck on to this young nurse, who had already had so much to deal with. I let him take that on, in the moment. It was the right thing to do. And, I am grateful for that young man's courage and competency.

Gary's funeral, at the chapel in Forest Lawn, in Los Angeles, is seared in my memory. The soloist sang, "When the Storm Passes Over." How we longed for that storm of unrelenting AIDS and death that was taking the Garys of this world with it, to pass over.

In Salvation Army tradition, a nod to the church he had loved in his youth, we "promoted him to Glory," at the closing of the service.

Sweet Hour of Prayer

I met Evelyn Kinser when I became pastor of MCC Los Angeles in 1986.

At the time, she was an auditor for the Bank of America, specializing in bankruptcies, driving all over Southern California. She was a serious person, good at what she did and not someone to mess with.

Evelyn, who went by "Ev," was an old-style butch. She drove a big car, and she always drove. She had been a Four-Square Gospel Minister decades before, in another life. She and her partner Betty had been co-ministers and were deeply closeted in that fundamentalist church founded by a woman, Sister Aimee Semple McPherson.

It was a denomination known to have a lot of closeted gay men and lesbians, but later became publically hostile and homophobic. Sister Aimee, the founder, had a lot of Hollywood friends and followers and apparently escaped to Palm Springs and elsewhere to party from time to time. Scandal followed her. She didn't have a lot of room to judge, and those who knew her, knew that. Her theatrical tendencies made her a favorite of sexual non-conformists.

I am not sure exactly how their ministry ended, but I know it broke Evelyn's heart. These two women made their way to the very first MCC Church in downtown Los Angeles.

This was a church hungry for experienced clergy who would sacrifice and go start new churches. That was Evelyn's dream, after her Four Square vocation had been crushed. She and Betty saw themselves as the "barren women" in Isaiah 54, who would have a slew of spiritual children!

Ironically, this new MCC, in 1969, was not really sure about ordained women or ordaining them. It's hard to believe, but true.

Evelyn was rejected by the new ministerial credentials board.

Betty passed away, and Evelyn drifted away from MCC. She would visit from time to time but just for old time's sake.

When I became pastor, she reappeared, and stuck around. It was a time when MCC Los Angeles itself was drifting and lacked leadership. Evelyn offered to serve on the new board that was forming as I began, and I jumped at that offer.

I got to know Evelyn well. She was full of faith, very loyal to me, and to MCC. She was also somewhat un-reconstructed in her fundamentalism, and was no particular fan of my eclectic, liberal, feminist, liberation, theology! Somehow she thought I was salvageable. She liked that I preached from the Bible. I took it seriously if not literally (Marcus Borg's phrase), and that was better than some preachers.

I really could not have her preach, except at small or special services. She did do some Bible study and tutoring. For those who wanted to delve into it, she was very knowledgeable. I had to trust that on the balance of everything they learned, they would take her theology with a grain of salt.

But, damn, she could pray.

I asked her to be my prayer partner. Every week, for many years, she would come to my office, and pray, and pray and pray. She wept when she prayed, she labored over me. She prayed until I squirmed. I grew to dread and love her prayers all at the same time. Many times, I believed her prayers covered me, saved me, got me through AIDS and moving the church a dozen times, financial chaos, and denominational drama. Her prayers were well-anchored, and they soared. They were generous, and they were demanding. Most of all, they were thorough! Very little was left on the field after one of those prayer sessions. We covered it all.

As I learned more about evangelical and charismatic gifts and graces, the kind of deep piety and connectivity of her prayers was nurturing, it was food and drink.

Sometimes, it still made me squirm. Over time, it made me a better pastor.

Evelyn did other things — balanced the church books, lead the search committee for at least one or two new buildings; she answered the phone, did weddings and funerals, minded the office, supervised the deacons whether they wanted it or not. She did endless hospital visits.

Some of her contradictions showed up in her love life. For a fundamentalist, she dated quite a bit, even as a senior. When we would drive around Los Angeles, as we frequently did, going to hospitals or looking for buildings to buy or rent, she would say, "I lived there with my partner," so many times, I finally said, "Either you moved around a lot with the same woman, or I might be shocked about how many girlfriends you had!" She just chuckled, blue eyes twinkling, leaving no doubt in my mind.

She was the person who, in 1989, told me that I had to stop my fast. I had been fasting for 32 days or so, in an effort to call attention to how banks were red-lining churches, especially ours. Even though we did not yet meet the goal of having a new lender at a decent interest rate (which we got three weeks after I ended my fast), we had enough cash to last us a couple of years, which was really enough.

Evelyn told me that in the Western migration in the US, there were some who came to beautiful valleys and plains, where they could finally settle down. But others had become addicted to pushing on, farther and farther west, beyond their goal. Some were greedy or just unable to stop. She looked at me with firmness, with those steel blue eyes, and said, "Time to stop." So, I did.

Early on, I learned of the injustice done to her in the early and sexist days of MCC leadership. Several women clergy joined me in making an appeal on her behalf to grant her credentials, to overturn that decades-old bad decision. The committee heard our argument, read our appeals, and offered Evelyn Kinser ordination in MCC. She had not been willing to make the appeal on her own, but accepted our efforts. We had a wonderful celebration at MCC Los Angeles, and "Rev. Ev" became our term of affection for her.

She liked to say, "I can do anything Nancy Wilson thinks I can do."

It turns out, that was quite a lot.

I celebrated her wedding to her beloved Viva, the first same-sex wedding my parents attended, just a few years before my Dad's death.

Her last years were tough, and she did not accept disability or diminished capacity well or gracefully. I had moved to Florida, but she had a loyal crew of younger lesbians from MCC Los Angeles who looked in on her and Viva in those last years. I visited her when I made it back to town. On one of those trips I preached her memorial service.

Relentless, Evelyn pushed me to preach past the "defensive" position on homosexuality and the Bible, to a more positive and pro-active hermeneutic. Her challenge was the inspiration for my book *Outing the Bible*.

But, most of all, I miss those prayers that made me squirm.

Babies, Kids and Angels

From the earliest days, Metropolitan Community Churches asserted that "all are welcome," and that included children and teens. That was not an easy stance in a time when homosexuality was a crime and considered unnatural and immoral. The prevailing public view was that gays were child molesters.

Some MCC churches quickly embraced offering Sunday School for kids, and welcoming parents, most of whom were lesbians. Other MCC churches, reacting out of internalized homophobia, were afraid to welcome children, or their parents. When I became a pastor of MCC Detroit, they insisted that only people over 18 were welcomed, because someone might accuse us of child endangerment. I said that if people under 18 were not safe or welcome, then neither was I.

Sometimes LGBTQ people, in those days, expressed their negative reactions to kids as a negative reaction to heterosexuals. But, as we pushed through the irrational fear, children always blessed us. There are kids who grew up in MCC being the only kid, or consistent kid, in their church. Other MCC's had many children and programs for them.

Initially, the only people who had kids were those who had been heterosexually married or partnered. Many did not have full-time custody, or struggled through ugly custody battles.

But, by the late 80s or 90s, at the height of AIDS in the United States, the LGBTQ community started experiencing a baby boom. Couples found ways (artificial insemination, surrogacy, etc.) to physically bear children, and many more fostered or adopted.

The first baby I baptized was Eric, in 1972, in Boston. I will never forget the joy of that moment, for me, and our brand new MCC.

Nothing makes people in MCC more emotional than a baby baptism, or the growth of our very diverse families. Children in MCC have sometimes not had all the resources that a large church could offer, but, they are included in communion, worship, and are celebrated. Gradually, we made important commitments to child care and programming at conferences, and found ways to support parents of kids and teens.

Most of all, we hope that kids growing up in MCC felt and absorbed deep spiritual values of justice and inclusion, while embracing diversity and hope. I know that especially in my pastoral ministry, I learned so much from the kids who were part of our congregations.

Jamaal's Bread

Jamaal was about ten when I met him. He was the biracial, autistic son of a white, lesbian mom who started attending MCC Los Angeles when I was pastor.

Jamaal had extraordinary social skills, contrary to the stereotype of an autistic child. He was a member of the "Kid's Club," and later, in his teens or early adulthood, he would leave worship with the kids and assist whatever teacher was leading the program that day. He felt like a founder of that Club, in the days when there were fewer kids.

When Jamaal and his mom wanted to join the church, I visited them in their home in Pasadena. It was their new home, and I blessed it for them. We also shared communion, and that's how I learned that Jamaal could not tolerate the communion wafers at church. The sensation was disagreeable to him, a barrier to participation. So, that day, at their home, we used grape juice and real bread.

I made Jamaal a promise that evening, that if he came to communion at church, we would have a reserved, small, piece of fresh bread for him at the table, and make sure that servers knew where it was if he was not coming to me, or I was not there.

So, that came to be "Jamaal's bread" at our table on Sundays. There were times we slipped up, but, for many years, he could come to church confident that he could access communion without the extra anxiety of ingesting what felt like a strange substance. For autistic people, life itself is filled with things to be anxious about, so it was helpful to accommodate him.

Over time, Jamaal, his Mom, and her new partner, were a part of our lives and our church community. Jamaal hosted an annual tree-decorating party at his home just before Christmas that I attended several times. He loved music, and knew hundreds of song titles and musicians.

Eventually, Jamaal decided he preferred the MCC Los Angeles evening service — it was more gospel, more African-American, really, and less formal. Sometimes I would drive out to Pasadena after three services in the AM, and hospital visits in the afternoon, to pick him up. I did that because I liked Jamaal, and I knew he loved coming in the evening.

We always had a great chat on the way to church. When I dropped him off in the evening, I would have to allow a little extra time — good-byes always took longer than hellos. He would ask over and over again if he would see me next week, if I would pick him up for church. I would say yes, and assure him, as often as I could.

One Sunday, I had a runaway teen in my office in the late afternoon. Joshua was seventeen, homeless at the moment, from a strict Pentecostal background. He was still very naïve, just coming out, and agonizing about his faith, family and sexuality. His homelessness had forced him to trade sex for a place to stay, which freaked him out.

I was concerned about him, and did not want to kick him out of my office. So I asked him to come with me to pick up Jamaal.

On the way there, Joshua slept the sleep of the exhausted. He felt safe with me, in my car, and just could not help himself. He was sleeping in Jamaal's seat, in the front of the car, and assumed I could just have him move when we got there. But Joshua was so tired he didn't wake up when we got to the house.

I explained what was happening to Jamaal, and he graciously got in the back seat (small changes in any routine are not easy for someone with autism). Joshua stirred briefly, and I introduced them. Jamaal told him that he was very lucky to find MCC Los Angeles, that it was a great church, and there were so many nice people. Jamaal was instinctively trying to reassure this young man that he was safe, and would be okay, a generous thing to do for someone who had taken his special seat in the car. Joshua slept all the way back to church, and Jamaal and I rode in a sweet silence.

Joshua eventually reconciled with his family, and enjoyed becoming a part of our young adults group, The Tribe. Jamaal moved in with his Dad as his Mom gradually lost her battle with cancer. We went through that altogether, as a church family. Jamaal's Dad was very supportive of his church connections, and to this day, Jamaal sometimes finds his way to church. Jamaal's Mom lived to see him graduate from high school and get accepted to college, quite an achievement.

Sometimes, in my mind, I still see his bread on the table.

Easter Inclusion

During the years I was pastor at MCC Los Angeles, I had the honor of becoming a friend to Judi Longman, and a godmother to two of her child, and an "auntie" to others in the Longman clan. Often I would bring some of the Longman kids to church we had a Kid's Club that had a pretty decent program.

One Easter, I had godson Jody, age eight, and cousin Matt, age six in the backseat of the car on the way to church.

Matt had told me recently that he liked going to MCC, because "gay people have a lot of fun in church."

This Easter, Matt was excited about the Easter egg hunt, until he learned from Jody that two other boys would be there who had serious behavior problems and often made things difficult.

"Oh, no," he said, "Jim and Tommy will be there too?"

To which Jody responded, in that oldest child, teacherly way, "Yes, Matt, it's just like communion at MCC, everyone's included."

Matt, thought for a minute and then challenged him, "I get it about communion, but the Easter egg hunt too?"

Caring for Babies with AIDS

MCC Los Angeles (now, Founders' MCC) lost our building in the Northridge Earthquake of 1994. We had bought the place in 1988. Besides the church itself, on our property was the first residential home and care center for infants and children under the age of five with HIV/AIDS. The organization that ran the shelter was called "Caring for Babies with AIDS (CBA)."

They rented the large house we owned behind the church building, which was surrounded by a fenced in yard, with large hedges, for privacy. CBA had been desperate to find a location. No one else wanted the CBA house in their neighborhood, and being on church grounds was a shelter for them. We were not sure what we were going to do with that house, and now it was clear. For the first two years, we charged them no rent. As the years went by, they were able to raise funds and pay us rent.

For several years, there was little progress with mother-to-infant transmission of HIV, and only a few babies that were sero-converting and becoming HIV negative. Eventually, mother to infant transmissions were nearly eliminated. But at this time, in the late 80s and early 90s, there was little hope.

Word of the home for these children spread fast. One morning, my assistant pastor, Rev. Danny Mahoney, was alone at the church office, and a car pulled up in front of the church office, another smaller separate house on the property. As Danny opened the door, they thrust an infant into his arms, and sped away. She became the first client of the first such place on the West Coast of the US.

Danny was himself HIV positive, and was so overwhelmed to receive her and welcome her into our community. This little baby girl struggled for a while, but survived and came to thrive.

Two twin boys came to live there too, as toddlers. Every morning a caregiver would bring them in their strollers past my office, and I would invite them in to feed my fish. As a church, we felt like it was part of our destiny to be a shelter for these very vulnerable children, whose parents could not take care of them. In a time when most of the persons with HIV/AIDS we knew were gay men, it expanded our awareness, sharpened our politics and opened our hearts to know these babies and toddlers.

Bless the women who founded CBA, and all the men and women who were caregivers and volunteers who fed, clothed, loved, rocked and helped those children survive and have a hope of growing up.

The Eagle's Center

When MCC Los Angeles was still at the location in Culver City, about a year or so before the Northridge Earthquake of 1994, we learned that there was a special high school in Los Angeles, called Eagle's Center, started for LGBTQ kids who would otherwise be at risk for quitting school. These were kids who could not or did not want to pass for straight, and who were bullied, harassed, beaten, and teased every single day in our schools.

Other groups, like Project 10 and the Gay/Straight Alliances sought to make schools more accepting by providing a supportive, onsite support group, but those programs were not in every school, and they did not help these kids. These were kids who could not blend in. They were targeted daily.

The Eagle's Center was not given a space by school officials. The staff resorted to meeting in the living room of a foster home that catered to LGBTQ foster kids. The program was supposed to have a sponsored location, and once that was in place, the school district would provide a teacher, teacher's aide, transportation for kids who needed it, and lunch, but that was all; no arts, gym or other amenities. Meeting in the living room of a foster home was pathetic.

We offered them space at MCC Los Angeles. We had almost finished renovations on our building in Culver City. They met in the social hall, which was a much larger and more appropriate place than a living room. We had just finished putting in restrooms in the building, and had an occupancy permit — not easy to get. For a year or so, these kids met in our building five days a week, and we got to know them.

There were adjustments and always challenges, but we felt like it was a good arrangement. These kids and their teachers needed us to be on their side to help pioneer what would become a model for schools all over the country and in other countries as well.

They had to have social workers as well as teachers, several lived in foster homes, and some had multiple challenges and disabilities.

Then, the earthquake happened, January 17, 1994. School did not happen that day, nor for many days.

Rev. Ken Kerr, on my staff, along with volunteers, had opened a youth/young adult drop in center in West Hollywood which we called "Back of the Bank." It was located in the back of the Bank of America on Santa Monica Boulevard. They owned the storefront and generously leased the back room to us for next to nothing, as a sign of their support for the program. We were reaching out to kids and young adults who needed safe space. Kids were coming out as LGBTQ and were at such a high risk for suicide and for HIV/AIDS infection. This place was a life saving ministry. We connected young people to social workers and agencies that could provide help. It was also a social space which was safer than many gay bars in the neighborhood, some of which were famous for pimping kids to an older clientele.

The space was only used in the evenings, so Ken and his crew worked with the Eagle's Center staff, and moved both programs into West Hollywood for the daytime school program, as soon as they could after the earthquake. This arrangement worked out well, for several years, as we ended up purchasing a couple of buildings in the West Hollywood neighborhood for the church and MCC headquarters.

Over the years, the Eagle's Center focused more on LGBTQI kids who also had disabilities which was a huge need. We worked it out so they could come to our sanctuary, where we had a grand piano for music lessons, and to the gym next door for recreation.

In an amazing twist, the fact that we had opened up to the Eagle's Center, just a year or so before the earthquake, we received an unexpected, material blessing.

FEMA was working with all kinds of organizations with damaged or destroyed building from the earthquake. They did not restore church or religious buildings, unless you could prove that the buildings had other, civic uses — like, say, a school.

When we learned this, it was a source of hope that we might be able to recover a little of what we lost. We did not have earthquake insurance. Our building was too old and simply not eligible. Even if we had been eligible, the cost would have been prohibitive.

We lost our building. For the moment, we could only recover the cost of the land. We eventually sold it to the group, Caring for Babies with AIDS.

Meanwhile, we had to pay the mortgage on a building we couldn't use and then had to tear down! We also had to look for other places to move our congregation and ministries, and find the time and energy to figure out if we were eligible for FEMA.

This was a journey I took with attorney Carol "Woody" Wood, a church member, who had been a board member and very generous with her time and legal services. Woody had been a Methodist, like me, in her early life. She had actually been a missionary to Korea, with a powerful vocation.

The first thing FEMA wanted to know was how much space The Eagle's Center had used in our now destroyed building. Then, they wanted us to do architectural drawings of what the building would look like *if* we rebuilt it, and *if* the Eagle's Center would meet there, neither of which was probably going to happen.

We did everything they asked. Then, we answered reams of questions, or Woody did, at least. Year after year this went on, until we were in our new building in West Hollywood.

Months and months would go by with no response from FEMA, even to simple questions. At the fifth year, they asked us to fill out one more application. Woody and I looked at each other, and I said, "This is their last chance; it is now in God's hands."

Finally, quite remarkably, they awarded us a substantial sum — enough so that we could refinance our new buildings with global MCC, and make our joint mortgage much more manageable. By this time, Woody's billable hours, that she and her law partner had donated, probably exceeded any award from FEMA. None of this would have happened without her partnership, loyalty, and perseverance.

Some people had worried that offering hospitality to the Eagle's Center would cost us something we could not afford. The opposite turned out to be true. Their presence, at our invitation, made it possible for us to survive the earthquake and move into a new era of outreach in West Hollywood, including our work with young adults at the Eagle's Center.

The Baby Rescue Relay

In the early 1980s, while working fulltime at MCC Headquarters, I started a ministry with some women from MCC Los Angeles for women in jail or prison. It started when a friend of a friend was in jail, then prison for vehicular homicide. She was driving drunk at the time.

While she was there, she met some lesbians at Sybil Brand County Jail who wanted visits. So, we formed a team, and just started. We followed some of those women to California Institute for Women, and we eventually had services there once a month. They formed an MCC church there and met for many years.

Our mentors in this work were a group of women called "Friends Outside," who worked with women in jail and prison. We were especially blessed with support from Joyce Ride, whose business card said, "Mother of First Woman Astronaut!" She was Sally Ride's mom, and the mother of Presbyterian clergywoman, Rev. "Bear" Ride, also a friend.

Joyce was a lay Presbyterian, feminist, and activist. She schooled us in how to help without enabling and in the politics of women in prison and jail. We learned this was a tough and heartbreaking assignment.

In addition to working with women in jail and prison, this work put us in touch with others doing amazing things for women caught in the criminal justice system. For a while, a couple of us got involved in volunteering for a group of women attorneys who helped women as they were leaving prison in Northern California.

It seems that women who had families, children in Southern California ended up in prison in the North. When they got out of prison, they did not have funds to return south, or even to bring their children to be with them. Returning to the place in which they were involved with drugs, or abusive partners, etc. was not good either.

Women attorneys commuted from Los Angeles to Sacramento. They hatched a plan to transport babies and toddlers back and forth. What they needed were people to actually fetch the babies, and that's where we came in.

It seems surreal, now. We volunteered to go to the homes of strangers, without a single piece of authorizing paper. These were not kids in the foster system, or being tracked by the state, just kids dumped off at relatives' homes. We took them to the airport and met the attorney who would transport them. We were like a relay, an underground railroad of sorts, trying to unite babies with their moms who were trying to make it in a new environment.

Connie Bilow was a deacon at MCC LA, when we volunteered for this program. We used her van, and headed to an unfamiliar and impoverished neighborhood, in South Central Los Angeles.

We knocked on the door, but no one answered. I am not sure when it occurred to us that the people in this house might not want two white women taking the baby, especially with no paperwork.

Then, we realized the door was open. It was pretty dark inside, and a couple of kids, ages three to six, were on mattresses on the floor. To my right was a crib. I saw a cockroach and froze, and then I saw the baby, about a year old. He pulled himself up in the crib, and lifted his arms up for me. I took him in my arms, and he held me tightly around the neck. I was struck by how strong his grip was, this little baby, grabbing on for dear life.

Then, someone, I presume his grandmother, stumbled into the room, high on something. She was smoking, and said, "You here for the kid?" I said, "Yes," and she said, "Well, I don't have anything to send with him."

So, we left.

The baby clung to me. I tried to put him in the car seat in the back seat, but he would not let go. When we tried, he protested. So I just sat in the back, and Connie helped strap us in. I was his car seat on the way to the airport.

Nothing, he had nothing. Not an extra diaper, a toy, or any clothing other than the shirt on his back. No shoes, nothing.

As we drove to the airport I don't remember him making a sound. I think he was sleeping. He was warm and continued to hold tightly around my neck. I didn't even have a blanket to put over him — lessons learned for the next time.

We parked, and found the airport lounge in which we were told the attorney would be waiting. She saw us first. She was an attractive, African-American lawyer, very sharply dressed. Connie made her show us her ID before we gave her the baby.

She smiled and complied. For Connie, it was a matter of honor and dignity. No one at that baby's house asked us for ID, or seemed to care what happened. We were going to do this right. We made sure we sent him with the right person, on his way to his young mother. He deserved an ID check.

The time came, and I apologized that we had nothing for the baby to take with him. The attorney was prepared, though, with a diaper bag, a blanket, some clothes and a toy. I felt a rush of relief and gratitude. Here was parental competence. He saw her, and in an instant, he let go of me and easily scrambled into her arms.

Connie and I touched him, blessed him, and told him to have a good life.

The Miracle of Miles Isaiah

Once in a while, not very often at all, my wife Paula will tell me to do something in relationship to ministry.

Deacon Pam's grandson, Miles Isaiah, was born prematurely, and was struggling in an incubator. He was unable to go home with his mom and teetered on the edge of life and death.

Paula said, "You have to go lay hands on him, right away!" I took her push as a prompting from Above, and called Pam.

I wasn't quite sure how to lay hands on a struggling newborn who weighed less than three pounds. Pam and I got there together, and went to see him. Miles Isaiah had not yet opened his eyes. He was so tiny, and vulnerable. I was almost afraid to touch him.

The incubator had a kind of glove like thing that you could put your hand in, and touch him without actually touching him directly. They were very concerned about germs and infection, of course. Pam and I prayed, and I put my hand in that glove like thing, and did not lay my hand on him, my hand was too big. I took my index finger (sort of like Michelangelo's God with Adam!), and touched the middle of his chest, the place I know is the center of one's immune system. I pressed just slightly, and as we prayed, pop!!! His eyes opened, just like that for the first time, looking at me and his grandma!

We were both astonished, laughing, with tears in our eyes.

It took many days and much care, but he got out of that incubator, out of the hospital, and grew up strong and healthy.

The Christmas Gift

Our AIDS hospice visitation team at MCC Los Angeles often visited on Christmas Day or Christmas Eve, a time when few churches are making the rounds at such places.

I remember a woman in a nursing home-cum-hospice, in a dark room, which you just knew had few visitors. It was Christmas Eve. She was a drug addict, had been infected by a dirty needle, was in a lot of pain, withdrawn, and not really in the mood for church people to be visiting. She was not a church person, at least not any longer.

We were visiting with beautiful, new plush bears. A member of our church worked in a department store that was going out of business, and got us about fifty of these gorgeous, white bears with big red bows. We were very careful to try to discern how to even offer them, to people who were dying. They were comfortable to hug, and we hoped might provide some comfort to them.

When we offered one to her she started to turn to the wall, and said, "No." But, then, "Oh, wait!" When she turned back to us, and we gave it to her, she began to sob.

We knew there was more to this story, so we waited.

Then, she told us, that tomorrow, Christmas Day, her mother was bringing her six year old daughter to see her, and she had felt so awful that she had nothing to give her for Christmas, but now! Now, she had this beautiful bear — for her child! Her whole being just beamed with gratitude and dignity, in her ability to give to her child.

That child would be at least twenty-six today, I wonder if she ever wonders where on earth her mother, on her deathbed, got that beautiful, soft, new Christmas bear with the big, red bow.

If this woman, who was so damaged, so wounded and beaten down by life and illness, could summon the energy to love her child enough to think of her first, how much more does the Creator of the Universe love us, and care for us? That Christmas, a broken, dying drug addict, who was a mother to the end, was a powerful reminder to us of a God that loves each of us like a mother.

If You Could Love Johnie

Johnie Matthews was one of those characters at MCC Los Angeles who had been there from the earliest days. Johnie defied categories. She used the female pronoun, but, today, night consider herself to be a female to male transgender person. She was probably at least in her late 70s when we met.

She wore a yarmulke on her head, and men's clothing. She had a cleft palate, a serious speech impediment, and by the time I met her, a serious hearing problem, which meant she shouted much of the time. She was emotional, often looking for attention in a child-like way — definitely an "extra grace required" person.

Johnie would usually come into church late, carrying huge shopping bags. In them were precious things she had picked up along her way, and brought as gifts for specific people. Though she was late, she wanted to sit in the front. If an inexperienced usher tried to dissuade her, or ask her to sit in the back, she would whack them with the bags!

She would then slowly and noisily make her way down the aisle to her preferred seat. A few times, she pulled out a newspaper, and begin to read. Songleader "Pappa Jimmi" Irving would dance down the aisle, while leading the song, and snatch the paper right out of her hands, it so annoyed him.

After church, she made a beeline to the prettiest new woman in attendance that day, many of whom assumed she was this sweet, old, Jewish man. And, whoever was the last person at church was obligated to take her to her home, no matter which direction you thought you were going. Half the time, that was me.

One time on the way home, she told me that she wanted to become a ventriloquist, and the picture of that made me nearly drive the car off the freeway.

One Sunday she showed up with "Bible" fortune cookies. These were from a fundamentalist bookstore that did not think Chinese fortune cookies were a good idea, and promoted this substitute — fortune cookies with Bible verses instead! Johnie handed them out, including one to me, that I stuffed in my drawer.

A few months later, she died. Her funeral was packed with so many people who had Johnie stories; we laughed and cried together. At the time, the windows had broken out in the dome, and we had plastic on them. The plastic came loose in a storm, and the plastic rattled, like her bags did coming down the aisle!

An attractive, heterosexual woman who had joined the church spoke of her first Sunday, and how warmly Johnie had greeted her. Then she said, "I knew if you could love and accept Johnie, you would probably love and accept me."

A month or so later, I was in my office. It was one of those days. People were ill and dying, one of my staff members was sick, the offering on Sunday had been poor, it was raining, and there were two leaks in the roof.

You know, that kind of day.

In desperation, I took out the Bible fortune cookie. I took a deep breath, and cracked it open, it was so stale it turned into powder!

As I unfolded the little paper messages, it said, "Cast all your cares upon God, for God cares for you." (1 Peter 5:7). I chuckled thinking of Johnie, and suddenly I was flooded with tears of comfort and peace.

The message was as subtle as being hit upside my head with one of her bags.

Brighter Days Are Coming

Every now and then an angel appears who is rarely recognizable right away.

At first, my tendency is to feel annoyed by someone who is just a little odd, who is getting on the plane, and then they sit next to me. Then, very early on, like a tap on the shoulder, I have the awareness that this person is no ordinary person, but, possibly an angel of sorts, a test for me. When that happens, I relax, and try to let go and let God.

One time it was Alice from Dallas. She bumbled onto the plane just before the door closed and sat in the middle seat. She was disheveled, with a husky smokers' voice, and before we even took off she was trying to interest me in sharing a couple of little bottles of whiskey, passing them to me like contraband. When I said no thank you, she tried the guy next to her, 30 years her junior, and flirted with him. When he looked horrified, she turned her attention back to me.

She made me laugh throughout her very eccentric monologue. Something about her, though, made me suspect she was just a naughty angel, testing our forbearance. We ended up talking about marriage equality and politics. She was vulnerable, open to a fault.

***

On long flights, I do not really care to talk with strangers, or even relish coming out or talking about what I do for a living. Sometimes, a long plane ride is a time to get caught up on reading, work, or news, or just rest.

On one long flight, I had managed not to talk with the woman next to me until we were starting to circle Chicago, getting ready (I thought) to land. Then they told us our flight would be delayed. For some reason, we had to keep circling for a while.

With that, the woman next to me burst into tears, apologizing. She was on her way to see her father, who would be going in for surgery, and she was afraid she would not get to see him, and it was very serious. The flight delay might mean she would not see him again.

I took a deep breath, and said, "By the way, I am a clergyperson, and if you would like, I can say a quick prayer for him and you right now."

She took me up on it. Then, asked what church? I told her about MCC, and she cried again. It seems that her next door neighbors are lesbians, and they were the ones who got her the plane ticket, that she could not afford.

"It's a sign," she said.

***

A few years ago, on a long domestic flight, a man started to get into my aisle, but looked at me a little desperately, and said, "Do you think I have time to go?" like I was an authority. So, I said, "sure, go now!" He did, and was almost there when the flight attendant started to reprimand him. I stuck up for him, "He really has to go," I said, so she let him be.

He rushed back to the seat. I found out his name was Jim, and he looked at me and said, "Brighter days are coming!" All buckled in, he nervously told me that his wife of five years had just died, and he was on his way to his sisters. His family reached out to him so he thought he should go, even though he was dreading it.

Apparently they had not approved of the marriage. I could tell Jim was special in some way (other than possibly being an angel unawares). I listened, he relaxed. He would tear up, then say his mantra, "Brighter days are coming!" I found myself smiling, and taking that promise in.

Before we landed, he touched my hand and said, "I thank the Lord for getting to sit next to a nice lady like you."

Brighter days are coming, an angel told me.

Below left: Rev. Ann Montague. *Below middle and right:* Rev. Elder Freda Smith. *Middle:* MCC Los Angeles after earthquake in 1994.

Right: Rev. Dr. Nancy Wilson speaks with Haitians at ICM Santo Domingo, Dominican Republic. *Far right:* Carol Wood speaks at the dedication of MCC Los Angeles in West Hollywood, in 1999.

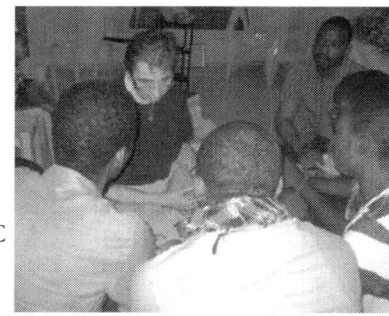

The First Decade

STORIES OF JUSTICE, INCLUSION AND HOPE

When I came into MCC, in 1972, it was already 4-years-old, and full of stories, heroes and legends.

But, I have my own origin stories from that first amazing decade. It was a time when you had to be prepared for anything.

In 1974, Rev. Beau McDaniels was conducting services for the new MCC Indianapolis in a private home, when, in the middle of one of those very first services, there was a loud banging at the front door, as the police tried to enter. Suddenly, as congregants were running out the back door, the police were bursting in.

Indiana law, in those days, said it was illegal for homosexuals to assemble. They had heard rumors about a "church," but figured that was unlikely, and instead assumed the gathering was a cover for illegal activities.

Rev. McDaniels stood up to them, shamed them in fact, and they left.

Later on, after being interviewed on the radio about the new MCC in town, a truck pulled up next to hers, first seemed to be racing her, and then shot her tires out. Welcome to one of the places outside of the south where the Ku Klux Klan had flourished!

These things happened. Often, the MCC clergy in town was the only person who was out of the closet and could speak publicly, and we could not go to the police for help; they were still, usually, the enemy. We had no colleagues nearby. Maybe a closeted clergy from another denomination who would have lunch with us, in an out of the way place.

I remember being on those late night radio talk shows — we helped boost their ratings, because our topic was so sensational. Only drunks or fundamentalists would call in, but we always hoped someone who was LGBTQ would be listening, and sometimes they were.

Advertising MCC services was a challenge. Mainstream newspapers would not accept ads. The "gay rags" reached only a portion of the sub-culture we were trying to reach.

I had two tactics for outreach in those very early days. I would find the local "dirty bookstore." Gay people always worked there, even though the books were not necessarily gay. I would leave cards on the bookshelves or at the counter.

Then, I would go to the Christian bookstore, usually fundamentalist. I would find the really awful books on "homosexuality is a sin," and put MCC pamphlets and cards in them. Only gay people or their families looked at those books anyway! With no Internet, getting the word out was a challenge.

The vast majority of LGBTQ folks then were closeted to a degree that is not imaginable today. People lived divided lives. For some people, the gay subculture was alienating, and finding a friendly church seemed safer. But often,

MCC churches met in places that were hard to find, perceived as dangerous, or just unfamiliar.

Few people used their last names. Sometimes you would know people for years, without actually knowing their last name, or their real name.

I came out just as that culture was shifting, breaking, coming apart and coming out — when we began standing up to the bullies, be they police, churches, psychologists, television personalities, politicians, or others with power. Not enough has been told about that first wild decade of our movement and our church.

Outed by a Gay Pioneer in 1972

I first met Barbara Gittings in about 1971, when she and Frank Kameny spoke at Allegheny College in western Pennsylvania, where I was a junior. They were Gay Liberation speakers of that pioneer generation, who had protested at the White House in the years before Stonewall. Barbara and Frank were invited by the college chaplain's office to tell their story, and to give people a visual of "normal" homosexuals who only wanted to not be harassed, and to live lives openly.

I remember the build-up to their visit, how controversial it was for conservative, Methodist-affiliated Allegheny College. There were a couple of more-or-less openly gay students, Susan Day, a lesbian was among them. After graduation she went and worked at the Oscar Wilde Memorial Bookshop in New York. To me, that sounded so amazing and romantic! But at Allegheny, as with most colleges at that time, homophobia reigned supreme.

They spoke at Ford Chapel. The place was packed. I sat all the way in the back, transfixed. I was still not really out to myself. I had been very involved in liberal causes, the anti-war movement, and was learning about feminism. I had been a complete failure at dating men. But, I still had not crossed over to that conscious moment.

Frank and Barbara held my attention completely that night. Barbara told the story of cross-dressing as a teen-age runaway, and all the ways she had tried to cope with her identity and sexuality.

I contacted her later in the year, hoping perhaps to set up another time that she could come and speak — I thought we needed to hear more of her, in particular. This was in the spring of 1972. She asked me a question, since my parents lived on Long Island, if I had ever been to such-and-such a place.

Only after I hung up did I realize that she must think I am a lesbian, and the place was probably a gay club of some kind. I wondered, almost aloud, "I wonder if other people think I am a lesbian?" It was not very long after that,

that I woke up one morning, and looked deep in the mirror and said, "You are a lesbian." I broke through to a realization that I had feelings for one of my housemates that I had been suppressing. Not long after that, I summoned the courage to tell her and we came out together.

I wrote to Barbara through that spring, and told her that I had come out to myself at last, and with a partner. She was very kind, and wrote back. I went home after graduation, still not out to my parents, and worked that summer to earn money for seminary. I was separated from my first love, and continued to write to Barbara.

One Sunday in June 1972, my friend Jean invited me to my first Pride Parade, in New York City. It was an amazing, gorgeous day. We marched with Isabel Miller, the author, and Jill Johnston of Lesbian Nation and the *Village Voice*.

We were in a bookstore after the parade, and there was Rev. Troy Perry's book! Jean tried to tell me this was her new church, and how great it was. I had seen the crazy queens from the Beloved Disciple Church in the parade, in their purple outfits and church drag, and assumed that was what she was talking about. What a silly idea. She invited me, and I turned-down my very first invitation to an MCC service, even though she said it was not so different from the Methodist Church we grew up in.

I took the train home, walked in the door to my parent's home, and my mother was ready for me. I knew she knew. My life did, more or less, flash before me.

At first, I thought I must have been caught by the cameras. But, no. Barbara Gittings had been on the David Suskind show that night, and as fate would have it, I had a letter from Barbara sitting by the table at the front door, where we kept all the mail.

My mother confronted me, and I confessed. It was awful, and she gave me chances to recant. I didn't. My Dad was in the hospital, with back surgery, I had to pedal my bike there and come out to him. He was calm about it. But, it was devastating for both of them, for quite some time.

It was awful for weeks, and then I just left.

I continued to stay in touch with Barbara, occasionally saw her at events over the years. Things got a lot better with my parents. They stretched themselves, accepted me, and attended MCC. Later, they stood on the sidelines and cheered, together, at the first Pride parade on Long Island. They snuck out of church a little early, my mother told me, and cheered as if I were marching in the parade!

In 2003, in Dallas, at our MCC General Conference, we gave Barbara Gittings our Human Rights Award for her amazing contribution to our movement. By that time my Dad had been gone for a decade, but my mom was there, and we all sat at lunch together, including my friend Jean who had invited me to that parade thirty-one years before. Hard to believe we were all sitting around a table, celebrating such progress.

Thank God for all the people like Barbara Gittings of that era, for their courage. She gave me hope, at such a young age, for who I might become.

My first MCC service, October 1972

The year 1972 was a big one for me. I came out to myself, met my first partner, was accepted to seminary with a Rockefeller Fellowship, and could choose any seminary I wanted. I chose Boston University; it was Martin Luther King, Jr.'s school, it was Methodist, and had a good- reputation.

I had no clue as to how I was going to navigate being out and being at seminary. I knew I could not lie, but was not sure how to tell the truth.

Three weeks after I started school, my roommates were listening to one of the first gay radio shows in the country, "Gay Way," hosted by out lesbian and Emerson Professor, Elaine Noble, who later became the first openly gay person elected to public office in the United States, even before Harvey Milk.

My roommates yelled for me, and I listened along with them, to Elaine interviewing Larry Bernier, who was starting an MCC church in Boston. He said, "And, if there is a woman out there, preferably one in seminary, who would be willing to pastor this church with me, so it will be welcoming to men and women, please call me at this number." I called him. He had forty calls, he said, one from a woman — me.

The next day, in the pouring rain, Larry came knocking on my door, and we went to a nearby restaurant for some chowder and coffee. He told me the story of MCC, and handed me a copy of **The Lord is My Shepherd and (He) Knows I'm Gay**. He told me the story of MCC, and what he envisioned for MCC Boston, and I heard myself saying, Yes, I will pastor the church with you.

On Sunday, Jim Hayes, a shy, Irish Catholic law student, picked us up for church: me, my partner Gerry Azzata, our roommate Greg Ford. We went to the Hunnewell Chapel of the Arlington St. Unitarian Universalist Church. About thirty people were there, in that tiny chapel. The pulpit was one used by William Elery Channing, the leading Unitarian minister of the 19th century.

Larry was in some kind of cassock and surplus, like the one Rev. Perry wore in the early days. I didn't know that he was not yet ordained, or even licensed by MCC. He was an "exhorter," student minister, of MCC Los Angeles at that point. But he was preaching, doing communion, and was clearly in charge. That was good enough for us.

Gerry, Elaine Noble and I were the only women at the service that Sunday in early October, 1972. Elaine did not attend regularly after that. It took a while for women to darken the door of that chapel. Feminism was in full bloom, and the year before, Mary Daly had led women in a march out of the chapel at Harvard University, and out of the church.

I would take courses from Mary Daly, who, though a feminist, taught more like a fascist. She tolerated no other opinions.

I had found the first church I knew would accept me as a lesbian and feminist, and she was furious with me for making that choice. She was not out at the time, as a lesbian, and had no tolerance for my romance about this new church. Church was patriarchal to the core, every church, and the sooner I accepted that, and left, the more correct I would be.

But, back to my first MCC service.

We opened with Larry inviting us to recite the Lord's Prayer. I started to cry, and knew I was hooked. At the announcements, he said, "This is our new assistant—or—er—co-pastor, Nancy, may I use your last name?" I said, "Yes."— "Wilson." Applause. That awkward introduction was it. My baptism into MCC as a pastor!

Before the next Sunday, Larry had taken me to Jordan Marsh department store to get me a clergy shirt and collar, and had found a cassock and surplus for me as well. At this point, I had no idea what the process was for becoming clergy, or even if there was one.

We just made it up as we went along.

The third Sunday I preached, and the church started to grow. We were on the front page of the local section of the Boston Globe, in an article by Kay Longcope. Kay was a closeted lesbian, respected religion journalist, and partner of Elaine Noble, for a time.

That third Sunday, a young man who was Seventh Day Adventist, told me he was having surgery the next day, and needed me to pray with him. I realized he meant "pray out loud, in a spontaneous way," something I had never really done. Until that point, all my prayers were scripted, except the desperate, private ones!

So, I just did it. I prayed aloud. I don't think he knew I had never prayed for someone, like that, out loud before. I was wearing a collar, for Pete's sake, but this was the "seat of the pants-on-fire" school of ministry.

Larry decided I needed a stipend, so by December, I was making $10.00 a week to be the co-pastor of MCC Boston. I am not sure what Larry was earning, it was probably not very much more than that.

I was working at a hospital, going to seminary and helping to start this queer church.

A few weeks later, my friend Jean, who had tried to get me to go to MCC New York in June, called, and chewed me out. I had turned her down to go to MCC New York, but now I was co-pastoring MCC Boston? Truthfully, I had no idea they were part of the same outfit.

In six months I came out to myself, started my first relationship, graduated from college, came out to my parents, started seminary, came out at seminary, started co-pastoring MCC, preached at Harvard Divinity School, and landed on the front page of the Boston Globe. It took several years for me to absorb all that transition.

Meeting Troy Perry in 1973

I met Troy Perry at Arlington Street Unitarian Church the first weekend in February of 1973. He was in the little parlor just outside the small chapel in which MCC Boston worshipped.

Troy jumped up — he was tall, and big, and filled the room. He had Elvis Presley sideburns, and an intense Southern accent. He embraced me, really enveloped me, saying it was nice to meet me, etc. I was overwhelmed, at first. I had such Yankee prejudices about Southerners. And, I was very ignorant about Pentecostals and people from more conservative Christian backgrounds. So, this was a challenge for me. All my suspicions were aroused, but I was intrigued.

When he preached that night, I was inspired. The way he blended activism, liberation theology, and good old fashioned gospel preaching gave me a glimpse of what MCC could be beyond our little church. What I had heard, I now saw for myself. There was something authentic, down to earth, and full of a passion in Troy. I had never seen this passion in church. And, honestly! Oh my. Sexuality, spirituality, church, and justice was all there. He was clearly the engine behind this big vision. I could see how he could inspire intense loyalty.

Our very young movement needed someone we could trust. Some called him a prophet — and I had to really contemplate what that meant.

Troy was with us only one week after the Mother Church of MCC in Los Angeles was burned to the ground by arsonists. I was so impressed that he would leave them to be with us, in Boston, at MCC's newest church.

That Sunday, he took me into membership, as we received our charter as an official MCC Church. At the same time, he made Larry a licensed clergy, and me an "exhorter." I had no idea what it meant, except it was some kind of step towards being licensed, and then ordained.

Neither Troy nor I knew that he was taking into membership a future pastor of the church he founded, and his future successor as Moderator of MCC.

I saw him one other time that year, at a clergy conference in Boston, but I do not recall that we spoke.

At the General Conference in Atlanta, in 1973, at a break, I snuck alongside him on our way to the MacDonald's for lunch. I felt shy, but pushed myself to make conversation. I have no memory of what we talked about. It may have been small talk, or about the business of the day at Conference. But I remember how privileged I felt to have those few minutes of private time with Troy Perry.

He was a hero for this lesbian. He was an unlikely prophet — one with a heart and personality confident and humble enough to manage the tumultuous founding days of MCC.

The Homophile Community Health Service

It may seem so hard to imagine now, but in 1972, when I came out and started seminary in Boston, Massachusetts, we lived in a country where there were very few options for psychotherapy for LGBTQ people. If you were fortunate, you lived in a city where word might spread about one or two licensed, competent practitioners who did not treat being gay, or transgender, as a mental illness. There were a lot of quacks. Some people exploited our community, but most counselors just parroted the bad psychology of the time.

There was not an enormous amount of so-called "reparative therapy" at the time, just damaging ignorance. The trend for a while, in the early days of our movement, was to form our own clinics, or group practices, opened by LGBTQ persons or allies.

In Boston, a group of clinicians, gay and straight, opened the Homophile Community Health Services (HCHS) in the early 70s. It was the very first licensed mental health clinic focused on the needs of LGBTQ people, and staffed mostly by LGBTQ practitioners.

"Homophile," as opposed to "homosexual" was the lingo of choice in 1972.

There was also a Homophile Union of Boston, a political action group that most of us belonged to, led by working class Irish Bostonian, Bob Dow. Bob always wore a suit and an enormous campaign button that said, "I AM A GAY AMERICAN." He was relentless in working at the Boston State House for basic gay rights in those days.

Bob never seemed to be in it for the power, or recognition, or even notoriety. He was just a driven, passionate, true believer. He didn't always have the greatest social skills, and never seemed to know what to do with lesbians, but, he is an early unsung hero, now forgotten by all but a few of us.

Rev. Don McGaw, a Methodist minister, gay, and a clinician himself, was the director of HCHS. Dr. Cal Turley, the President of the Swedenborgian Church, was straight and amazingly open and accepting. Besides the clinic and his private practice, Dr. Turley ran the Swedenborgian House at Andover Newton Theological Seminary.

I went to the clinic first, for myself, in 1973, in my coming out process and in response to the break-up of my first relationship. I was devastated and saw a therapist there named Gail King, who was in a wheelchair with multiple sclerosis. She was wonderful and very funny.

She decided I was being too nice about the break-up and said, "Don't you really want to see her in 100 lbs. of cement in the bottom of the 'Chahles'?" That was how she pronounced "Charles," as in Charles River, with her very New England accent. She worked hard to uncover my anger. It was buried very deeply, for safekeeping. Anger was not a very allowable emotion in my world, but she helped me break it open.

Gail had a doctorate in literature from Amherst — focused on Emily Dickinson's work. But, instead of seeking an academic position, she devoted herself to this ground-breaking clinical work. A white, working class Bostonian, she was in love with Helen, an African American, former nun, who also served at the clinic.

Then, there was also clinicians Andy and Jane Graham. Andy was gay, married to Jane, who was, well, I was never sure. She was a lot butcher than Andy, or me, or any lesbian I knew. They were funny, smart, and courageous.

In the process, I learned that I could do a year of clinical work there through my Boston University School of Theology Field Education program, so I signed up, with Dr. Turley as my supervisor.

One of my first clients was a woman I will call, "Meg." Meg was an ardent feminist, and involved in women's mental health. Like LGBTQ people, women had been pathologized for ages by the male-dominated mental health system.

She helped to found the Elizabeth Stone Center, which still serves women and their families.

As I got to know Meg, I realized that something was terribly wrong. I did a lot of work with Dr. Turley on this. Meg even seemed to have some homicidal and suicidal thoughts, though nothing concrete. Clearly, I was over my head.

Meg called me in-between sessions. I was in school, working twenty hours a week at the rehab hospital, and doing several hours of clinical work as well. And, I was helping to start MCC Boston! I was young, so, mostly I managed. But extra phone calls were another level with Meg.

Then, suddenly, she didn't show up for her session, which she never missed. I called her. Nothing. This went on for a few days, and I was very worried. So, I crossed a boundary, and went to her house, and knocked on the door. Nothing. I then called the police, suspecting that she could have killed herself.

They burst in the door, with me behind them. Meg was laying in her bed, holding a bottle of lye, unable to speak, or respond to me or the police. Since she was not dead, or apparently dying (her eyes were open), they left.

I spoke to her, and suggested that maybe it was time to check in at the hospital, which we had spoken of before. With that, she bolted up, and ran to the kitchen. Now I was really regretting sending the police away.

When I got to the kitchen, she pinned me up against the refrigerator with an enormous butcher knife that was big enough to slice me in two.

It is true that your life flashes before you, as did all twenty-three years of my life.

I threw up my hands in a gesture of surrender, and said calmly, "Meg, you don't have to go to the hospital if you don't want to. Just put the knife down, and we can talk."

Her eyes fluttered, I could not really tell if she could hear me, and the knife was not just pointed at my stomach, it was pressing in.

She dropped the knife, and sat down. I sat down next to her, and we were able to talk. She agreed to go to the hospital, and I did not see her any more at the clinic.

A year or so later she contacted me, thanked me, and let me know that she had been diagnosed with a rare form of epilepsy that produced the kinds of behavior and symptoms she had.

That was a tough way to learn about boundaries with clients, and psychotic behavior. I know now, as I knew then, that it could have gone another way.

The First Pride, Worcester, Massachusetts

In 1974, the gay organization and the MCC in Worcester, Massachusetts, decided together that we were ready for our first Pride Parade. We were relentless with the city, got a permit, and the grudging cooperation of the very homophobic police department.

Members of MCCs from Hartford, Boston, and Providence, Rhode Island, showed up to support us. With all our out-of-town help, we still had only about seventy-five or eighty people marching. We were able to persuade the Red Cross to send a van in case anyone had a health issue — and frankly, so if anyone was injured by homophobic attacks, we would have help.

Night after night, in the weeks before, we had been challenging the patrons of the only gay bar in town, The Port's O'Call, to have the guts to march in the daylight. There were only a few takers; most of them were our church members.

It was a bright sunny day. We had instructed the marchers not to fight back if assaulted, and not to hurl insults back, either. We had our proud banners and signs. As we walked, to our shock, thousands of local people, coming out of church along Main Street, or out of their homes, lined the streets.

Mostly they stared, some jeered. A few kids started to throw rocks and cans, and a police officer said, "Hey, cut it out, don't you know it ain't okay to throw stuff at queers no more?" Progress! Enlightenment!

Then, we got to the end of the parade route. Our plan was to march into the park and begin our picnic with hotdogs and coleslaw, etc. The police understood that they were to take their leave of us as we entered the park — we thought, or hoped, they would remain just a little longer. They did not.

Teenagers, mostly grubby looking boys, climbed every tree hanging over or near our hot dog roast, jeering and pointing at first.

We just keep cooking the hotdogs, serving up the potato salad, buns and chips, sodas. Slowly, they got quiet, and slid down the trees. The bravest ones took a couple of steps closer to us. We could see that they were, in fact, hungry and tormented about asking us for a bite

Rev. Joseph Gilbert sweetly offered the hotdogs to them, which they took gratefully, and ran off. That was the end of that. No police needed, grilled hotdogs were the best defense.

The next day, we were in all the papers, including the *Worcester Telegram Gazette*. On the front page were photos of me, in my clergy collar. Being a public queer, especially a public queer preacher, was who I was, and who I was becoming. But, something inside of me had not entirely caught up with that new identity. After a whole day of bravado, confrontation and having my photo taken, I crashed the next day into vulnerability.

I had forgotten that I had a dental appointment that day.

When I got to the office, my internalized homophobia was in full gear, especially as I saw the newspaper with my photo in the waiting room of the office. I did not know this dentist. I had a bad molar, and no money or insurance. At that point I should have rescheduled, but my tooth was killing me.

I was seized with fear as he opened my mouth and began working. He made no comment about the paper or the march, but I did not feel safe. The molar was bad, and needed either a root canal, or just to come out. I had no money for much of anything, and taking the tooth out was the cheapest option, which is what he did. Even with anesthesia, it hurt like hell, probably more, because of my fear. I was afraid he was making it more painful because he had targeted me. That was probably paranoia, but it was painful nevertheless.

To this day I have no molar there, no implant or bridge. It is a hole in my head that reminds me of a time when I could not negotiate for safe dentistry! I learned never to allow anyone to treat me without being completely sure of my safety. I can't say I have always stood up for myself as well as I should have, but I never subjected myself like that again.

I was fortunate for many years to have a lesbian dentist in LA, whose partner was the receptionist. As a person working for a church that was still in its formative years, who did not have dental insurance, she worked with me to allow me to make payments on work that needed to be done immediately. I will always be grateful to her for that, for her kindness and skill. It was a luxury to feel entirely safe in her hands.

Women, prisoners, people with HIV/AIDS, so many others, have had to fight to be treated fairly, even humanely, by doctors and practitioners. This is true for LGBTQ people as well. In time, I would have the privilege of training hospital chaplains not to assume that everyone was straight, and strategies they could employ to offer signs to patients that they were inclusive, non-judgmental and open as professionals and ministers.

Elected Elder 1976

The MCC General Conference in 1976 was the Conference during which, at 26-years-old, I was elected an Elder, the youngest person ever to be elected to that office in MCC.

In those days, a nominations committee came up with a slate of nominees right there at the general conference.

I was surprised, and not surprised, in a way, to be nominated, but I was shocked to be elected on the first ballot, along with Rev. Charlie Arehart.

I replaced Rev. Elder John Gill, who was just a few years older than me. He sent me a huge bouquet of flowers not long after the results were announced. I never found out exactly how he accomplished that.

John was our Princeton "guy," from an upper class background, who found his calling and passion in MCC. He was always the "gentleman," and an opera aficionado who loved Mel Brooks movies. His sense of humor was flawless, and he was one of those people who, when he stood up to speak at Conference, everyone hushed, because we knew he would make sense, in a centrist, calm and authoritative way.

John was one of the young MCC pastors present in the aftermath of the New Orleans fire, sharing MCC's compassion with a hurting community, and insisting on justice.

When they announced that the Board of Elders was having a quick meeting, from the podium, I just went to lunch, because, how could I be an Elder? It took me all week to get used to it.

I remember asking the silver-haired, confident Rev. Elder Jim Sandmire, "What do I do now?" There was no training, no orientation, nothing to read, only what I had observed, to help me figure out what to do now. He replied, "Just go home and pray."

The other operating factor of the 1976 Conference was Kerry Brown. Kerry was an outspoken, brilliant lay leader of MCC Washington DC, who was, let's say, very resourceful and quite a character. She discovered a month or so before the Conference that the hotel manager had run off with his secretary, and no one was really managing the hotel. So, Kerry simply moved in and took over. She managed the hotel (which was torn down not too much later) for the weeks leading up to and during the Conference.

I remember a sermon she preached, not long after that, in which she said she almost never said, "Thy will be done," when praying the Lord's prayer, because she was so willful herself.

Kerry and her partner, Rev. Nancy Radclyffe, were the force behind MCC clergy getting a supplemental pension plan, in the United States. They came up with the proposal, which included requiring all churches to contribute, and got it through the 1983 General Conference, in Toronto.

Kerry also managed the MCC headquarters in Los Angeles for a while, during a time of difficult transition. She made many contributions to MCC in our first two decades. She died of cancer in 1988. Kerry was a special person, whose gifts met our needs in those early years.

Elder's Meeting, Troy Fast, Jeff's Couch and Sweatshops

My first Board of Elders meeting, in late 1976, was overwhelming. They mailed me a plane ticket, and that was all the preparation I got.

I asked my friend, Rev. Jeff Pulling, if I could stay with him. Jeff had come into MCC within a month of me in late 1972, when we were both in seminary. He was a sweet man, deeply faithful, and committed to MCC. He and Larry were together for some years, but by now they were parted, and Jeff lived in his own apartment in Hollywood.

I slept on the couch in his living room. Jeff got up at 4AM to go to his job as a phlebotomist. After eight hours of that he would go to the MCC Offices where he would teach at our fledging school, Samaritan College. He was the Dean, probably a volunteer at that point.

Jeff had an overbite and slurped his cereal, which woke me up every morning at four. He didn't have a car, but he told me how to take the bus to downtown LA to get there for my first meeting.

The meeting was on the 9th floor of an old office building that mostly housed sweatshops, so when you got in the elevator, there was usually room for one or two people, and all the clothing racks.

Present at that first meeting was Troy Perry, Jim Sandmire, John "Papa John" Hose, Freda Smith, Charlie Arehart, Carol Cureton and me. As the youngest person there, I was very quiet at that first meeting, taking it all in, looking at the packed agenda. The meeting flowed with agenda items, finances, appointments, pastoral sharing (sometimes gossip), and lots of fires to put out.

I remember going to Olvera Street, in downtown Los Angeles, and having lunch with the Elders and Troy's Mom, Edith, who I had met at conferences (she attended every one for many years). I had never eaten an avocado, or tasted Mexican food. I was always trying to cover my inexperience and tried to find my way to fit into this high powered group.

Troy had us over to his home one evening. I appreciated the lunches and dinners, because at the time I shared a salary of less than $7,000 per year with my clergy partner. I had very little money with me to pay for meals, and MCC had no budget for that. We just managed.

It was a steep learning curve. I did an ordination in Washington DC (Larry Uhrig), and brought a church charter to MCC in Ottawa. It was travel on the cheap, by hook or by crook.

Troy had not even been paid a salary for the first two years he was Moderator, which took a huge toll on him and his mother. This was a time of sacrifice and the ingenuity of youth. We were creating a movement and a church from the ground up. It took everything we had.

NO ON 6

My third Elders meeting was in Los Angeles, in 1977. It was a heady time in the LGBTQ movement, with Anita Bryant, and huge challenges to our early successes. In California, the big news was Proposition 6, the proposed law that would outlaw LGBTQ teachers in California. When it was introduced, no one thought we could win a public referendum and defeat the law, except one person, Troy Perry.

A large national LGBTQ meeting had recently decided that it was too expensive and we would be stretched too thin to fight every state and municipal battle for equal rights, for non-discrimination.

When it became clear that this horrific law could pass in California, Troy broke ranks with national leadership. At our Elders meeting, he told us that he was going to raise $100,000 to do the first poll of Californians on Proposition 6, the first poll of its kind in history. And, that he wanted to work with other Californians to defeat this, and would be putting all his efforts into that for the next several months. To raise that amount of money (today it would be worth about one million dollars), he was going to leave our meeting, and go to the federal building in downtown LA, and fast until we raised the money.

"We" meant the Elders.

And then he left. Our primary job, whether we said so or not, was to support him and his prophetic voice and ministry. These were his instincts, born of prayer, and we knew it came from his heart and his guts. So, we had to work with our churches and anyone else we could to raise that money.

Few of us had experience in raising this kind of money, except those, like Sandmire, who were politically active.

We had no staff for this, and no fund development experience. We did not have the Internet, so we sent a letter to all the churches, and began calling.

The national and even California LGBTQ political leadership were divided at this point, so we really couldn't go outside of MCC. For the rest of the time we were in LA, we were calling churches and individuals, trying to get to $100,000.

Meanwhile, I had ended a relationship, and meant to tell the Elders. But, events took over, and I returned to Detroit having told no one of my personal pain and struggle.

Every day, between making phone calls, we visited Troy on the steps of the Federal building. We had a prayer service every day; I had to lead one of them. He took communion, the only thing he ate while fasting.

The fast lasted nearly a month, and we raised that money. Troy broke his fast.

I went home to a lot of crisis and drama around the breakup, and to a political community that was angry about Troy's decision. I learned a lot about who to trust and how to manage difficult choices.

The amazing thing was, of course, that we won that fight. No organization helped. The poll was paid for by MCC members, and provided the marching orders and strategy to an amazing group of activists and leaders in California who defeated Proposition 6. They even got Governor Ronald Reagan to come out against the proposition.

It was an amazing lesson in leadership instincts and trusting the Spirit.

Let My Books Go

In the early 70s, in the Public Library in Los Angeles, and, many other places, books on homosexuality were placed under lock and key, to be guarded by the head librarian, as if they were valuable "rare books," or more likely, as if they were pornographic, a danger to decent people and children.

If someone wanted to read a book about homosexuality, even for research (what LGBTQ person has not done that!), they had to go and ask the head librarian, who I am sure would give them a funny look. Most people wouldn't have the courage to do that, which is why they locked the books up, to assure they would be rarely read.

Ann Montague was a young MCC clergy, or student clergy. She had very leftist politics (still does!), and was horrified by this treatment of "our" books at a public library, which we all pay taxes to support, including LGBTQ people.

So one day, wearing her collar, Ann strode into the Los Angeles Public Library, took a hold of the locked bookcase, and started shouting, "Let My Books Go, Let My Books Go!"

And from that day on, the books went back on to the regular bookshelves, at least in Los Angeles.

A Queer Christmas Dinner 1975

In 1975, as the new co-pastors of MCC Detroit, my partner and I decided that, on Christmas day the church would open its doors, and have a dinner for anyone who needed it. In those times, lots of LGBTQ people did not go home for Christmas, or did so reluctantly.

So, about twenty of us gathered in the social hall of the Methodist Church we rented in Highland Park. Then, we had an idea. We got in a couple of cars and drove up and down Woodward Avenue, looking for people on the streets who might need a meal. It took a little talking to encourage them to walk the few blocks, or get in our cars. That far up Woodward there were not many on the streets that day. Our guests were pleasantly surprised, and that is how the only Christmas dinner open to the public in Detroit began. What we discovered was that many places were open on Thanksgiving, but, few volunteers were available to do anything on Christmas.

That year, we managed to "compel" a few folks to come. The following year, in a new location, downtown Detroit, we had more takers, and more participants, about 80 people. The following year it swelled to a couple of hundred. Our reputation began to grow.

After we left, in the late 70s, our host church downtown and other community groups took over the dinner, with MCCers still helping and staffing on Christmas. For decades, they fed over 1,000 people every Christmas, as grocery stores and other businesses chipped in.

Few remember that the only Christmas dinner open to all in Detroit started with a bunch of gay people who couldn't go home, who needed a place to be and a greater cause. Later, those LGBTQ people who were still avoiding a family gathering would simply say they were needed to help at their church's Christmas Day dinner!

For some people, it was simply the best place to be on Christmas Day.

To Retreat or Not Retreat

In 1979, we had serious turnover in the Board of Elders, the top spiritual, pastoral, and at that time, fiduciary leadership of MCC worldwide. We added two women, Rev. Jeri Ann Harvey, pastor of MCC Los Angeles, and Rev. Jean White, from London, England, our first Elder from outside the US. With Rev. Freda Smith and myself, there were a majority of women on the Board for the first time.

One of the puzzling aspects of being an Elder in this time period in MCC's life was that it didn't seem to me that we spent much time praying, or in "spiritual formation," as the Catholics would call it. Maybe I noticed this more because I was just graduating from a Catholic seminary. In those days, they had a corner on the market of spiritual formation issues and expertise. I had been profoundly impacted by the ways they opened up prayer and "spiritual practices."

It seemed to me we prayed mostly in crisis, governed in crisis, and were always on the run. Once or twice, in dire moments, we had all gotten on our knees, to beg for help, for courage, mercy, for resources, for wisdom. But mostly, as Elders, we thrashed out policies, talked endlessly about pastors, churches and crises. We worried about money. We laughed, and gossiped, and told stories. It felt like we rushed from one burning building to another.

We followed our leader, Troy Perry, who was always on the go. Always. He was the kind of person who filled a room when he entered it. He was the classic extrovert who heard his own ideas as he said them out loud. He was always in a hurry, catching the next plane, making the next phone call, starting the next rally, or leading a March on Washington.

In the days before the Internet, when Troy needed something, usually money for some project that was not in the budget, or if he needed support for an idea, he would call each Elder. There were seven of us, and he would call in alphabetical order. When he had four votes, he just stopped calling, and went on to the next thing. Sometimes, months later, those of us on the end of the alphabet would hear, second hand what had been decided. He didn't mean to exclude us, really. I don't think it was conscious or deliberate, but, he would say, "I got my four!" which included him, so that was enough to move forward. On to the next thing.

There was no time for lots of debate or conversation. That was the thing that would irritate him about other configurations of MCC leadership structures over time. Anything that slowed things down, that got in the way, annoyed him if he felt passionately about whatever it was. This is classic entrepreneurial leadership. And it shaped our first two decades.

I had some sensitivity about that. I believed in dialogue, conversation, discernment and good process for decision making. That caused some conflict from time to time. Mostly, though, I went along with the older Elders, who were just trying to keep up with Troy. It took a village of us to do that. He had unbelievable energy, resilience, and good humor. Even when you disagreed with him, he loved you and was loyal, and the love and loyalty was returned.

The fact was, we needed to make many decisions quickly. No question about it.

After the 1979 Conference, with some traumas and changes in leadership, I finally voiced out loud that I thought we needed an Elders Retreat.

Just to humor me, I think, Troy consented to that idea. I was thrilled!

We arranged for all the Elders to drive up, in two cars, to Mt. Calvary Retreat Center and Monastery in Santa Barbara, California. This was a gorgeous, well-appointed, Episcopal Retreat Center, run by Episcopal brothers. I had a gay friend who had joined the order and moved there, who said, "If this is poverty, I can't wait to see chastity!"

My idea was that we would gather on Friday evening, and that Troy would lead us in a retreat on Saturday, and we would return to Los Angeles Saturday afternoon, go to church on Sunday, and start our meetings. In those days, Troy led everything, I would not have dreamed to assign this to someone else. He was our prophet, our spiritual leader.

I arranged for the retreat center, for our rooms and meals.

There was perfect Santa Barbara weather for the weekend. We arrived before dinner and walked the grounds, looking at the amazing sunset. Everyone seemed thrilled to be there, and were looking forward to a new start with a new Board of Elders.

This was something I had longed for and anticipated for months.

At dinner, the monks read and everyone was to keep silent. We participated and enjoyed a lovely meal. We hung out in the common area until 10 PM, when there was to be lights out and the Grand Silence. No talking.

Jeri Ann, Jean White and I were in one room. We whispered a little, for a while, then, in obedience, turned out our lights.

At 10:15, there was a knock on our door. It was Troy.

He was bored and not ready to sleep. So, he kept us up until about 2AM in the morning, telling stories, making us laugh. We were like guilty kids at sleep away camp, breaking all the rules. We laughed until our sides hurt, and the tears were rolling down our faces. Troy was amazingly entertaining, and Jeri Ann followed suit. Jean and I participated, loving the intimacy and revelry. I believe cheap wine was also involved.

The stresses and pressures we faced were so overwhelming at times, misbehaving in this kind of way, bonding with the Founder of our movement was a momentary privilege we could not pass up — not the three of us, anyway. We were at a monastery where silence was the law and we were, once again, outlaws after all.

When the bell rang for breakfast at 7 AM, we were really dragging, all four of us, and several of the others looked at us, accusingly. I guess our efforts to keep it down had failed.

As we ate in silence, the monks read again.

We went to our rooms, made sure we were packed up to leave later in the day, and at about 9AM, gathered in the common room for what I believed would be several hours of retreat, prayer, time for reflection, "holy conversation."

Instead, when we were all there, Troy said, "Well, there's nothing else to do here, let's go!"

Nothing else to do here?

Half of us seemed very happy with that suggestion. I was appalled, to the point of not being able to speak.

So, we all got in our cars, and drove back to Los Angeles.

Jean White commiserated with me — "What did he think there was to do here?" She said, "I thought you had asked him to lead a retreat for us."

"I did. I guess he had no idea what I meant by that. Or he forgot."

He was so hard-wired for action, for pressing the agenda of civil and human rights, for meeting the urgent needs of our congregations, he didn't see any point in being silent, or slowing down enough to reflect, or listen to this remarkable group of leaders, who loved him and would follow him anywhere. He didn't know that we were right on the precipice of a disaster that would threaten the very mission and leadership of MCC — AIDS. How could he have known then that this life and death challenge would require a level of spiritual maturity and endurance for which we were not really prepared, but which came barreling down towards us?

The day did come, years later, when he was ready for that retreat, and we were too. AIDS slowed us down, pushed us to our limits.

We were privileged to have actual retreat time with bishops, seminary professors, civil rights leaders and church leaders from other denominations who prayed with us, offered their wisdom and encouragement, and met us in our exhaustion, and our deep need for God's healing presence and direction, but not in 1980.

In some twist of terrible irony, our slogan for the decade was, "The 80s Are Ours!" This was the decade in which our true metal was tested, and in which we were needed by a community reeling from AIDS more than we could have ever imagined. But the sunny slogan disappeared early on, and got replaced with the assertion, "God is Greater Than AIDS." Our prayer then was, "God, you had better be."

MCC Places and Spaces

Sometimes I think we could tell the story of MCC by telling the story of our buildings. The ones we rented, borrowed, bought or built. The humble ones decorated lavishly. The ones that were arsoned, vandalized, and repainted many times. The ones that were destroyed in earthquakes. Ones that now grace many neighborhoods, unmolested.

The first building owned by an MCC church was MCC Los Angeles, in 1970 or 71. It was an abandoned church building on 11th and Hill street in downtown LA. It was full of trash and garbage, and the new congregation raised a whopping $10,000 in one offering. People who were there tell of people throwing in diamond rings, giving over and above what they could realistically afford. Those were not realistic times, they were times of miracles.

A film of the dedication of that building exists. It was the first property owned by a group identifying with the LGBTQ community ever in history. Some say it was the first place gay people met, with others, in the daylight.

That beloved building, so lovingly restored, the site of the first General Conference of Metropolitan Community Churches, was burned to the ground, by an arsonist, in late January 1973. That Sunday, 1,000 people gathered in the street, in the parking lot, as church was held next door to the church building. Rev. Willie Smith famously said, "God burned the closet down!"

For many people, it was the first place of belonging and healing, it was their first church home as adults. That Sunday was the first time many of them stood, fearlessly, in anger and defiance, in the daylight, with the media present, to claim this community as their own.

That story has been told many times, in many ways. MCC Los Angeles itself had lived in many buildings before it owned that one: in a home, a women's club, in theaters. Over the years they met in other churches, a former chicken restaurant and skating rink, They met in a synagogue that they had helped found years before. They met in a sound stage, in a public auditorium, in a converted furniture design store in West Hollywood, and eventually, again in a church building they purchased.

Nowadays, in Cologne, Germany, the church meets in a garage in an industrial park. You roll up the front door, and, there is a lovely sanctuary! After church they set up the barbeque right in front of the garage door, everyone hangs around and shares some food.

In Jamaica, in Kingston, the MCC there met on the lawn of the AIDS Service Center, under a tent. The center was a large building, and it was surrounded by a huge hedge, which gave it some privacy. Nevertheless, as we sang, and prayed, and preached at that place, every car backfiring put us a bit on edge.

In Chicago, Church4me met for a few weeks in an off/off/off Broadway theater, that was entirely black on the inside, had stage lighting and stadium seating for 50 at the most, in very close quarters.

The church in Pensacola lost their building to a hurricane, and met temporarily, for over a year, in a Bingo Hall, that reeked of cigarette smoke. I coughed through most of my sermons when I preached there as a guest minister.

Many MCC's have to have a "church in a box," in other words each week they bring all the elements, worship and fellowship materials, in a box or two to set up at a space they rent, where they cannot even store things for the next week.

We have churches that have won architectural awards and spaces that challenge the heartiest of seekers. Each is a story of hope and promise.

Quaking in Los Angeles

The Northridge Earthquake happened on the Martin Luther King, Jr., holiday, on Monday, January 17, 1994, at 4:31AM. I know that because for years, I would wake up at that time, even just for a few seconds, and see the time on my bedside clock.

That weekend we hosted church growth workshops at MCC LA, in Culver City. I remember on Sunday night asking the question, how were we going to really accommodate growth in this sanctuary? We already had four services per Sunday, including the Spanish language service. The foyer was cramped, we had maxed out the seating, including a small balcony.

The next morning, my question became irrelevant.

Paula and I were violently shaken out of a sound sleep that morning. It was probably the most frightened I had ever been in my life. For a minute or more, I wondered if the house would fall on top of us, or the earth swallow us up.

It didn't, and finally, the shaking stopped for a bit. A few things had toppled in our living room and kitchen, a few cracks appeared in some walls, but nothing disastrous. An hour later, we were on our way to the church in our car, through the back streets of Los Angeles, with Norm Mason. Norm had worked on the building, and served as my administrative assistant off and on for some years. We got a firsthand view of the city along the way.

A church member had called us at about 5:30AM to tell us the church dome had fallen into the street, and that the church was very damaged. This, after we had invested a lot of money in earthquake proofing our building.

When we got near, we saw sky where there had been a church dome. Lots of folks were gathering. It was a mess. We were half a mile, at most, from the 405 Freeway, which had been destroyed. The church was on La Cienega Blvd., which means "swamp" in Spanish.

The earth was still shaking.

The board gathered. That night I was supposed to be on a flight to South Africa, to a World Council of Churches Central Committee meeting, and to meet with LGBTQ Christians in several cities. This was right before the end of apartheid, and while there were lots of flights to London, there were still very few to South Africa. If I missed the flights and connections that night, I would miss the meetings, and the opportunities to connect for the future of MCC.

We were all in a daze. The board, though, unanimously decided that I should still go, if I could get out of LA that night. I was ambivalent. How could I leave my home, my church, my partner at at time like this? She was supposed to join me a week later, for the second part of the trip. Everything was so uncertain.

I got on that plane that night. LAX was operating, and I made my connections. I was so torn throughout the flight, and, it was hard to connect back home, because so much infrastructure was damaged, and communications were impacted.

In our church, few of the members lost their homes, though many were traumatized. Some slept outside, afraid to go into their homes. In the San Fernando Valley, it was the opposite; the church was not damaged, but many lost their homes, and were so traumatized they moved away. This was a factor, I believe, in the decline of that church in the next decade. The Valley itself still struggles to recover from the effects of that earthquake on residents and businesses.

I went to South Africa with others of us from MCC, and made a powerful witness to the World Council. We had a chance to meet with Bishop Desmond Tutu, who became a powerful ally to the LGBTQ community.

LGBTQ Churches in South Africa invited me to preach, and some of those congregations eventually became MCC churches. I met people of faith and passion for justice who were doing the same things we were doing in MCC all over the world.

We held an impromptu seminar one night for all in the WCC who still believed that homosexuality was "unAfrican," and that LGBTQ issues were a Western import to Africa. We brought together about 25 people from the groups we met — truly multiracial, lesbian, gay, bisexual and transgender people, with people who cross-dressed. We were all there!

The testimonies were passionate. For the first time at a WCC meeting, we shared about our faith, our struggle for human rights, our struggle for acceptance and hope in a New South Africa that was on its way right at that moment! A number of communion heads, WCC officials and church leaders attended that evening, and, I believe, were amazed at what they heard.

It was an honor and a joy to bring together people who were new sisters and brothers in faith and struggle, and to hear their powerful testimonies. That evening, in 1994, still shaken from the earth moving, I had a vision of the emerging LGBTQ global struggle that would be the next challenge of our movement world-wide.

What a blessing for a church and a partner, who encouraged me to go. Our church was in shambles with the dome in pieces but we were alive! We were still the church!

Where Do We Go From Here?

I returned to Los Angeles a little over two weeks after the Northridge earthquake. By that time, commuter patterns had changed to accommodate repair of the biggest freeway in the world, and other repairs of hospital parking structures, roads and buildings were under way.

When we arrived at the airport, Rev. Lori Dick, my friend, and colleague, who had done so much to hold the church together in my two week absense, met me at the airport with directions to where the church was meeting the next morning, and keys to my new, temporary office.

The drive to church the next morning was strange. I struggled to learn that we were meeting at a sound stage in Culver City, not far from where the church had been. Someone had a friend who knew someone, who found this space. Someone used our brand new church sign (ouch) to tell everyone the address of where we were currently meeting. I had been so excited and proud of that church sign. Now, it seemed to mock us — or, at least, me.

The sound stage was a huge, cavernous warehouse, several stories high. There were some temporary rooms we made into offices and a social hall of sorts. And, this sound stage happened to have the Christmas/church backdrop, set design from the TV show "Home Improvement." So, presto! Instant church. An altar area with folding chairs in front of it appeared.

In a room where there were fire trucks, other huge vehicles, and large set designs, we had a little area that was an instant church.

I preached there that morning. Loyal church members, now in their third week out of church, were there as usual. We had a birthday celebration for someone.

The Spanish language ministry suffered the most, as people who had only known MCC in the Culver City space could not find this new location since it had no church sign out front.

That afternoon, I did a memorial service at another MCC, in Atwater Village because the sound stage was not appropriate for funerals or weddings.

So, we borrowed the Episcopal Church, and I conducted a funeral of a community leader who had died of AIDS.

Seven years later to the very day of that funeral, I was at a community dinner in Los Angeles. The man next to me was very touched to see me, and told me that I had done his partner's funeral 7 years ago to the day. When he said that, I was puzzled, and could not remember it. Then, I thought, well, he probably knows who did his partner's funeral.

As he talked, it all came back to me, through what seemed like shards of broken glass. I remember being in that Episcopal church, and though I was present performing the funeral, I evidently was still in shock.

Leading up to that funeral, in a space of one month, my father died, my assistant pastor Danny died, friends had died, the church building was destroyed in the earthquake, and I had been to South Africa, returning the night before the funeral of this man's partner. It was probably then that I realized why the year 1994 was often such a blur for me. I had a form of PTSD, I am sure, from all the years of AIDS deaths, and these multiple losses in such a short space of time. I am just grateful I got through it. I know it was friends, family, Paula, and so many people praying for me — for us — that got us through.

In those weeks after the earthquake, we had to put our grand piano, and whatever else survived the earthquake, including remnants of our gorgeous granite and marble memorial wall, in storage.

All we brought with us were hymnals, some folding chairs, the altar and some altar ware. Later I learned, members had risked themselves to rescue those things from the shaking building in the week after the earthquake. Lori had been the arbiter of who got to go in the building and for how long. They saved old records, my damaged ordination certificate, and some furniture. So much was lost, forever.

When we left the sound stage, Penny, a woman who had found us while we were there (one of the few), was upset the day we loaded the truck, much of which would go into storage. We finished up but did not load the churchy backdrop from "Home Improvement." Penny was shaken. "But that's my church!" she cried. We had to explain that it was from a TV show.

We smile at this story but it is more poignant than funny. We who were condemned by our church families are like abandoned children who finally find what it feels like to have a family. Penny was losing a symbol of the first church home she had ever had. It made me so conscious of how quickly MCCer's attach meaning to symbols and rituals — even if it is just a TV prop.

From the sound stage, where we were for only about 5 weeks, we went to Congregation Beth Chayim Chadashim, the synagogue that MCC had helped to start decades before. Their Rabbi was so kind to offer the space to us on Sunday mornings. It was a beautiful sanctuary, but too small for us.

While we were worshiping in the synagogue, I invited some new folks to train as deacons, including Alex Escoto. Alex had struggled with many issues, sexual abuse, acting out, HIV. I learned later that he had prayed for a "path," and the very next week I had asked him to consider training. Alex had to come out to us about all his issues, but I saw God at work in him. Today he is an ordained MCC clergy, pastoring our Spanish language ministry at Founders MCC and helping other churches to do outreach.

Also, while at the synagogue, a man who was in our grief group came to church with his family, and asked for prayer. It was the first Father's Day without his Dad. I prayed for them, and then blurted out, "It's my first Father's Day without my Dad as well," and to my surprise, he then prayed for me. It was one of those humbling moments. I had not mentioned my father during the sermon, and was probably trying to exercise control, and then, I blurted it out, in my humanness and need. The prayer was so sweet and appropriate, and I remember yielding to it in that moment.

From the synagogue, we moved on to a Junior High School, located nearer to South Central LA, right off the freeway. Though not in a familiar a neighborhood such as Culver City, the auditorium/gymnasium was large enough, and I think they had folding chairs that we set up every week. We had a little closet where we kept our hymnals, an altar, a large silk flower arrangement for the altar, and banners which we hung over the basketball hoops.

The toilets were usually less than clean, and had to be cleaned before we started church. A crew came every Sunday morning to do all of this. We set up a crate for mail and messages for all the church leaders. These were the days before email.

The best feature about this location, I thought, was the huge parking lot. Almost all our members drove, and there was not a lot of street parking there. This was perfect, and would be an encouragement. And, it was, for three weeks.

Then, one Sunday morning, I arrived to find the parking lot totally torn up, bulldozed. Gone. I stood there, and thought, well, I could just get in my car and drive. Drive far away, where no one would ever find me. I had talked church members into this location, hoping we could be there until we were in our new building. I frequently mentioned the generous parking lot. Now it was gone, and everyone who came to church that day would have to scramble for parking somewhere.

Then, Rev. Barbara Haynes arrived. She just broke into tears. We hugged each other, dragged out the church sign, met the crew who set everything up, and went on. The parking lot was never resurfaced but we were there over a year before we moved to Plummer Park, starting with a very, very rainy Easter Sunday.

Plummer Park was on the edge of West Hollywood. It had great parking, nice and clean bathrooms, and even a place we could fix some food. We grew there, and people found us again, including some who couldn't figure out where we had gone (even though we told them dozens of ways).

It worked so well, except for a couple of Sundays a year, when they rented that space to other groups. Then we had to cram ourselves into a small classroom for two or three services. People mostly stayed away those Sundays, except hard core members.

Those years were the refiners' fire for me and the members of MCC LA. I am forever grateful for those who persevered, and saw us through those times of wandering.

Devastation in Haiti

In January of 2010, a terrible earthquake rocked Haiti.

Just a few years before, MCC had planted a new church in Santo Domingo, in the Dominican Republic, which shares the island of Hispaniola with the much more impoverished Haiti.

Our church in the DR, founded by native Dominican Rev. Tania Guzman, and pastored by Rev. Wilkin Lara, was made up of about 30% Haitian refugees, many of them seeking an education and a new life.

When the earthquake hit, our young church sprang into action. MCC churches around the world eventually raised about $50,000 which we used to bring help to people in Haiti, to the families of our church members, and to LGBTQ and AIDS activists in Haiti, who were not necessarily being served by other groups. They were courageous and relentless in giving of their time and resources. They were the hands and feet of an increasingly global MCC.

The Haitian members of our church in Santo Domingo, are a persecuted minority in the DR. In a powerful way, it was the moment in which they knew that the church really cared for them as family and community. The church and MCC globally did not shrink from risking themselves to help the families and community in Haiti.

Rev. Tania, Rev. Wilkin, and volunteers from the church in Santo Domingo made three trips that year.

In order to fill the trucks with a maximum of food and supplies, the pastors had to go to very tough, dangerous neighborhoods to get things at the lowest cost. They chose food that would be familiar comforting, and nourishing to those who needed it so much.

Eight people went on the first trip, including three Haitian members.

Their method, in the midst of the chaos of those early days, was to ask the families of members to choose one person to meet the truck to get the supplies.

Rev. Tania wrote, "We took those cell phone numbers with us, and contacted them as we were approaching the area, having bought Haitian calling cards at the border. When we got to the point of delivery, the person was waiting for us. We had only seconds to get all the food and supplies out of the bus and leave before desperate crowds would gather. Each person receiving the food and supplies was in tears. It was bittersweet for the Haitians who were with us, because they would only see their loved ones for seconds as we unloaded. Sometimes it was parents who wanted to hold their children. We made deliveries to 22 families, and then just handed out what was left over to the people on the street."

Though she had been following the story on CNN, nothing prepared Tania or the MCC church members from the DR for the terrible conditions. There were tents everywhere, including on busy streets. They were not real tents, just sheets and sticks holding them up. There were thousands on the street, people who were injured, children who seemed to be orphaned or alone. There was the overpowering smell of decaying flesh, and flies were hovering over the rubble. Tania reported that the team was shocked to see human remains, body parts just lying on the heaps of destroyed buildings.

The second trip was in April. This time they gave out food and hygiene products to forty families. They also brought 16 sturdy tents which could house 8 to 10 people. They had made contact with POZ, an HIV/AIDS organization, and brought desperately needed medication and special tents for patient consultation, to set up a makeshift clinic.

POZ was the only open organization that also worked for LGBTQ rights in Haiti. This is often true in the Caribbean, that HIV/AIDS clinics and programs are also a "cover" for LGBTQ human rights work. In the earthquake, the POZ building was destroyed and leaders died. This was a terrible blow for the LGBTQ community.

Our church also wired money to some families and groups that were hard to get to, praying that there were things they could buy in their neighborhood.

The third trip was in June 2010. By this time, the devastation was wearing on everyone, the shock was wearing off, but the impact was dire. This was a more dangerous trip. The chaos was breeding crime and violence at an unprecedented level. Our pastor and church members narrowly escaped, at one point, with their lives and their trucks.

On this trip they were able to continue offering help to the POZ group, a school that had been destroyed, and families of church members who were running out of everything.

With our relatively small resources, and the courage, commitment and creativity of our members, we made a difference in the lives of many people, straight, LGBTQ, children, our families, and people whose names we will never know.

National Cathedral — MCC for a Day — then and now

In *Don't Be Afraid Anymore*, Rev. Troy Perry tells the story of how and why he vowed never to enter the National Cathedral, in Washington DC ever again.

It was 1970, a time when any mention of LGBTQ (then termed "gay") issues that was not hateful, whether it was accurate or not, was a victory.

Rev. Paul Breton, our pastor of the new MCC Church in Washington DC, had rented an Episcopal Church for the evening of Rev. Perry's visit. Unfortunately, word had gotten out in the *Washington Post* that right after the service, Rev. Perry was going to do a gay wedding, we called it a holy union, then.

The Episcopal Bishop, the Rt. Rev. William Forman Creighton read this story in the Post, invoked canon law, and ordered that the church be locked with MCC on the outside, on what was a freezing cold afternoon.

So with seventeen church members and a lot more press than that, they held a quick service on the side lawn of the locked church. People knelt in the snow to receive communion from frozen fingers.

Rev. Perry, in a moment of inspiration, (or as he says it, "off the top of my head!") remembered the National Cathedral, an Episcopal Church, was open to the public. To Rev. Breton's surprise, he told the press that he and MCC members were on their way there now to pray for the Episcopal bishop!

The short story is, the Cathedral was being used that day for a memorial service for a prominent leader and there were huge crowds. As the service ended, a young seminarian, who would one day be an MCC minister, had the keys to the high altar. He let Troy into the high altar area.

Elder Troy, kneeled again and prayed in front of TV cameras, for the bishop's homophobia to be healed — and vowed not to return until it was.

Fast forward to 2005, the year Rev. Perry was retiring as MCC's First Moderator, and I was elected as his successor.

As we thought it through, the leadership agreed that the General Conference in Calgary would be the venue for my election, but the main focus would be on an amazing good-bye to Rev. Perry in his history-making role.

We decided that my installation as the new moderator would occur a few months later. Troy had the idea to do it at the National Cathedral.

The cathedral states as part of its mission that it will be a cathedral for the nation and that if a denomination holds an event there, it would be a church of that denomination for the day!

Troy had a very highly placed Episcopal "mole," Dr. Louis Crew, founder of Integrity for LGBTQ Episcopalians, a professor at Rutgers University, and a member of the General Board of the Episcopal Church.

Louie was knows to us, as "Lula Belle," his drag name. He was a mover and a shaker, and in no time at all, the National Cathedral was ours for the day, October 29, 2005.

I knew Louie from our adventures at the WCC General Assembly in Zimbabwe, where he and I led the nightly gatherings of LGBTQ Christians, several hundred strong at the height of it, as we made our presence known and worked to support the embattled gays and lesbians of Zimbabwe. Louie loved to confuse and torment the Zimbabwean secret police that attended every meeting by referring to himself as Sister Lula Belle.

The installation service in October was designed by a team, and executed by our own Rev. Grant Ford. The Sunshine Cathedral MCC choir sang, I preached and consecrated communion. Hundreds participated as readers, singers, servers, ushers, and security. More than 1,500 people attended from all over the United States and several other countries as well.

Paula, my mother and many members of our family were there. I was installed by the leadership of MCC, with Rev. Perry praying the installation prayer. This was the first time he had returned to the Cathedral in 35 years.

An enormous procession included hundreds of clergy and lay leaders, the Rev. Elder Pat Bumgardner swung the thurible with incense wafting over the crowd. MCC vergers trained by the Cathedral vergers were in place, and banners designed by Rev. Phyllis Hunt flew from the heights of the Cathedral. People of color, people in leather, a seminary president, a rabbi, other ecumenical and inter-faith friends, young people and people representing the diversity of MCC installed me that day.

For that one day, that wonderful, very 21st Century Cathedral belonged to the people of MCC, and all the people we have ever touched.

Novenas on Santa Monica Boulevard

In many ways, the stories of our Latin Ministry at MCC Los Angeles are illuminated by our building struggles.

In the very earliest days of MCC Los Angeles, there was a very successful outreach to the Latino/a community, and a Spanish language ministry and service, which we shortened to "Latin Ministry" to avoid the dualistic "Latino/a" gendered language. Fernando Martinez was the young, charismatic leader. The group grew to over 200, meeting in the cramped chapel at MCC LA, when it was in downtown Los Angeles, on Hill Street.

The group grew and grew, and the mostly white, Anglo leaders of MCC Los Angeles did not really know how to handle this growth. Racism and other issues caused increasing conflict, and Fernando left with his 200 Latino/a members and formed an independent Latino/a LGBTQ church — probably the first in the world.

On its own, the church thrived for while. In the early 80s when AIDS hit, it hit them harder than any other group. They had already been struggling, in terms of affording a place to meet and other expenses.

Eventually, Fernando himself died of AIDS, and the church dwindled and died.

Meanwhile, MCC Los Angeles had many Latino/a members, most of them more assimilated, who spoke English. But every year at Pride, we encountered hundreds, even thousands of Latino/a LGBTQ folks who wanted church.

We tried ways to be inclusive, and failed, for five years. My most promising young student clergy left to become a Presbyterian. Other attempts failed.

Finally, a trio of folks, a young, former Franciscan priest from Chile who spoke almost no English, a Cuban lesbian and her Anglo partner, who was an evangelical, former missionary, started a prayer group. They told me to stay out of it! So I did. They thrived and outgrew the little prayer chapel they were meeting in on Sundays.

They wanted to have one service per month, which quickly grew to two, and then one every week.

Most of the people attending were newer immigrants to the United States. Many were undocumented, many were HIV positive. They were from 14 different countries, and cultures. There were struggles with Puerto Ricans (technically from the United States) dominating the leadership with a mostly Mexican and Central American congregation. It was a big day when we made Alfredo a deacon, the first from Mexico!

We tried squeezing them in-between the two English services, so that we could see them and come to know them. But, that meant pushing up the time of the 11 AM service to 11:15, and you would have thought I had spit on the cross!

I was not above shaming the English speaking folks at 11:15 saying, "I know it is a terrible sacrifice to get to brunch 15 minutes later, but I know that you want to be gracious and welcome our new ministry — don't you?"

And, when the Latinos ran overtime, since starting on time was a challenge, white board members got angry or impatient as 11:15 folks wanted to get into the sanctuary. It got ugly, fast.

Some people at the 9 AM or 11:15 AM services thought this was an "outside" group that was renting from us, so why couldn't we reschedule them?

I was so shocked that we had been talking about this for months, and that people could still think that *our* Latin Ministry service was *them*. I was very naïve, about racism and culture clashes.

So, we moved the Spanish language services to 1:00, where it has stayed for nearly 25 years! That ended up being a much better time frame for the Latino/a Ministry, as it gave them lots of time and space Sunday afternoon for programs and celebrations.

I attended that service a lot, and sometimes just enjoyed the music and worship. Sometimes I served communion, once a year or so I would preach. I was always so blessed to attend a service I was not leading, that fed me in a different way. And to feel the power of that community in the lives of so many who had nowhere else to turn.

We learned to have bi-lingual congregational meetings, which had a bi-product of shorter reports and comments! We had all-church celebrations that were bi-lingual in various configurations. Those of us who were English speaking learned now culturally conditioned we were, and the Latinos had to learn to trust us, even when we failed at times. And we all had to forgive, ourselves and each other.

When we moved so many times after the earthquake, our Latino/a ministry members were often confused and lost. If the folks who spoke English struggled to keep up with us, how much more for those who were just coming to this country, whose lives were complicated by families back home, by immigration anxieties and HIV. Sometimes only a handful would find us, and when everyone finally found the new location, we would move again.

When we moved to the junior high, Proposition 209 was on the ballot. This was a highly punitive piece of legislation in California. I had preached against it, quite strongly, in the English services. But, apparently, we had not done enough to ease the anxieties of the Spanish service.

By that time, the Spanish service was at 1 PM We had use of the sanctuary, but not great facilities for socializing after service. We had gotten permission that week from the school to use a picnic area in back of the gym for the Latin Ministry, because often their social hour was also a fiesta, birthday or anniversary celebrations, and they lingered a long time, and it would be better to have tables, and more capacity, we thought.

The problem was, the new location was behind the gym, and the old coffee table had been in the front, by the street.

On the Sunday after Proposition 209 passed, we moved the Latinos behind the building for socializing — and the rumor quickly spread that we did this because we were either ashamed of them, or trying to protect them from being seen by the police.

Of course, none of this had occurred to us, or to our Latin Ministry staff. So, I had to have an emergency time with the Spanish speaking congregation to reassure them that neither of those things was true. I listened to them, and how this new law impacted them.

It humbled me to realize how little we had done to anticipate the fears and the rage, and how easily trust was breached.

When we moved into West Hollywood, it was not a Latino neighborhood and we were trying to be welcoming by making our sign include Spanish.

Our mostly white and English speaking board was freaked out, and pushed back. When I tried to get them to say why, they just kept saying the logo was confusing, etc. The real reason was that Spanish language on a sign in Los Angeles was a "class" signal that they didn't want to give off in West Hollywood. In other words, racism and classism combined. The board backed off when I confronted them, and, it caused us some serious tensions for a while.

I wanted the Spanish speakers at the church to see themselves on the very front of their new building. The sign was welcomed with tears of joy.

Some of my own happiest memories in ministry are some of those first few years in West Hollywood. Our Latin Ministry paid and volunteer staff was growing, and one day, I was alone in the building with all of them.

I had eaten a chocolate ice cream bar, and dropped a big piece of chocolate on my shirt, high up by my collar bone. Throughout the day, I greeted or hugged them all. Then, I noticed, all of them had this strange brown mark on their upper right shoulder.

Finally, I looked in a mirror, and figured out the problem, went to their office and meeting room, and say, "What gives? No one could tell me I had a huge chunk of chocolate ice cream on my shirt?" They all laughed sheepishly, and said that they felt it was not polite to say anything to me, since I was the pastor. We laughed about that for a long time.

I came to appreciate that people who were so emotional in their relationships and conversation, so passionate, could also be so formal and polite, to a fault. I learned so much from all of them. We had weekly lessons in cross-cultural communications that were alternately funny and painful.

Even months after we moved into our new building it was clear to me that the message that this was *our building for all of us, Latin Ministry included,* was not entirely received and internalized.

The Latin Ministry leadership thought they had to go to the board (on which they had representation) each time to ask to use the building for special events. Again and again, I would say, but it is your building, just put it on the schedule, no special process required!

Finally, they took me at my word that they could just put themselves and their programs on the church calendar and building schedule. In December, they scheduled a novena to the Lady of Guadalupe in the chapel, which had store front windows on Santa Monica Blvd.

This went on night after night, with the chapel filling with flowers and fruit, and lots of bright lights, so it smelled like a florist/funeral parlor and looked a little like Tijuana. I cannot report that no MCC members complained, I can tell you it did not matter. It was their church. We were celebrating this novena together, learning how to be community, and this felt like a breakthrough.

I can still smell the fruit and flowers, and hear the mariachi's that came the very last night. And see the joy on Deacon Alfredo's face, who, when he recovered from a near-death experience with AIDS, promised the Virgin this novena.

Rearranging the Furniture

When MCC Los Angeles moved into the old "Gina B" building in West Hollywood, it was a huge box, a big empty space, with a spiral staircase that some of the more flamboyant members of the church would have liked us to keep.

We did our best to carve out a space on the first floor for the sanctuary, leaving a large entry area that was very attractive.

But, the sanctuary space was oddly shaped, and we weren't quite sure how to make it work. We did the best we could, and started holding services.

We pulled our grand piano out of storage, and an organ, and not much else. One of our members worked at a local hotel and sold us their ballroom chairs for a song, it was really more like a donation, and we were thrilled!

Maybe a year later, a newcomer in the line on Sunday morning, told me he had an idea for re-arranging the sanctuary that would be a much better use of space, and would feel so different, he was a set designer, etc. etc. So, as many pastors do, I nodded, said it sounded great, call me, etc.

The following Sunday, I was up in my office, which was on the second floor. I bypassed the sanctuary since I came in through the stairs from the garage below.

Garret, the worship leader who organized and lined up all the worship participants, came rushing into my office, waving his arms, all upset. "How could you do this without telling me?" On and on he hyperventilated.

"What are you talking about?" I asked.

We went downstairs, and, lo and behold, the entire sanctuary had been re-arranged — chancel, piano and organ, chairs, pulpit, lectern, altar, and banners.

It looked gorgeous! It felt totally different — more open, and spacious. Your eye was drawn to the altar and the entire place was serene and beautiful.

All I could think of was how upset the choir director, musicians and usher would be!

There was Bryan, smiling.

He thought my head nod, smile and, "okay" on the Sunday before was a permission slip. So, on Saturday afternoon, after all the 12 step meetings were done, he brought in a couple of friends. Since Bryan thought he had permission, the custodian thought so too, and let him in! They worked for hours.

Although the choir and whole church were shocked, they quickly warmed up to this arrangement.

If he had gone through our normal channels, God only knows how long it would have taken, and Bryan might, understandably, have moved on.

It just goes to show you that if you invite new people to your church, they just might rearrange the furniture! And, it could be fabulous!

I confessed in church that morning what had really happened, just in case anyone thought this was really my bright idea. The church got a good laugh, which was probably a product of enduring so many changes for so many years. This change was par for the course.

Sexuality, the Vatican, the World Council of Churches and Other Ecumenical Adventures

MCC claims as part of our mission to preach and teach "the holy integration of sexuality and spirituality." I am not sure that we always take in the ways in which that flies in the face of millennia of Christian history and theology. There has always been a vein of "integrative" theology in the church, but it was never the dominant voice.

When we experience violence, it is because we dare try to live into this vision. A vision of the wholeness and holiness of bodies, of sexualities, and diversities of gender. It challenges the power structures, the mind-set of domination. Christianity has served colonialism and the politics of domination for most of its history, in shameful and puzzling ways.

MCC has been a David to the Goliath of church power structures and sexuality. We are the ones who insist that sex is God's idea, and that until the church heals of its sexism, homophobia, transphobia, and binary vision of gender and power, the world cannot heal. Our role has been to tell some truth, expose the lies, and insist on radical inclusion. Mostly, we have been resisted and hated for that by other churches. But, change is coming.

Rage, Obscenity and the King James Bible

In 2009, a King James Bible, was put on display at a museum in Glasgow, Scotland, by Metropolitan Community Church (MCC) minister Rev. Jane Clarke, with pens and an invitation to anyone, but especially queer people, that said, simply, "If you feel you have been excluded from the Bible, please write your way back into it."

It was part of an art show called "Made in God's Image," sponsored by the Glasgow Museum of Art. For Jane, it was a pastoral use of art, a way to be a bridge between Christianity and a queer community whose religious wounds are so great, just being an MCC church in Glasgow has been a challenge.

What ensued was international and ecumenical media frenzy. Many people took advantage of Jane's invitation, writing rage, fury and obscenity into the sacred text, in addition to the poignant and moving comments.

No one was prepared for either the intensity of participation in the art project, or the intensity of the public response. Though a majority of Scots thought the project had merits and should not be censored, the media and religious frenzy took up all the airspace.

Jane, said, naively perhaps, that she assumed people would have at least some respectful boundaries when writing in the Bible. But they did not, which, in some ways, made it more significant. The sacred, deep rage of so many who felt alienated, but who also bothered to participate, was the great surprise of the exhibit.

The outrage was so intense that the Glasgow Museum of Art eventually removed access to the Bible, put it under glass, and offered separate paper and pens to all other participants in the future.

There were many public critics of the show, including Pope Benedict XVI. There were death threats, and hysterical articles, and outcries. And there were some defenders, including those who pointed out some of the intense rage at God in the Bible itself. None of the critics seemed to think the death threats, inspired by their over the top language, were troublesome enough to mention.

Jane articulated it this way, "The most difficult thing for me was the hostility of the Christian community. There was, I felt, a deliberate attempt by the more right-wing Christians to misunderstand and misrepresent what we were trying to do. It became about graffiti and vandalism, not about anger and marginalization."

She was trying to give those who had been oppressed and excluded by the church and its Bible a chance to engage with it, viscerally, directly. Her intention was to provide a vehicle for the suppressed rage at the church to surface and be heard.

It was heard alright! All the way to Rome.

Benedict called it "disgusting and offensive." Funny, he never used those words to describe pedophile priests or their supervisors, like Cardinal Law. Not with the same kind of indignation. Writing one's rage in the Bible, even if it offends one's sensibility, did not steal anyone's childhood, or cause a lifetime of mental and physical suffering. Really, is there any contest here? Where is the sense of proportion and justice?

The Bible in question had to have security and be insured! It has traveled to Berlin, Hamburg and Stuttgart, in addition to being on display at the Anglican Sheffield Cathedral as a part of the celebration of the 400th anniversary of the King James translation of the Bible.

Four hundred years earlier, people had an interesting way of referring to the two monarchs, Elizabeth the first, and James the first, a Scot: "Elizabeth was king, but James is queen!" Their gender queer natures were well known.

Yes, ironies abound when it comes to the Bible. The authorizer of the King James Bible was known for being homosexual. It always amazes me that the Bible that is the preference of Protestant Christian conservatives was made possible by a generous, gay, lover of the Bible. The very Bible with which, for centuries, they beat us (literally and figuratively) would not have been possible without a queer, royal hand at the helm.

Sexuality Seminar — World Council of Churches in Brazil

During the WCC Conference in Brazil in 2006, there were some special, by-invitation only seminars, one of which was on the topic of Human Sexuality. I was one of the few invited from any of the LGBTQ identified groups.

Sexuality is always a hot topic at the WCC and one that they often seem to want to avoid. Our MCC and European Forum and other organizations that offered workshops at the World Council Assembly always had standing room only — especially when we were talking about human rights, justice and sexuality.

The two-day seminar started with some folks giving some lectures on the Bible and sexuality, etc., from several theological viewpoints, all of it pretty good, I would say, if tame. But then, they asked us to get into small groups, react, and actually talk about sexuality from a personal and church perspective.

My group included all men of color, clergy, from countries and cultures in which even husbands and wives don't talk about these things. And, now, we were just all supposed to open up in a very Western-style kind of format in front of strangers, women, and men. I felt bad for the men. I have so much practice in coming out matter-of-factly and talking about sexuality while keeping my boundaries. Our group was mostly very quiet. There was a lot of staring at the floor.

But after that awkwardness was over, we were asked to do another exercise: there was newsprint all over the walls, and we were to write words about sexuality, sexuality and church and faith on the walls.

When we finished, one man, who works in HIV/AIDS prevention in Egypt thanked the WCC for bringing up these topics, for mentioning homosexuality. He pleaded with them to write a book or pamphlet on homosexuality and the Bible, since such a thing did not apparently exist.

At first, I felt like, "Are you kidding me? MCC and others have been writing books and pamphlets for 40 years (grumble, whine, grumble)." However, just because we have done that, does not mean it reaches most of the cultures and countries in that room, and their own indigenous scholars were not engaged, or found it too risky to engage these topics. After everything, I realized how amazing it is that it took only 40 years from Troy Perry's living room to this room in Porto Alegre, Brazil, for someone to request what we have been working on for so long.

Dr. James Forbes, former pastor of the Riverside Church, preached an amazing sermon at MCC's 2013 General Conference in which he said, "MCC, today you have the sublime satisfaction of knowing you are the answer to the question people are finally asking!" That was the perfect description of my feeling in that room.

On the newsprint in that room were many, many words of fear, anguish, conflict — a thorough "problematizing" of sexuality and spirituality. I thought of MCC's vision, our mission to "integrate sexuality and spirituality" which was needed so much, right there, in that moment. The level of fear, pain, and alienation in that room was unbearable at times.

I spoke up and observed that as far as I could see, I was the only one who put up words like, "intimacy," "love," and "erotic power." My years in MCC gave me the gift to not see sexuality as a problem, but as a gift of a good God. I felt so grateful in that moment.

I asked the WCC participants to imagine if the WCC called for a Sunday every year that we would celebrate the good gift of sexuality in our churches. There were a few positive noises in the room, and then, silence, as people imagined the consequences of proposing such an outrageous thing in their context, in their local churches.

Until we de-problematize sexuality, and begin instead with its goodness, we can never solve the conflicts and struggles it also brings. The church still needs to learn this, to heal from the millennia of oppression around sexuality. Forty years is not enough time...

The Future Pope and I

In 1987, Pope John Paul II came to the US, and celebrated a special service with Protestants and Orthodox Christians. Rev. Troy Perry was invited to come by the Conference of Catholic Bishops in the US, and he invited me to accompany him.

In 1987 AIDS was still not spoken about very much in polite company, or in church circles. We wore our "God is Greater than AIDS" buttons, and for about five hours we were cooped up with 400 church leaders in the US, waiting for a Pope who was detained by a hurricane in Miami. We experienced a lot of homophobia in that room, as I am sure people were thinking of Troy and me, "Who let them in here?" We never got to meet the Pope himself, but we did socialize with a number of Catholic cardinals who greeted us. Troy seemed to know which of them were gay.

But that was not the only story of that trip.

The next day, I got invited to the 40th anniversary of a Lutheran-Roman Catholic Dialogue on reconciliation of the two churches. Their topic for the day was sharing the Eucharist, and the historic, ecclesiological and theological barriers to joint celebration.

I was invited to the event by Rev. Jeanne Audrey Powers, a United Methodist Church leader, an ecumenist and a closeted (in those days) lesbian.

Jeanne was a member of the World Council of Churches Faith and Order Commission, and had been involved in ecumenical issues all her life. She might have become a Methodist Bishop, but I assume too many people knew her not-so-well-kept secret.

Unlike other closeted church leaders, she reached out to me, and was not intimidated at all to be seen with me in public. That was a great gift. She was helpful to me many times at National Council of Churches (USA) meetings, as a mentor who would strategize about MCC, and our inclusion in the ecumenical movement.

I think she also got a kick out of inviting me to this high level, exclusive, even stuffy ecumenical event. She liked to make the very conservative and proper men, in particular, squirm. And, so she did.

Halfway through the day, she took me by the hand to introduce me to one of the conveners and speakers, Cardinal Joseph Ratzinger. I knew of the Cardinal because of his attitude towards theological liberals in the Catholic Church, especially liberation theologians, and anyone speaking up for gays in the church. He had been involved in what became a persecution of Jesuit John McNeill, a courageous gay Catholic theologian. Many saw him as the force behind the conservatism of John Paul II, and as someone bound and determined to undermine the progress of Vatican II.

We got near the front, and Jeanne Audrey engaged him in a little small talk. He looked happy to see Jeanne, she obviously knew him well. Then she piped up, "Cardinal, I would like you to meet Rev. Nancy Wilson, a leader in Metropolitan Community Churches, you know, Cardinal, the gay church. She will one day succeed Rev. Troy Perry as their Moderator — sort of like their Pope!" Ta da! Just like that, she prophesied!

I smiled, and put out my hand. He looked at me with a look of pure malice, as God is my witness, and with all great reluctance, gave me his hand, which was cold and limp. I squeezed it with both my hands and said, as cheerily as I could, "Delighted to meet you, Cardinal!" "Oh, yes, yes," he said, looking frantically at Jeanne Audrey and away from me. He rushed off to another encounter.

I could not have imagined then, nor could most of us, that he would actually become Pope himself one day.

The one thing that most amazed me at that Lutheran Catholic Conference was the halting conclusion made by some of them: that maybe, actually, the separations and divisions over the Eucharist (what is said, what it means, who can preside, etc.) are not of God's making or design, but are "man-made." Duh. That took 40 years?

By that time, MCC had been celebrating an open communion in our churches, every week for twenty years, with people from every conceivable

Christian background. We knew that God was uniquely present in our communion, precisely because it was radically open, and not limited by our own human imagination.

People in our world are sick to death of divisions among Christians, especially over things that do not matter much to 21st century people. In fact, no one cares particularly anymore, if Christians can get along or celebrate communion together. It is the bigger issues, of inter-religious dialogue, of peace and justice, that the world really hopes religious leaders will focus on together.

The Women of Bucharest

In 2012, I had the great privilege to visit our MCC operations in Bucharest, Romania, which included meeting with the staff of ECPI, the Euro-Regional Center for Public Initiatives. This NGO, founded by MCC leaders, promotes human rights and law reform for LGBTQ persons, women, and people with disabilities.

While I was there I was pleased to meet the U.S. Ambassador, and his staff. ECPI and the U.S. Embassy held a recruitment event to ask law firms in Romania to provide pro bono legal assistance to those individuals who needed assistance. Pro bono legal assistance is not something that has been a tradition in Romania, or much of Eastern Europe, as they are still in the process of developing civil society institutions in a more open, functional democracy.

The ambassador and his wife march every year now with the Pride marchers, in Bucharest, and open their home afterwards as an act of solidarity with LGBTQ people.

We were also thrilled to meet openly LGBTQ people on the Embassy staff, who worked with ECPI, and other LGBTQ friendly organizations to continue to foster progress.

One of the most moving experiences for me was to be invited to speak to a Women's Studies class at the University of Bucharest. I had been invited to speak as a woman religious leader on the topic of reproductive rights and women's moral agency.

There were about thirty-five women in the class, most of whom were heterosexual — there were a few lesbians, who came out to me later.

They were shocked, of course, to see a woman in a collar, who was also an out lesbian, and, who could speak about sexuality, reproductive rights, from a feminist and progressive point of view. My main points were that women have a fundamental human right to adequate reproductive healthcare, to insist on respect for our own bodily integrity, and to assert our independent moral agency and capacity.

I told some stories and watched them warm up to me and the topic.

When I finished my lecture, we began to really talk.

For at least another hour, these women opened up, talking about their own experiences, their marriages, their struggles to be respected as women in their culture. They talked about how they had no spiritual home — that the Orthodox Church was so misogynistic, so dismissive of women, that they did not feel like it was their spiritual home. They told stories of priests who were at the best insensitive, at the worse, bullying and violent in their approach to women.

It occurred to me then and there, that MCC could start a church with these women, mostly heterosexual, who were so deeply alienated from their church by a patriarchal, outdated leadership. They needed a spiritual home, to feel a connection to God, in community. They deserved that. I was amazed that it took no time at all for them to trust me with stories and secrets and their desire to be free and whole as women.

When I think of MCC's mission and future, I think of these women, and the men in their lives who clearly grasp the fullness of the Gospel.

There is a sleeping, hungry giant of spiritual pain and rage, and spiritual yearning that needs to be awakened, all over the world. The Jesus who loved women, who respected their theological integrity and their moral agency, who offered non-judgmental healing, who was willing to be corrected by women, is with us as we pray for this awakening. I am convinced.

Calvin *Vas* Not Smiling! My Adventures in Catholic Seminary

I attended Boston University School of Theology, a Methodist school, from 1972 to 1974, and then dropped out. I had been going to school all my life, I think I was tired, and I was already deeply involved in MCC ministry. Having an M.Div was not required, so I let it take a back seat. I moved to Worcester with my partner, and we started a church there, and I never returned to Boston University.

Boston University School of Theology was a very homophobic place when I attended, as were most seminaries. I was very out, in the school, in the city, in the newspapers. And, since I wasn't a Methodist anymore, they left me alone. There were professors who were supportive, and others who were not.

The Dean in particular was known for raging about the school becoming a "haven for queers." Students who were gay but trying to stay in the Methodist Church were outed. They dropped out, some attempted suicide, some lived in the closet for many, many more years.

Years later, I saw that Dean at a World Council of Churches meeting. I reintroduced myself, but I knew he knew who I was. He asked me, no kidding, "How is your work going in San Francisco?"

"I have never lived in San Francisco," I replied, not really wanting to make it more comfortable for him.

I guess all queers live in San Francisco. The conversation fizzled after that.

Several years later I had moved to Detroit. The church was growing, and I had already been elected an Elder in MCC.

The pastor of the Methodist Church told me, one day, in his office, to go back to school and finish my degree. He told me that I would need to have that degree because I was destined for leadership in MCC, and to be in places where having that credential would be an important element of succeeding in the mission.

I had never had anyone say that to me, push me, offer me correction like that, in the context of having faith in my future. I was still somewhat alienated from my parents at that point, but that was not their style anyway. I will always be grateful to Rev. Dick Devor for taking the time and trouble to care about my theological education. Dick had been the chaplain at my alma mater, in the years just before I went there. We had an Allegheny connection.

So, I started to look for a place to finish up my M. Div. I had about a year of classes to complete, I thought it would be no big problem, except for time and money, which were in short supply.

I applied to the Methodist seminary in Dayton, Ohio, the nearest Protestant seminary, but they rejected me because in the meantime, the Methodist Church had passed their new, homophobic, social principles, in 1976.

Later, that seminary would open the doors wide to MCCers, and look upon the time they rejected me as a bad chapter the life of their seminary.

Meanwhile, a Methodist pastor friend, Ken, was teaching at the non-diocesan Roman Catholic Seminary in the Detroit area, and he suggested I apply there.

This was a Polish Catholic school attached to St. Mary's College. The Dean, Fr. Anthony Kosnick, was President at that time, of the Catholic Theological Society of America, and had published a controversial, more open, sex-positive (for its time) book on Catholic theology and sexuality.

Several years later, he would be silenced because of it, and never permitted to teach on the topic of sexuality again.

But, at that moment, the Vatican had not caught up with him. Fr. Anthony, and the assistant dean, Sister Anneliese Sinnot, were very kind to me. They admitted me to the M.Div. program and accepted all my courses from Boston. They exempted me from Advanced Pastoral Polish, from Canon Law and Priestly formation! I took amazing classes in the history of the Eucharist, in the Reformation, and in spiritual formation. I had the great privilege of reading the documents of Vatican II, which, though so embattled in recent decades, are works of theological genius yet to be lived into fully.

I loved the Reformation class from a Roman Catholic perspective. The professor had a wonderful sense of ecumenical humor, and a heavy Polish accent, and said that Luther and Calvin were very similar in their thoughts, but that "Calvin *vas* not smiling!" Luther preached a more earthy, and, comparatively cheerful faith than John Calvin offered, and was happier to have thrown off the weight of celibacy.

How honored I was to be the first Protestant woman pastor to graduate from the school, and, of course, the first open lesbian! Among the alumni list, you can still find a Wilson, among all those Polish names.

I will always be grateful for the courageous people who offered me hospitality when my church of origin was pushing people like me away. Who could have guessed it would be a Catholic seminary? I am proud of my eclectic road to a theology degree, and grateful for those who pushed and pulled me along.

Charismatic Renewal and Sexual Healing

In the 1980s, MCC Long Beach, California, experienced a charismatic revival, mostly occurring at their Wednesday night services. Later, they offered an annual conference, which people from MCC, and beyond MCC attended, from around the world. Many speakers from denominations that would have been hostile to MCC came to speak, to witness the ministry of MCC, and to have their hearts and minds opened and changed.

It provided a bridge for many who had no bridge from one world to another. And, it enriched and deepened MCC's range of spiritual experiences. MCC was founded by a Pentecostal, but Rev. Perry did not want all the fundamentalist baggage that came along with that way of worship many times, the narrowness and pettiness. It took others to reclaim those dramatic gifts of the Spirit.

This particular manifestation was lead by Rev. Dr. Dusty Pruitt, who became my friend. We pastored the two largest churches in the Los Angeles area.

I was not very familiar at all with charismatic worship — I had seen it at some MCC services, and Conferences, but not so much as a part of regular worship in most MCC churches.

One Wednesday night, Dusty invited me to come and share the Word in Long Beach, and to experience their amazing revival. I brought my friend Phil, who was newly diagnosed with AIDS, and my partner Paula, who was just curious, I think.

In fact, when we got there, and sat in the second row, Paula, ever the skeptic, said, "I'll believe all this stuff if Phil goes up there to be prayed for by you, and falls down (i.e., rests in the Spirit)."

What we knew and had heard was that after the sermon, Dusty would open the altar for prayer, and people would stream forward, ministers and deacons and others would lay hands on people, and whether they were kneeling or standing, they would fall back, into a kind of special sleep, a resting in God. Miracles would happen, healings, sometimes loud shouting, release, very emotional, as it is every Sunday in many Pentecostal and Holiness Churches.

Now, some in MCC were skeptical, and even made fun of Dusty and MCC Long Beach. But I was curious, and eager to understand how this could be a time of breakthrough for people who were hungry, even desperate for inner healing, physical and emotional and spiritual healing. Our community, then in the early days of AIDS, still hurting from so much lethal homophobia, was ripe and ready for dramatic, breakthrough leaps towards wholeness. Maybe this was one way God would provide some of that.

Dusty was also doing some doctoral studies, and exploring the relationship of authoritarian religion and child abuse, especially sexual abuse. This, of course, was before the current scandals around pedophile priests exploded. But, many of us knew, even then. It seemed to us that many people in MCC, maybe more LGBTQ people, had been targeted for sexual abuse as children. Rather than seeing a causal relationship (child abuse caused homosexuality), what if it were actually true that those who perceived that we were LGBTQ saw our vulnerability and targeted us.

Dusty was someone who understood this very early on. In the middle of the charismatic renewal of the 70s and 80s, many people were uncovering nightmarish histories of abuse. She came from a Southern Baptist background but was not a fundamentalist — but understood people who were and how they could be manipulated to blame themselves for the harm others inflicted.

She encouraged those whom prayer had opened to seek psychotherapy to work on long term healing issues and new coping skills. It was also clear to Dusty, and many of us, that the addiction that was rampant in our community was an attempt to medicate the pain away.

It was our role to facilitate healing, and to help our people regain health.

After I preached that Wednesday night, I took my place for the first time behind that altar, and offered myself to be used by God for healing. Phil, my friend newly diagnosed, came up, knelt down, and before I could even touch him, he fell back. I just stared at him. I had always wondered if people pushed people to send them sprawling, but, today, I felt this amazing wall of energy and love and power that just laid people out, hundreds of them, in the front, the aisles, even in their seats. God was up to something.

After Phil went back, I looked up, and Paula was shaking her head. I am grateful to have been allowed to leave so many things on the floors of MCC churches, or on the carpeted ballrooms of hotels where we were holding conferences and prayer services. I left so much grief, pain, disappointments, hurts, betrayals there that would have kept me from living fully, from ministry. Thank God for those generous floors, and for the Spirit who put many of us there, time and time again. That allowed us to rise renewed and refreshed. In our bodies, whole and ready for the next day.

So many times since that first Wednesday night at MCC Long Beach, I have availed myself of that kind of prayer, and offered it to others. In the right setting, with the right Spirit, it can do so much. I have witnessed it over and over again.

God, Grace, Sex and Porn Stars

We met Craig when he was dying in a hospice. This particular hospice was located in a hospital, on the west side of Los Angeles. They had converted one of the wings into an AIDS hospice, and struggled to find clergy to come and visit the patients housed there.

Someone referred them to us. We simply never said no to any request for a visit for anyone, especially someone dying from AIDS. I asked Deacon Alex to be my partner in this relationship with Craig, as I had my hands full.

Our building had been destroyed in the earthquake, and we were trying to decide whether to rebuild or move. We were operating our offices and ministry out of a trailer on the property. So, when I said yes, "we" would do this, it was always a royal "we," although lots of staff, volunteer deacons, and other lay people helped out.

Also, I have to admit that I loved visiting people in hospitals and hospices, because I was pretty good at it, and people were mostly glad to see me when I showed up. That was not always the case in other settings!

With all the things I could not fix, including a building, I believed I was useful to God in this way. I took refuge, right or wrong, in visiting a lot of people who were dying or very ill. Probably church growth experts would say I should have done less of that, and more of many other things. They may be right. But, at the end of the day, sometimes a hospital visit that was right on time, or well-received, made me feel like it was worth it all. It probably saved my self-esteem, and made me feel like I had accomplished something. I could not heal them, but, I could be a compassionate, familiar face, a hand to hold, a prayer to comfort, a shelter in a storm.

I visited Craig first, and then asked Alex to follow up. Craig was even well enough to even come to a couple of church services. But soon, he was too sick to leave his room. After visiting a couple of times, Craig opened up to me.

His day job was in a hotel in Hollywood, but, in his other life he was a model and a porn star. In fact, he gave me his headshot photo which was gorgeous! It certainly did not look like the ravaged man I saw in front of me.

And, then, we went deeper. He was in a moral quandary. He knew that his unsafe sex practices, related to starring in porn, had caused his sickness and would kill him. He had terrible, gnawing guilt about that, because he had been in denial for so long.

On the other hand, this was the part that was hardest for him to tell me; he loved the kind of sex he had in those contexts, and missed it. It was the most transcendent experience of his life, even though most people would think of it as debasing. But, for him, it was not. And, he needed me to hear his conflict, and not to judge him.

He did not regret the sex he had. He felt guilty that his denial contributed to his contacting AIDS. He did not want to die, but he did not want to live without being able to experience the kind of sexual connection and ecstasy that was so meaningful to him.

He asked for forgiveness, and I tried to help him be very clear about what he was and was not asking forgiveness for. Not for being gay, for loving men, for loving gay male sex.

It was not easy. And, he had not had an easy relationship with God most of his life. His very religious family had rejected him, and he never tried to renew his own connection.

Upon reflection, if Craig had not been on his deathbed, I might have asked him to think about the difference between his experience of sex, and sexual addiction. Truthfully, I have no way to know if Craig's desire for this kind of sex was coming from addiction. Or if his denial contained veiled suicidal tendencies. I know that risking one's life could be a clue that it was. But I don't think Craig knew anything about sex addiction.

Even now, I am haunted by his very innocent, in my view, and poignant conflict. How could what gave him pleasure, joy, something he had a gift for, in fact, be so deadly and so wrong?

Craig continued to decline, and I prayed for him every time I saw him, I know he was grateful for the chance to be honest, for our consistency and faithfulness to him. He had a special sweetness. I looked forward to visiting with him. I knew that God loved him, and I hoped he could see that love in me, in us.

Alex and I did a memorial service for Craig, at the home of one of Craig's friends, in Beverly Hills. It was the oddest memorial I think I ever conducted, and that is saying something.

We selected a few readings, had a nice picture of Craig, probably the headshot. We all sat around in the living room. But, you could cut the air with a knife. Everyone there, almost all men, had a deer in the headlights look.

As we were starting, I realized, oh. These are not Craig's friends from the hotel, or his family, who had nothing to do with him. These are his friends from modeling, and the porn industry. There were many very handsome young men, but, some of them looked a little too thin, and some were perspiring.

They were quiet. I imagine they were hoping they would not be next. It was probably amazing they came at all. Fear can paralyze.

Alex and I did all the talking, and praying. When we did what we often do, at MCC funerals, and invite people to share, no one said a thing.

No one.

I felt this terrible despair and loneliness for Craig.

I wanted these men to be angry, to be sad, to express their fears. To do some AIDS education, or testing. Anything to make it real. This was way before anyone in LA, or anywhere, was trying to regulate the porn industry for safe sex.

But, no. We ended the service, people were polite, and went their way.

The Dance of Healing

A young man, a gifted dancer, in an MCC I pastored, was in a terrible car accident, breaking his leg in several places. He had many surgeries, and still, there was a gap in the bone in his leg that would not heal.

To keep himself occupied, he taught Japanese. I asked him to teach me to celebrate communion in Japanese, and in turn I visited with him and praying with him.

One time when I came to visit, he told me that he was very nervous about his father coming to visit him. I probed just a little, and he broke down and told me that his father had abused him when he was young. He was still very angry, sad, and afraid to see him. He poured out his heart to me that day, crying and shaking.

As an MCC pastor, I had seen so much of this kind of abuse. Of family and clergy abusing children, adolescents. Long before anyone else seemed to know of the pedophile priests, we knew. We heard it often from people who grew up Catholic. And, the Protestants seemed no better.

This untreated sexual abuse had impacted him all his life. It made it hard to accept himself as a gay man. Sometimes his sexuality seemed so damaged by the abuse. All the shame of the abuse spilled over into his own sexual self-image.

I took a risk, and suggested we pray a prayer of trust in God, and forgiveness, to allow him to see his father without the burden of fear.

In addition, I asked him to consider that his unhealed leg was an outer manifestation of his unhealed heart. That perhaps he was being given an opportunity to heal two things at once.

He wept and wept. We talked about how he could take care of himself. That he could keep his boundaries with his father, now, as an adult, in a way he was not able to as a child. He could generously offer his father his time and his forgiveness, and that it would heal him as well.

He was able to see his father, and have some peace and reconciliation with him this time, which was so important. His father died just a year later. There was such a sense of relief that he had completed an important part of his healing before his father died.

His fathers' death made him the head of a large family, spread out over many countries and cultures. Before his healing, he felt unworthy of fulfilling that role in his family, and afterwards, he took it on with joy.

But, perhaps the most amazing thing was that two weeks after he had opened his heart about this deepest of sexual and emotional wounds, his leg was finally healed. He is able to walk, and today, he dances.

What Would Jesus Do?

In 2012 I had the privilege of visiting MCC churches in Europe, and connecting with our human rights workers in Romania and several other countries.

One evening, several of us visited ACCEPT, the LGBTQ and Pride organization of Bucharest, Romania. For years, MCC had worked with their leaders, and had been present for breakthrough events in LGBTQ rights.

We gathered in the office to offer an MCC style communion, and to listen to young LGBTQ persons who were struggling with faith and their sexuality. We sang, shared, and prayed for a bit, when one young man, Cosmin, said he just had to tell his story.

He was twenty-two now, but five years before, when he was only seventeen, he was in love with the Orthodox Church, its liturgy, and its faith. He was very impressed with the young priest who served his parish. One day, he decided to tell the priest that he was gay. The priest took it very badly, to say the least.

His hateful response was to tell Cosmin to go home, to take a poker and put it in the hot fire, and to grasp it with his other hand, and burn it. Then he wanted Cosmin to return to him and show him the scars. The priest said he could then tell Cosmin how not to have his soul and body thrown into hell.

Cosmin went home, totally distraught. He prayed and wept all night. Sometime, early that morning, he came to believe that Jesus would never want him to hurt himself this way. He then came out to his mother, who was more accepting than he thought she might be.

At Easter, he went back to church. When the priest saw that he had no scars, he refused to serve him communion.

Cosmin never returned to church until he came to that service at ACCEPT. He took communion that night, and afterwards, we talked for hours at a local restaurant.

Cosmin stays in touch with MCC clergy and leaders, and is active in human rights work. He still struggles with his faith, but he knows he has a community he can turn to in the process.

Lesbians on Yang Tse River

In 2011, I had the wonderful opportunity to tour China with a lesbian tour company, Olivia, owned by Judy Dlugacz, who was the cousin of my best friend in high school. Her mother taught at my elementary school.

Recently, I saw Judy at the White House gathering in which the President signed the bill eliminating discrimination in hiring of LGBTQ people at the federal level, including federal contracts. Of the 200 or so people there, I think Judy and I were the only two activists from the seventies. There were very few from the eighties or nineties either. I guess we have worn well!

In the seventies I became an MCC pastor and activist, and she created the first Women's Music recording company that morphed into an amazing lesbian tour company and enterprise in more recent decades. Here we were at the White House 40 plus years later.

On the China tour, I asked Olivia if they minded if I did a little side work for MCC while there. Using our MCC contacts, we went to visit the AIDS clinic in Beijing. And, we met up with some lesbian activists for dinner.

The next day, I spoke at the LGBTQ Center in Beijing.

(China, oh my. Learning to be post-colonial in our partnerships with LGBTQ activists is a huge shift and absolutely necessary.)

It reminded me of how much mentoring and support of the Beijing Center has been extended from the LA Gay and Lesbian Center, under the leadership of Lorri Jean, the executive director. I teased Lorri Jean, who in her pre-lesbian life was a Southern Baptist Christian educator by asking if her global aspirations are just the baptist missionary urge in disguise?

Years before I asked Lorri to preach at MCC Los Angeles, once I found out her Southern Baptist secret, and she was more nervous than I have ever seen her. And, what a preacher! So many LGBTQ leaders have religious skeletons in their closets. Some are PKs (preacher's kids). When we wonder why our movement has been so religiously phobic, it is no wonder.

During my 2011 trip to China, I spoke to a group of about 50 in the small center. Hard to believe that in a city of millions, the only dedicated space for LGBTQ folks was the size of a small apartment.

Gay bars in Beijing were always moving around, or switching up nights with straight bars. The LGBTQ film festival had been shut down the week before — but, they just move it, and texted everyone. The police cannot keep up with them!

That night, no one was arrested, but the censorship laws are still quite extreme. They wanted me to speak on religion and homosexuality, and, I knew that I would not be allowed to preach, so I took a somewhat academic approach.

Pretty soon, it was obvious that there were a lot of Christians at the Center to hear me, and that the academic stuff was not working.

So I began to tell my story, and the story of MCC. People began to ask questions, Christians, Buddhists, people of no faith. One young man was furious, talking about his parents and church that had rejected him. His face was contorted in pain. He said he no longer believed in God, and hated the church.

Another young woman talked about not wanting to shame her parents, another was afraid to alienate her friends at Bible study.

So, I talked, like I might preach, without preaching, of course.

Afterwards, the young man came up to me, crying, putting both hands on my shoulders, and choking the words, "Do you really, really, really believe there is a God who could love even me?"

How amazing, there I stood in Beijing, China, offering the testimony I had given all my life, to this young gay man, "Yes, yes, I am very sure. I know this God with all my heart, don't be afraid, let that God love you and heal you!"

Later, we cruised down the Yang Tse River. All 250 lesbians on the trip were very out of the closet. Most of the time, no one seemed to notice or care that much. As the crew and cooks came forward at the end of the cruise for us to thank them, the lead cook said, "We just want you to know that from now on we are only working on lesbian cruises!"

Later that week, in the south of China, in a smaller, mountain town, a young man got on our bus who was to be our tour guide. My gadar went off! Then, as he settle in, he told a heterosexist joke, which let us know he did not know who we were. Someone clued him in, and then, he threw up his hands and shouted, "I am also gay!" Tada.

Then, he proceeded to tell us his story, his woes, that his boyfriend had dumped him, and that he was afraid to come out to his parents. We had way too many therapists on the tour, so they spent the day taking care of him, counseling him. We are everywhere, no kidding.

Clockwise top right: Rev. Dr. Nancy Wilson reads Scripture during President Barack Obama's National Prayer Service in 2013. (© Donovan Marks, All Rights Reserved.) *Middle right:* President Barack Obama, First Lady Michelle Obama, Vice President Joe Biden and Dr. Jill Biden pose for a group photo with Rev. Dr. Nancy Wilson prior to the National Prayer Service at Washington National Cathedral in Washington, D.C., Jan. 22, 2013. (Official White House Photo by Pete Souza). *Bottom right:* President Barack Obama greets Rev. Dr. Nancy Wilson as he drops by a meeting on trafficking with the President's Advisory Council on Faith-based and Neighborhood Partnerships, in the Roosevelt Room of the White House, April 9, 2013. (Official White House Photo by Pete Souza) *Bottom left:* Rev. Dr. Nancy Wilson and her mother, Barbara Wilson, attend the White House Holiday Reception in December 2012. (photo courtesy of Nancy Wilson)

White House Encounters

STORIES OF JUSTICE, INCLUSION AND HOPE

Over the last 40 years or so, one of the signs that the clout of the LGBTQ civil rights movement increased was in access to the U.S. political halls of power, particularly the White House, to the State Department, and to the halls of Congress. But, within that story, and sometimes beyond it, is also the ways in which LGBTQ people of faith have participated, lead, and expanded that influence and inclusion.

For twelve years, during the Reagan and Bush years, we were all but shut out entirely from the White House and those administrations. Our only access was through some friendly faces in the Congress. We worked ecumenically, through the National and World Council of Churches.

In recent years, it has been the White House, the State Department and the Supreme Court that have really led the way in creating more equality for LGBTQ persons and our families.

Through the decades, MCC has been in the mix, present at the table, and working from behind the scenes. Here are some untold stories.

Bullet-proof Vests, 1976

In 1976, when I was elected to the Board of Elders, at MCC's General Conference in Washington DC, we planned a demonstration in front of the White House for what we then called, "gay rights." It was the bi-centennial of the Declaration of Independence, and we wanted to publicly demonstrate that our human rights should be the law of the land.

Gerald Ford was President, AIDS was still a long way off. Gay rights was very new, and off the charts controversial. Very few people thought of gay rights as human rights at all.

In a much more low-tech era, we had a simple soap box, across from the White House, and a simple mic and loudspeaker of sorts. Maybe a bullhorn.

Hundreds in attended, not the thousands we would have three years later at the first National March on Washington for Lesbian and Gay Rights. By that time lesbians were included in the title itself.

Right before that 1976 rally in front of the White House, someone told me that I was expected to speak that day, and by the way, did I want a bullet proof vest to wear when I stood on the soap box?

I am not sure if I said the obvious, such as, "Do you think I need one?"

It was a very sobering reminder that being an MCC clergy and a newly minted denominational leader meant I could also be a target.

I have no real idea if there was any "intelligence" saying we were being threatened, though, come to think of it, we had had a number of bomb threats all week at our conference. We had our own kinds of security in those days.

People who had been police officers, or had some kind of security training volunteered for Rev. Perry, primarily.

I did not wear the vest. I think I might have even tried it on, and it looked ridiculous. Maybe it did not seem like a very brave, lesbian MCC minister thing to do, to wear such a vest. I couldn't really even tell if anyone else was wearing one. So, I passed that day.

I have no idea what I said at the rally, people seemed reasonably pleased. Maybe a little surprised that I could get that worked up! At some level, at age 26, I was in shock, there on a soapbox, in front of a White House that was not paying attention in the slightest.

Three years later, they would.

Jimmy Carter's White House

In 1976, Rev. Troy Perry was a delegate to the Democratic Convention, and supported Jimmy Carter. Troy liked Carter because he was a progressive Democrat and a progressive Southern Baptist (who eventually left that church because of its sexism, racism, and fundamentalism).

Troy's support of Carter, not really the liberal choice in 1976, was good enough for me, a 26-year-old MCC pastor, in Detroit, Michigan, and an Elder in MCC.

I happen to think Jimmy Carter was an excellent President, who, with an engineer's mind, set to fix a lot of things. He was not a President for romantics, and, as much as I liked Teddy Kennedy, I think he did Carter in. Carter worked hard on complex issues. He told the truth unceremoniously but did not excel as a political communicator.

Then, Reagan just swooped in, on the backs of the Iran hostages, and a troubled economy. I will never understand the appeal of Ronald Reagan, who never even mentioned AIDS until his second term. Imagine if President Obama never mentioned Ebola through his second term! Tens of thousands dying! It was a time of deep political alienation for our young movement.

Jimmy Carter was the first President to notice LGBTQ people at all. He convened the first White House conference with LGBTQ leaders in 1977. White House staffer, former Rochester mayor Midge Costanza (who later came out) was there with Rev. Perry and I at that historic meeting. We were so excited!

Troy also told me that, in a time before AIDS, they wanted to ensure that LGBTQ (mostly gay, really) health issues were raised. They had asked George Reyes to do that. When George chose to bring up the subject of "anal worts" in the first ever, White House meeting, some were embarrassed and shocked!

Troy thanked George for being courageous and "thorough." The levels of body and sexuality censorship in White House conferences was pretty intense in those days, so even bringing a bunch of people who were open about their sexuality was a barrier-breaker of major proportions. And, helping LGBTQ leaders to get clarity on priorities, and to learn to educate leaders at that level was a challenge.

Troy also shared that Jean O'Leary, the lesbian co-director of the National Gay and Lesbian Task Force, was true to her reputation, and slept with Midge Constanza the night after the meeting, bringing White House pillow talk into a more gay-friendly era!

In our community, there are things that are said among us, "internally" but are not always said in "prime time." As leaders, we often had very different views on what was "appropriate," in more public spaces. Representing sexual minorities means bringing up sex in places people didn't necessarily want to hear about it.

When I was on the President's faith council, several decades later, at a White House meeting on human trafficking, a survivor told a room full of bishops and religious leaders about her story, and I was not sure the word "blow job" had ever been spoken openly in that setting before. She was matter of fact, oblivious to their shock. I did not dare look at a familiar face at the moment.

Three years later, I had the honor of leading the first White House meeting of religious LGBTQ friendly groups, with White House Religion Advisor, Robert Welch in 1979. There were just under twenty faith groups represented, Protestants, Catholics and Jews, as I recall. That was all the diversity we could muster then.

At 29-years-old, I led the delegation. I can still remember some of the names and faces there — Bill Johnson, the first openly gay UCC and mainstream Protestant clergy to be ordained, Adam De Baugh from our MCC staff, Robert Nugent and Jeannie Grammick from New Ways Ministry.

Our issues included working for legislation, something like ENDA, and concern about Anita Bryant and groups like the Moral Majority, religiously motivated hate and discrimination.

AIDS was still a few years away, and, trust me, no one mentioned marriage.

I am not sure anything at all ever came from that meeting, and Jimmy Carter was soon denied a second term by Reagan. The impact of that on us was costly. Carter was the first President in history who treated us like citizens who were a legitimate constituency. He has a place in history and in our hearts for that act of solidarity. Imagine if he had been President when AIDS came crashing down on us.

REV. DR. NANCY WILSON

The Clinton White House: On his right and his left!

President Bill Clinton was the first President I remember saying the word "gay" as if he had said it before, in a way that you knew he had LGBTQ friends. He was a baby boomer, so of course he had gay friends. I even knew some of them!

President George H. W. Bush, just a few years earlier, when asked about a lesbian being ordained as an Episcopal priest (he is Episcopalian), said, "I'm not ready for that!" Of course, recently, he and Barbara were witnesses at the same-sex wedding of close friends. Times do change.

Clinton was not known for LGBTQ progress as far as the law was concerned. His "Don't Ask, Don't Tell," was a disaster reversed in Obama's Presidency, as was DOMA (The Defense of Marriage Act). However, Clinton did show a strong interest in dealing with AIDS, which, in the early and mid-90s was very important.

By 1993, AIDS had been surging for about a decade. As the time of the annual World AIDS Day commemoration on December 1st approached, the Clinton White House called MCC headquarters in Los Angeles to ask if Rev. Steve Pieters, our MCC Field Director for HIV/AIDS, could attend the first White House breakfast and program for religious leaders working in the AIDS prevention and support services. This was two days before the event, and Steve and our staff scrambled to get him there.

Steve was the perfect representative for this event. In 1993, he was a long-term survivor with AIDS, who had written on spirituality and HIV/AIDS. He was an embodiment of hope, in a time when we were already quite weary, and in a time when AIDS still was a death sentence.

When the breakfast was served, in the family dining room, Steve was seated at the President's left, and across from Vice-President Gore. To the President's right was James Dobson, the Executive Director of Focus on the Family, a right wing organization that also did AIDS work, but with a very homophobic approach. It was the White House's way of giving "equal time" to both approaches, I suppose.

Clinton alternated in talking to both men throughout the breakfast. Steve felt acutely aware of how the President really had to shift gears to keep up both of those conversations.

As it turned out, the President knew something of Steve's story, and said, "I hear you are quite a miracle!" He then asked Steve to tell him his story, which Steve was delighted to do. Then he turned to Dobson, talked for a while, and then back again to Steve.

His final question to Steve was, "So what's the story about oral sex?"

Silence, for just a minute.

Steve took a breath, and then offered the President of the United States the unique opportunity to be personally, and clinically, educate him on the facts of HIV/AIDS prevention.

From Easter Prayer Breakfast to the March on Tolerance

In 2011, I was invited for the second year in a row to the White House for an Easter Prayer breakfast. This was a time for President Obama to connect with Christians who celebrate Easter — usually with an open and closing prayer, some scripture, and a local children's choir. In attendance were members of the President's Faith Councils, past and present, local religious leaders, people doing extraordinary work with the homeless, children, and people in need. Televangelists, a Papal ambassador (I was seated next to him the first year), denominational leaders, and ordinary people of faith, doing courageous things attended. White House staff, and also several cabinet members were there as well.

The President spoke simply and movingly about some aspect of faith and the message of Easter. There were moving testimonies, and then, the President asked us to remain at our tables. In a very unhurried way, he came to every table, to greet each person warmly.

He was the first President I ever met in person. Joshua DuBois, the White House Director of the Faith Office, introduced us. The second year, he tried to introduce me again, and the President said, "I know who she is, Joshua." I don't know if he did or not, but I liked hearing that.

One particular Easter, there were a fair number of LGBTQ folks at the Easter Prayer breakfast — Rev. Harry Knox, also an MCC minister, and former Director of the Religion and Faith Office of Human Rights Campaign, and Bishop Yvette Flunder, Presiding Bishop of The Fellowship of Affirming Ministries. Bishop Flunder is also a United Church of Christ minister, and had clergy credentials in MCC. I also have clergy standing in her Fellowship, another sign of our deep connection and desire to collaborate.

Without any coordination, all three of us, in succession, decided to have a sidebar conversation with televangelist T.D. Jakes. Some of his preaching I have enjoyed, and admire the work he has done on domestic violence and supporting women in standing up for themselves. To my knowledge he has never made a huge deal out of slamming gay people. But, I also knew that he has a huge following in Jamaica. I knew that I might never have this opportunity again to speak to him face-to-face.

So, right there in the East Room of the White House, I introduced myself, thanked him for his ministry, and mentioned his work in Jamaica. He smiled broadly, taking in my complement. Then I told him how much it would mean to people I work with, LGBTQ people and their families, if he would speak up again violence against our community. Even if he did not agree with us about scriptural issues, surely he did not sanction people being beaten or killed just for being who they were. One word from him could save lives, help families, give pastors some guidance and cover.

I took a breath, forced him to take my business card, and said I would love to talk with him further on this matter. By this time he was barely looking at me, staring somewhere over my shoulder, like a deer in the headlights.

I did not know that Harry and Bishop Yvette were on their way to talk with him as well. Poor guy, it isn't safe for televangelists in the White House anymore.

From there, that evening, I flew to Montego Bay, Jamaica. The next day, Jamaica attorney and human rights activists, Maurice Tomlinson, JFLAG and others were organizing a "March for Tolerance." Rev. Pat Bumgardner, pastor of MCC New York, Rev. Dr. Robert Griffin, who had helped to found the churches in Jamaica and support the local leadership, and Rev. Mike Diaz, from Sunshine Cathedral MCC were also there to march. We had dinner that night, a prayer service at the MCC in Montego Bay, and tried to get a good night's sleep.

The next day, we waited in the hotel lobby for hours. The march was to start at ten, and by noon, we had no word. Finally, at about 12:30, Devon, the local MCC leader, came for us in a van. He said about ten people were at the march site. I could feel my heart sink, and my fears confirmed that this might be a really bad idea.

The concept of the March was for LGBTQ people, those with AIDS, and sex workers to march together for their rights, and for toleration in a country that had been very intolerant to these three, different, but often interrelated groups.

When we got to the march site, there were more like 50 people. At 110 marchers, Maurice decided we should step off.

We were led by a teen band — comprised of kids who were themselves HIV positive, or whose parents had died of HIV infection. They had cute looking uniforms and the worst looking instruments you can imagine, but they made a great sound, nevertheless, and led us with great enthusiasm.

Only four clergy marched, all of them MCC. Every church in the area (and there are lots of them), had been invited to join us, not for affirmation of any "lifestyle," but for mere tolerance, a stand against violence. No takers.

We marched for several miles, handing out leaflets, with the band playing up a storm. Onlookers loved the music, but were a little confused about our group. Some stared quietly, some swayed and danced. No one rushed us, or tried to attack us, not for the whole length of the march.

Partway through, the young LGBTQ marchers, who had all been wearing surgical masks, began ripping them off. It was fascinating to me that the sex workers and AIDS activists did not seem to have the same level of fear about being identified. One tall, chubby young man asked me, "Do you think someone will think I am a sex-worker?" He laughed, but was only half joking. In some neighborhoods, being a sex-worker was much more acceptable.

As they took their masks off, newspapers took photos, and television cameras recorded their presence. After the march, a few had to go into hiding, but this time, no one was killed or "disappeared."

Some organizers were very quick to insist that it was not a Pride Parade — however, they paraded the largest rainbow flag I have ever seen outside of New York, it must have taken up 1/3 of the parade itself! There was a lot of pride, energy, joy, and determination to bring change to Jamaica.

We walked all the way down to the very place where, five or six years before, a young man that people just assumed to be gay, was harassed and driven into the sea to drown. That day, the marchers were reclaiming that beach. There was a huge press conference, and a rally, public, outdoors.

That evening, when I got on the plane back home, at the airport, those in the security monitoring area were discussing that I was, indeed, that "lesbian pastor," who was marching in the March for Tolerance that day. Mostly they seemed more curious than hostile about seeing a public lesbian.

I thought a lot about how things in my life turned upside down in twenty-four hours. From the relative safety, luxury, acceptance and privilege of being in the White House, to being on the streets of Montego Bay with people asking for the kind of "tolerance" we now take for granted in many countries.

A Kiss from Our President

By 2012, I was serving on the President's Faith Council, and had been to the White House a number of times.

One of those times, early on in the Obama Presidency, my friend and colleague, Bishop Yvette Flunder and I met with Joshua DuBois, the White House Director of Faith-Based and Neighborhood Partnerships. Bishop Flunder's spouse of more than 30 years is Shirley Miller, *the* Shirley Miller, soloist of the most famous recording of, "O Happy Day," a gospel classic. Joshua's eyes widened at that revelation, and I am not sure he heard anything else we said. Was he thinking, "Oh, my God, I can't wait to tell folks I met *the* Shirley Miller," or "Shirley Miller is a lesbian! WOW!"

At that same meeting, Harry Knox from Human Rights Campaign Faith Office was introducing all of us to the very young White House staff, and let them know that I had led a similar delegation to the White House in 1980, when Jimmy Carter was President (their jaws dropped, how old must that woman be!?!), and that I had founded MCC with Rev. Troy Perry, which was not true. Oh dear. I had come into MCC four years after it started, and to me that was a huge misstatement.

I did not want to correct him in front of the White House staff. Then, I realized that no one battled an eyelash, because, of course, no one else was around then, doing this work. For all they knew, I had been with Troy in the beginning. Close enough.

Of course, this meant that I really was a relic from another age. My previous White House visit was older than the White House staff standing in front of us. From the foggy, fairy tale LGBTQ pre-history days.

Later that year, I got invited to one of the many White House celebrations at the holidays. The invitation arrived early enough to be able to squeeze it in between two trips. I invited my Mom, who had campaigned for the President in the last election, and voted for him twice. Paula had been to one the year before, and was delighted for my mom to go.

She was thrilled. She bought an outfit and borrowed a really nice coat. We had to leave early in the morning, fly to DC, find a place for mom to change, (I just wore my clergy suit), have lunch, go to the party, and fly home that same night so I could catch a plane in the morning to my next gig.

I told Mom she was now officially a jet-setter, going from Florida to DC and back in a day. She just shook her head!

We got to DC and went to Kareem Murphy's office. He is an MCCer, activist, and member of our public policy team. He did everything to make my Mom comfortable in his lobbying firm's offices. We then went to lunch with his partner, DeWayne Davis (now ordained), and Rev. Pat Bumgardner, who was in town for meetings as well.

Mom and I got to the White House, and went through all the security hurdles. It was flawlessly decorated with over 50 Christmas and holiday trees, the U.S. Marine string quartet played. It was just lovely. Then, more food.

I knew the drill by now, that the President and First Lady would descend the staircase, speak briefly, and shake hands across the rope line. If you wanted to touch either of them, you had to push your way closer. So, we lined up early, and did just that. Unfortunately, for my Mom, it was way too long to stand. But, she held on to me, and leaned a little into others occasionally around her.

I knew this was probably the closest she would ever get to a sitting President.

Mrs. Obama came through the line first. Unlike the President, who is more low-key, she filled the room with her personality and charisma. She reached out her long arms, uncovered, into the crowd, and we both grabbed her hands. The President came next, and he saw someone he knew behind me, and shouted out. Then, he saw me, recognized me, and said, "Thanks for all your good work!" and smiled. He started to move on, and I did something I would not normally do, I reached out and grabbed his upper arm, hoping I would not be slammed to the floor by Secret Service (turns out, I probably had nothing to worry about).

He turned back, and I said, "Mr. President, this is my mother." He stopped, completely, smiled and said, "All mothers deserve a kiss," and kissed my mother on her cheek.

She turned to me, opened mouthed, a little teary, and in shock I think. People around us had just sort of parted to make all that possible. It seemed like it all took a really long time, though it was really a matter of seconds.

And, of course, no photos — I couldn't manage my phone and tap the President all at the same time.

I pulled Mom out of the crowd, so she could find a seat. We barely sat down, for a minute, when they began moving us along, and out of the White House.

At the airport, my Mom was so tired, she slept in the waiting room and then on the plane. I kept thinking about how much my Mom loved politics, and really loved this President, and how I never imagined, in my young life, that something like this could happen.

Later, my brother Dave joked and said, "Oh, man, no fair! Mark (my other brother) and I could never compete with that Christmas gift!" He was right.

Inaugural Prayer Service, January 2013

For a few years, I served on the President's Council on Faith-Based and Neighborhood Partnerships. It was a wonderful honor to work with men and women from so many different faith backgrounds on the issue of preventing and stopping human trafficking and modern slavery. We were part of a coalition of groups, and we have begun to make a dent in this domestic and global travesty. Our goal was to support the White House's effort to change the equation so that modern day slavery is a high risk, low profit business, rather than the opposite, as it is today.

Because of my participation, I got to know Joshua DuBois, the young and brilliant White House Director of the Office of Faith-Based and Neighborhood Partnerships. Joshua was from an African-AmericanPentecostal background, and had an openness to people of all faiths and sexual orientations that was encouraging.

Occasionally Joshua or his assistant would call, if we were working on a document, but, it was not every day that the White House called our office.

A couple of weeks before the President's second inauguration, Joshua called my office, and my assistant Linda interrupted me with wide eyes, and said, "The White House is on the line." Joshua was friendly and informal as always, although, he called me "Elder Wilson." I rarely use that title outside of MCC, usually going by "Reverend," or some more common title. In any case, the White House had two Elders on the Council, me, and Stephen Snow, an attorney and Mormon Elder. On the ecumenical and interreligious spectrum we were probably the two outliers. I enjoyed my connection to Stephen Snow, who was delightful and always kind to me.

Joshua started with, "Are you coming to the inauguration?" Well, truthfully, I was not planning to go. I did not have tickets to anything, or an invitation, and I am not great at standing for hours outside in the cold unable to see much. I didn't say that, I just hemmed and hawed. Then he said, "The President asked me to invite you to read the Old Testament scripture at the Inaugural Prayer Service the day after the Inauguration." I said, "Oh my, then I guess I am coming after all!" I told him I was honored and would be delighted to accept the invitation.

The word went out swiftly in MCC. Since the first Inaugural Prayer Service for George Washington, I would be the first openly LGBTQ person, and the first MCC clergy to be invited to participate. Our church in Washington DC, and our volunteers on the Public Policy Team sprang into motion.

There were a limited number of tickets we could distribute to other MCC leaders, and Washington DC folks, and local clergy. Rev. Cathy Alexander volunteered to coordinate — people would have to find her early that morning, in front of the National Cathedral to get their tickets.

My wife Paula came, and our friend Ann, we got to DC late the night before and managed to find room at the inn, at the last minute.

We were escorted that morning to the Cathedral by a local church member. It was so cold, and not just to us Floridians.

When we located Cathy Alexander, she had already been at her post a while, and was giving out tickets. People had to line up, in the sub-zero temperatures, for quite a while. Paula and I were fortunate enough to be able to enter early, as I was a participant. She was as excited as I was, and got a seat with families of participants, where she would be able to see me and take photos, and, also be able to see the President.

I was escorted to a place underneath the Cathedral, with the other participants. At the last minute, I had decided to borrow Rev. Elder Darlene Garner's MCC Elders robe. I thought that if MCCers were watching, on television, they would see the MCC emblem, the familiar vestment, and would feel a sense of joy and pride.

I had asked someone from the Cathedral about vesting and she said, "Oh, my, those men are going to dress, you ought to as well!"

We were downstairs for a long time. They had to sweep the church, security was very tight, since the President and Vice-President were both coming. I had some time with Dr. Serene Jones, from Union Theological Seminary, who, bless her, seemed more touched by the fact that I was participating than that she was! I also chatted with co-council member Dr. Katherine Jefferts-Schori, Presiding Bishop of the Episcopal Church. I was next in line, in the procession, after Dr. Adam Hamilton, pastor of the largest Methodist Church in the country, well-known writer, and our preacher for the morning. He was very gracious, familiar with MCC, and, what a sermon!

Then, after an eternity of waiting, and small talk — the President and Mrs. Obama, and the Vice-President and Dr. Jo Biden came into our waiting area. Not only did they greet each of us individually, but we had individual pictures taken with the four of them. The President and I already knew each other, but it was my first time meeting the other three. We snuggled up for a photo, and I felt so self-conscious. The President had his arm around my shoulder, and, he is so tall, I could only really put my arm around his waist, which was so small! It felt odd to do that, and sort of impossible not to.

Mrs. Obama was wearing the most gorgeous white beaded dress I have ever seen, and I rarely notice dresses.

Then, it was time to move.

The chancel of the National Cathedral was familiar to me — it was the place I was installed as the Moderator of MCC, in October 2005, about seven or eight months before Dr. Jefferts-Shori was installed there as the first woman head of the Episcopal Church.

Being on that chancel brought back so many memories.

There I was, sitting on the chancel with many religious leaders of my country, facing the President and Vice-President and their wives.

I was not nervous until the moment I had to climb up to the lectern to read. I tend to walk too fast, and, wearing all those robes, I did not want to stumble or trip. So, I had to slow myself down a little. I climbed to the top, and paused. I gave myself just a couple of seconds to breathe, smile, and savor the view. My wife Paula was seated to my right, camera in hand. The President and company were in front, with members of Congress and other leaders. My MCC colleagues, friends and church members were in the house, on the Internet and watching on television.

REV. DR. NANCY WILSON

I read a more inclusive version than had been provided of Isaiah. It turned out, I was not the only one who adapted their reading. There was an article in some journal about the fact that we had all done that in some way or another. But, since I was first, I did not know that. I enjoyed reading, slowly. My Mom said she heard my voice quiver, just slightly in the beginning. It was more emotion than nerves.

The service was long and full of fabulous music and preaching. We recessed and learned how powerful it really was. MCC people all over the country and the world, had seen it, and so many were touched, moved, and overjoyed to see me in my MCC robes (or, Darlene's). It touched a chord of pride, and made real and visible so much of the progress we were seeing.

I know that the President and Mrs. Obama were up very late, celebrating at home in the White House. Some said they were dancing with friends and family until 3AM I was even more impressed with their graciousness, not just in coming to the Prayer Service, an American tradition, but coming early, taking pictures with us, and greeting us individually. If I were them, I might have wanted to sleep in, just once. But, thankfully, we had the honor of praying with and for President Obama and the entire leadership of the United States.

Conclusion

Today, I am grateful for knowing so many dedicated and faithful people through our work in MCC. You have made me laugh, cry, protest, and act. You have humbled me with your courage, and inspired me with your determination. Together we have prayed our way into the future.

We have much work to do as so many around the world live in fear. We have much work to do everywhere as we face rising waves of hate driven by race, religion, gender identity and sexual orientation.

MCC is a small denomination — so small that when Pew Research compiles survey data, we are too small to be "statistically significant." But does that mean we are insignificant? No. It means, that MCC is a small, feisty, and loving denomination that has made history.

We were the first to marry, the first to have an AIDS day, and we were in the first LGBTQ delegation to the White House. We were the first to demonstrate at county clerk's offices for marriage equality, and the first to bring a law suit for marriage equality. We have risked our lives, and some of us have lost our lives. We are not finished, and we are not afraid.

Tell the stories. Live the stories. Be the stories. Be MCC.

About the Author
The Reverend Dr. Nancy L. Wilson
Global Moderator,
Metropolitan Community Churches

Rev. Elder Dr. Nancy Wilson was elected to the position of Moderator of Metropolitan Community Churches (MCC) in 2005, following the retirement of the Founder of MCC, Rev. Elder Troy Perry, and in July 2010, she was re-elected for a term of six years. She is only the second person, and the first woman, to serve in that role since the founding of Metropolitan Community Churches in 1968.

Rev. Wilson obtained her B.A. from Allegheny College, her M.Div. from St. Cyril and Methodius Seminary, and her D.Min. from Episcopal Divinity School.

She served as pastor of Church of the Trinity MCC in Sarasota, Florida, from 2001 to 2005 and was previously the pastor of MCC Los Angeles — now Founders MCC — from 1986 until 2001; the church founded by Rev. Troy Perry in 1968. Rev. Wilson joined MCC as Associate Pastor of MCC Boston in 1972 at 22 years of age. She served as Pastor of MCC Detroit from 1975 to 1979. She was elected Elder of MCC in 1976 and served as the denomination's Vice-Moderator from 1993 to 2001.

Rev. Wilson served as Clerk of the Board of Elders for ten years; and became MCC's first Chief Ecumenical Officer, a post she held for 23 years. She has been the official delegate of MCC to the World Council of Churches

General Assemblies in Canberra, Australia (1991); Harare, Zimbabwe (1998); and Porto Alegre, Brazil (2006).

Rev. Wilson is also an Associate Minister with The Fellowship of Affirming Ministries in which Dr. Yvette Flunder serves as the Presiding Bishop.

In 2011, President Barack Obama appointed Rev. Wilson to the President's Advisory Council on Faith-Based and Neighborhood Partnerships. Following President Obama's re-election in 2013, Rev. Wilson gave a Scripture reading at the Inaugural Prayer Service at the National Cathedral in Washington DC, and was the first openly gay clergy member to participate.

In 2014, Rev. Wilson was named as one of the spokespeople for Blessed Tomorrow, a team of twenty-one top ecumenical and interfaith leaders to spearhead an effort to mobilize religious communities to address environmental concerns. Blessed Tomorrow emerged from EcoAmerica MomentUs, a group that invited Rev. Wilson to join in 2013 as they began to formalize their strategy to secure grassroots support through faith groups to work toward climate solutions in their congregations, communities, and homes.

In May 2014, Rev. Wilson was one of four honorees to be recognized by Intersections International for her humanitarian work in the area of social justice.

In honor of International Women's Day in 2014, HuffPost selected Rev. Wilson as one of 50 "powerful religious leaders…making change in the world."

Rev. Wilson's published works include: Outing the Bible: Queer Folks, God, Jesus, and the Christian Scriptures (LifeJourney Press); Outing the Church: 40 Years in the Queer Christian Movement (LifeJourney Press); Nossa Tribo: Gays, Deus, Jesus e a Bíblia (Metanoia); Our Tribe: Queer Folks, God, Jesus and the Bible (Alamo Press); with Fr. Malcolm Boyd, Amazing Grace. Rev. Wilson's prayers and poems are included in Race and Prayer, edited by Malcolm Boyd and Chester Talton (Morehouse Press).

Rev. Wilson is frequently published in Huffington Post, and has been interviewed by various local, national, and international news agencies about matters related to the LGBTQI community and social justice issues. Rev. Wilson has spoken at colleges, national, and international conferences on the topics of eradicating human trafficking, a queer response to climate change, global LGBTQI human rights, religion and social change, and marriage equality.

Rev. Wilson is a popular preacher and speaker and was invited to preach at the Earl Lectures at Pacific School of Religion in 2002. She is also one of the founders of Trinity Charities, a nonprofit located in Sarasota, Florida, that provides support, education and intervention for those infected and affected by HIV/AIDS and for those in temporary crisis.

Rev. Wilson resides in Bradenton, Florida, with her wife of 37 years, Dr. Paula Schoenwether.

More from Rev. Dr. Nancy Wilson

The ministry of MCC depends on every MCC member. We must be committed to both our local congregations and our entire denomination. We have moved from a house church in Los Angeles to having growing ministries in dozens of countries.

Other books by Dr. Wilson:

- *Outing the Bible: Queer Folks, God, Jesus, and the Christian Scriptures,* 2013

- *Outing the Church: 40 Years in the Queer Christian Movement,* 2013

- *Our Tribe: Queer Folks, God, Jesus, and the Bible,* 1995

By Rev. Elder Troy D. Perry:

- *The Lord Is My Shepherd and He Knows I'm Gay,* 1973

Special Gratitude

To Ann Craig, for your partnership in the work of justice and for your skill and help with this book project.

To Linda Brenner, for your faith in this book and in me; and for your extra effort to get it done.

To my wife Paula, for your love and support, always.

To my friends Connie Meadows and Haviland Houston, for believing in the power of these stories and for your generosity and support.

Order your copy of

I Love to tell the Story

on

MCCchurch.org

If you liked the book, please leave a review on
Amazon.com
Also available in Kindle

Made in the USA
Middletown, DE
19 February 2018